Do not be afraid of presenting Christ to someone who does not yet know him. Christ is the true answer, the most complete answer to all the questions which concern the human person and his destiny. Without Christ, the human person remains an unsolvable riddle. Therefore, have the courage to present Christ!

Certainly you must do this in a way which respects each person's freedom of conscience, but you must do it. Helping a brother or sister to discover Christ, the Way, the Truth, and the Life, is a true act of love for one's neighbor.

— Pope John Paul II

Catholicism and Life

Rev. Edward J. Hayes
Rev. Msgr. Paul J. Hayes
and James J. Drummey

C.R. PUBLICATIONS
345 PROSPECT STREET
NORWOOD, MASSACHUSETTS 02062

C.R. Publications Inc.
345 Prospect Street
Norwood, MA 02062

NIHIL OBSTAT
Msgr. William E. Maguire
Censor Librorum

IMPRIMATUR
+ Most Reverend John C. Reiss
Bishop of Trenton
August 25, 1996

The Nihil Obstat and Imprimatur are official declarations that a book or pamphlet is free of doctrinal or moral error. No implication is contained therein that those who have granted the Nihil Obstat or Imprimatur agree with the contents, opinions, or statements expressed.

Third Printing August 1998

Cover design by Jeff Giniewicz
Printed in the United States of America

ISBN 0-9649087-3-5

Contents

Preface

In our times, a great number of people have put moral and ethical principles aside and seldom consider such norms in their daily decisions. Some have gone so far as to remove religion entirely as a factor in their lives. The tragic consequences of ignoring essential moral standards are all too apparent in the shocking headlines in our newspapers and the frightening scenes on television.

This book, in the section on the Commandments, explains the necessary place of moral and ethical principles in the life of every human being. In the section on the Sacraments, it shows how God helps us to follow those principles and to live a happy and fruitful existence by sharing in the divine life of the Blessed Trinity.

Catholicism and Life presents this information in clear and simple language, furnishing a year's course in a Catholic high school or college or in a weekly parish religious education program. Its popular style makes it interesting reading for almost anyone, and it would be appropriate for adult education and for R.C.I.A. programs for those seeking full communion with the Catholic Church.

The book is well indexed, and a catechist's manual, containing practical ideas and suggestions for presenting the material, is available. Catechists or group leaders will benefit from the sources included in the bibliography, as well as from the charts in the text that clarify various moral and religious topics.

The practical and popular style of the book is a reflection of the authors' years of experience lecturing and teaching on every level of religious education from grammar school to the university. They have used this material in the classroom and before larger groups, and they know that it has great appeal to a wide audience.

Those using this text should also be familiar with three companion volumes to this work. *Catholicism and Reason* explains the basic doctrines of the Catholic Faith by means of reasoned arguments and examples, *Catholicism and Society* applies Catholic moral principles to the areas of marriage and the family, womanhood, the aging, racial justice, and morality in public life, and *Catholicism and Ethics* offers sound guidance on such medical/moral issues as artificial nutrition/hydration, cloning, organ donations, mutilation, "test-tube" babies, and tissue transplants.

In *Catholicism and Life*, the authors show what God wants us to do or not do (the Commandments), and the helps God gives us so that we may live fully the Christian life (the Sacraments).

Other essential resources for presenting this material are the *Catechism of the Catholic Church* and Pope John Paul II's important encyclicals on "The Splendor of Truth" (*Veritatis Splendor*) and "The Gospel of Life" (*Evangelium Vitae*). The *Catechism*, the Holy Father said, "contains a complete and systematic exposition of Christian moral teaching," while his encyclicals set forth "the principles of a moral teaching based upon Sacred Scripture and the living Apostolic Tradition, and at the same time ... shed light on the presuppositions and consequences of the dissent which that teaching has met."

While explaining the Commandments and Sacraments in detail, the authors have put them into perspective and have stressed obedience and fidelity to the Church founded by Jesus to help us get to heaven. In the area of natural and divine law, the authors have been very realistic so that readers can frequently see themselves reflected in the text – sometimes perhaps a little to their discomfort.

The section on the sixth commandment is plain-spoken but reverent, firm but sympathetic, and has a particular appeal to the youth of our time. Additional information on sexuality as God designed it can be found in *Catholicism and Society*.

To those who say that Christian morality is too demanding, too difficult to understand, and almost impossible to practice, Pope John Paul responded: "This is untrue, since Christian morality consists in the simplicity of the Gospel, in *following Jesus Christ*, in abandoning oneself to him, in letting oneself be transformed by his grace and renewed by his mercy, gifts which come to us in the living communion of his Church" (*Veritatis Splendor*, n. 119).

BOOKS IN THIS SERIES

Catholicism and Reason
and
Leader's / Catechist's Manual

Catholicism and Life
and
Leader's / Catechist's Manual

Catholicism and Society
and
Leader's / Catechist's Manual

Catholicism and Ethics
(No Manual)

Additional books in this series may be ordered by writing to the address below, by calling (781) 762-8811, or by sending a fax to (781) 762-7890. There is a 20 percent discount for schools, parishes, and church groups, and a 40 percent discount for bookstores. Major credit cards are accepted. Otherwise, send check or money order (U.S. funds only) to:

C.R. Publications Inc.
345 Prospect Street
Norwood, MA 02062

Chapter 1

The Roots of Life

The beatitude we are promised confronts us with decisive moral choices. It invites us to purify our hearts of bad instincts and to seek the love of God above all else. – *Catechism of the Catholic Church*, n. 1723

The Catholic religion revolves around the fact that there are two avenues for a person. One is the way of life; the other is the way of death, the death of a soul who has lost the way to God. The first avenue has signposts along the road so that a person will not lose the way. Those signposts are the ten Commandments.

Toward the end of Christ's last year on earth, he spent much of his time teaching groups of people his doctrine. One day, when he was surrounded by several followers, an influential young man made his way through the crowd to Christ. He was a man with high ideals and a person of influence and wealth. The crowd recognized his status and made room for him.

After paying his respects to Jesus by getting down on one knee, the young man asked: "Teacher, what good must I do to possess everlasting life?" Our Lord responded in these simple words: "If you wish to enter into life, keep the Commandments." Which ones? the young man asked. Jesus replied: " 'You shall not kill'; 'You shall not commit adultery'; 'You shall not steal'; 'You shall not bear false witness'; 'Honor your father and your mother'; and 'Love your neighbor as yourself' " (Matthew 19:16-19).

The ten Commandments are a guidebook for the kingdom of heaven. If a person does not follow the directions of that book, he or she is not going to reach their destination. From the very beginning of creation, God imprinted the natural law on our hearts. A young child who has done wrong – lied, stolen, disobeyed – feels uncomfortable, ashamed, or even frightened, though he or she may never have heard of the Commandments. Even before the Commandments were given to the world, men and women could tell right from wrong; they knew that it was wrong to murder, steal, lie, or to commit adultery. But as they drifted away from God, the Creator saw the need of putting his law before them in a striking way, making it stronger and more explicit than the natural law (Do good and avoid evil) they already knew.

So God gathered the Jewish people at the foot of Mount Sinai as darkness covered the mountain. Taking Moses to the top amidst thunder and lightning, the Lord appeared and made known to him the ten Commandments to be followed by all people for all time. Here was the blueprint of what we must do to get to heaven. Here was a set of laws given by God himself to the world in order that we might know how God wants to be served.

The Commandments were written on two pieces of stone, indicating that they are a more explicit enumeration of the two great commandments later stated by Christ: "You shall love the Lord your God with your whole heart, with your whole soul, and with all your mind. This is the greatest and first commandment. The second is like it: You shall love your neighbor as yourself" (Matthew 22:37-38). The first three Commandments express our duties toward God; the last seven our duties toward our neighbors and ourselves.

The Way to Happiness

In the days before Christ, God found it necessary to put his law strongly and almost with terror before a people who had turned away from him to a life of sin. Today once again we see the need for drawing people back to God through the same ten Commandments. And just as the rich young man would not give up his wealth and power to serve Christ wholeheartedly (Matthew 19:22), so today we are tempted to compromise our service to Christ with love of worldly wealth or pleasure. At the very time when a person seeks happiness by violating any one of God's Commandments, then that person has begun to lose true happiness.

The Commandments as they stand are not a complete list of all the things that must be done or avoided. Rather they are a summary of each type of violation of justice toward God or others. The fact that only parents are mentioned in the fourth commandment does not mean the obligation of respect and obedience ceases there. On the contrary, it extends to all lawful superiors; parents are mentioned specifically because our obligations to them are the most obvious. So, too, the fifth commandment includes much more than just not killing someone; it also obliges us to respect the bodily well-being of ourselves and others.

The Commandments, then, are a summary of what God expects of us. He put them in that form to make it easier for us to understand what it means to love God and neighbor.

The Maker's Directions

The Commandments of God are his plan for guiding us toward heaven. They show us "the path to life and they lead to it," said Pope John Paul. "From the very lips of Jesus, the new Moses, man is once again given the commandments of the Decalogue. Jesus himself definitively confirms them and proposes them to us as the way and condition of salvation" (*Veritatis Splendor*, n. 12).

They are not meant to interfere with our liberty, but to guide us in the proper use of our freedom. A railing is placed on the side of a narrow path along a steep cliff, not to hinder the people who walk along but to protect them. They are free to step under or over the railing, but in so doing they only endanger themselves.

When the manufacturer of an automobile gives a set of directions and rules with each car, it is not done to hinder the driver or to interfere with one's pleasure, but to help get the best use out of the vehicle. The driver is free to tear up the manufacturer's directions, or to put sugar in the gas tank, but to do so is to harm the automobile. When a mother tells her children not to play with matches or not to lean out a second-story window, she is not saying it to suppress their freedom, but to ensure their safety and well-being.

The manufacturer knows what is best for his product because he made it. So it is with God's Commandments. They are not meant to hinder us or to make life harder for us, but in fact to make life easier by keeping us away from words and deeds that could get us into serious trouble. God made us and knows what is best for us. He has left us free to keep his rules or not. But we cannot ignore those laws without doing ourselves harm.

The Commandments are a set of our "Maker's directions" on how we can avoid getting into difficulty and best accomplish our goal of reaching heaven. Ignoring God's blueprint will have the same tragic results as a builder would experience by ignoring an architect's blueprint for a house.

We have God's word that the only way to attain happiness in this life, and especially in the next life, is by faithfully serving him. Many of the people in the world have tried to find happiness apart from God – in money, power, position, pleasure, material comforts, and sin. And that is why the modern world is so chaotic, with little sense of peace or security, and why people today are so discontented and disoriented.

God's way is still the best way. We cannot find true happiness by rejecting the laws of God. The ten Commandments are still the only sure way to reach God, for they are an expression of his will for us. They are his love letters to us, and we will never have peace in our hearts or in our world until we are at peace with God. "If you wish to enter into life," Jesus said, "keep the Commandments" (Matthew 19:17).

Why We Do Things

Our world is one of action, and we do not often stop to ask ourselves why we act in a certain way. Actually, though, we usually regulate our actions according to some standard – e.g., what we did seemed pleasant to us, or it was to our best advantage at the time, or our friends pressured us into doing it. If we pay attention, we will notice that people act differently because they are guided by different norms or standards.

Thus, many people's actions will be determined by what is useful for them at the moment, rather than what is objectively right or wrong. Perhaps one of the best examples of this false standard occurred nearly two thousand years ago, when a Roman governor sentenced a man to death, although he knew that the man was innocent of the crime. "I find no case against this man" (John 18:38), said Pontius Pilate, but he sentenced Christ to death because he knew that the people would try to remove him from office if he did not do their will. It was more advantageous for him to do the expedient thing instead of the right thing. This same norm governs the lives of many people in our own time.

Another rule by which people live today says that they should only do what is pleasing and enjoyable, and avoid what is unpleasant and difficult. For example, the person who has a bad tooth but will not go to the dentist knows what should be done, but also knows that the dentist's office is not a pleasant place. It is dangerous to apply this standard to God's laws, for it will cause us to take actions that are contrary to the teachings of Christ. Our Lord did not say that keeping the Commandments would be easy, but he did say that that was the only certain way to heaven. We must rise above our feelings and seek not what is pleasant, but that which keeps us most surely in God's friendship.

The Law of Love

For the follower of Christ there is no question about what ought to govern our actions in everyday life. God gave us the norm: "You shall love the Lord your God .... You shall love your neighbor as yourself." Our world is one which talks much of love and knows practically nothing of what love really is. Most of today's ideas about love are obtained from sleazy books, obscene magazines, or smutty television shows or movies where the notion of love has been reduced to sex.

Actually, true love is expressed more by deeds than by words. A husband and wife who really love each other need not be constantly saying so, and in fact they may not often express their feelings. Their love is demonstrated by the sacrifices they make for one another, by what they do for each other more than by what they say. And that is why, if a person truly loves God, the standard followed will not be what he or she wants to do, nor what is most useful at the moment, nor what is most pleasant, but what is right.

There was an incident not long ago where a 74-year-old man suddenly collapsed in his home. A paramedic team rushed him to the nearest hospital. After examining him, the doctors found that he had a ruptured blood vessel in his heart and that only immediate surgery and a supply of fresh, whole blood could save him. Over the speakers in the hospital went an urgent appeal for blood donors. Within seconds, nineteen hospital employees came forward to give blood. Not one of them knew the stricken man; all they knew was that he needed them. That is what love means. They didn't know the man, but they loved him enough to give him their precious blood, and they saved his life.

"If You Love Me, Keep My Commandments"

Love is not so much a matter of *feeling* but of *doing* what we know to be the right thing. This is not easy, for if love is *doing* and sacrificing for others, and not mere *feeling* or sentiment, then it is going to be difficult at times to perform deeds when they are contrary to our feelings. Many people today have unknowingly worked out for themselves a more pleasant and easier gospel to live by. At times we will have to go contrary to that easy gospel, and to our feelings, in order to do what is right.

When Christ gave us this standard by which to act, he did not mean it as a mere pious axiom; he wanted us to put it into practice. When he said, "Love the Lord your God," he did not mean that we should merely get down on our knees and tell him that once in a while. He meant that we ought always to do what he wants us to do. "If you love me, keep my Commandments" means just that. If we know the Commandments and do not keep each and every one of them, then we are not following the Christian standard of life, no matter how much we may speak of our love of God or neighbor.

How much do we love God? How much do we love our neighbor? How do we stand in God's sight? Are we on our way to eternal salvation or eternal damnation? These questions can only be answered by how faithfully we adhere to the ten Commandments, to the commandments of the Church, to the moral code that Jesus spelled out in the Sermon on the Mount, and to the corporal and spiritual works of mercy.

The Works of Mercy

The corporal and spiritual works of mercy are a concrete expression of our love of neighbor, which includes everybody in need of our help, as Christ made clear in the parable of the Good Samaritan (Luke 10:25-37). Recall the time that two followers of John the Baptist came to Jesus with the question: "Are you 'He who is to come' or do we look for another?" Our Lord replied: "Go back and report to John what you hear and see: the blind recover their sight, cripples walk, lepers are cured, the deaf hear, dead men are raised to life, and the poor have the good news preached to them" (Matthew 11:2-5).

Christ in his own life not only preached the works of mercy, but he practiced them as well. He relieved the suffering and the afflicted, aided the poor, consoled the outcasts, taught the ignorant, and gave himself entirely to others. His public life was characterized by works of mercy toward others, and such should be the most recognizable characteristic of our lives as Catholics and followers of Christ. We must follow the example of those Christians in the early Church:

"The community of believers were of one heart and one mind. None of them ever claimed anything as his own; rather, everything was held in common ... nor was there anyone needy among them, for all who owned property or houses sold them and donated the proceeds. They used to lay them at the feet of the Apostles to be distributed to everyone according to his need" (Acts 4:32-35).

To feed the hungry, give drink to the thirsty, and clothe the naked are corporal works of mercy. The saints busied themselves performing these loving services to those in need. Saints like Elizabeth, Queen of Hungary, who used to feed some 900 people a day at the palace gates. She chose to live on bread and water herself so that she could help her subjects. Though she could have lived a life of ease and luxury, Elizabeth spent hours making clothes for the needy with her own hands.

To shelter the homeless, visit the imprisoned, visit the sick, and bury the dead are also works of mercy that affect the bodily needs of others. We can share in all these wonderful works of charity personally, or through generosity to those who are engaged in helping others, bearing in mind the words of our Lord, that as long as we do these things for the least of our brothers and sisters, we do them for him (Matthew 25:40).

To admonish the sinner, instruct the ignorant, counsel the doubtful, comfort the sorrowful, bear wrongs patiently, forgive all injuries, and pray for the living and the dead are spiritual works of mercy. They are aimed not so much at the temporal welfare of our neighbors as at the eternal well-being of ourselves and others. They are concerned with people's souls rather than their bodies. They involve preaching the good news to people and letting them know that whatever troubles or problems they face in this life, there is another and greater life to come where every tear will be wiped away and we will see God face to face and rejoice in his love forever.

The corporal and spiritual works of mercy are not just holy deeds for those who feel like doing them. Every one of us has the obligation to perform them according to the circumstances that arise in our daily lives and the needs of our neighbors. It should be noted that not every time a person feeds the hungry, visits the sick, or comforts the sorrowful is there really a work of mercy being carried out; the motive behind the action is all-important. A politician may give out hundreds of free meals, visit many hospitals, or attend numerous funerals, but there is little merit gained as far as

God is concerned if these works are done solely for votes. The deeds must be done out of love of God and neighbor.

Christ's Program for Heaven

The natural law that is written in our hearts, the ten Commandments given to the world by the Father, the precepts or commandments given to us by the Church founded by the Son, the works of mercy – all these are ways of fulfilling in practice Christ's two fundamental commands to love God totally and to love our neighbor as ourselves. And we should stress the positive dimension of these commands by trying to serve God in a spirit of love, and not out of fear.

Everyone recognizes that we live in a world governed by physical laws. Fire will burn us, a stone tossed in the air will fall to the ground because of the law of gravity, we must eat in order to live. We cannot pick and choose among these laws of nature, observing some and ignoring others, without hurting ourselves. We can't get away from these laws, so we must act reasonably and accept them.

Isn't the same thing true of the spiritual laws that govern our lives? We are free to ignore these laws of God, just as we are free to disregard the laws of nature, but doing so will bring harm to us, if not in this life then in the life to come. The rejection of God's moral standards may give us momentary pleasure or satisfaction, but in the long run we will suffer the loss of true happiness and peace – and perhaps even our soul.

A news story not long ago related that a burglar who had broken into a house and stolen a wallet containing ten dollars had inadvertently dropped more than a hundred dollars from his own pocket. Those who violate any of the Commandments will find themselves in a similar situation; they will have gained some slight pleasure, but will have lost far more in breaking their relationship with God. We cannot reject the laws of God without damaging ourselves severely.

All that has been said so far may sound like a formidable and even impossible blueprint for life, but it has its purpose and its rewards. Ralph Waldo Emerson and Thomas Carlyle once were walking through the countryside in Scotland. "What do you raise here on land like this?" Emerson asked as he noticed the poor soil and the rocky terrain around Ecclefechan. Carlyle replied: "We raise men."

Living the Commandments to the fullest in whatever walk of

life we find ourselves may at times require heroic sacrifice, but it will produce men and women who are loyal to God and who will have a significant and positive impact on the world, despite sometimes having to work with poor religious soil and on rocky moral terrain.

The history of God's people is replete with examples of heroic sacrifice, of a willingness to die as martyrs rather than deny the Lord. Think, for instance, of Susanna in the Old Testament, who refused to yield to the sinful passion of the two unjust judges (Daniel 13); of John the Baptist (Mark 6:14-29) and St. Stephen (Acts 7:54-60) in the New Testament, who gave up their lives to profess their faith in and their love for Christ; or a modern-day martyr like Maria Goretti, who was canonized in 1950 because this 11-year-old Italian girl preferred death to committing a single mortal sin.

Contrary to popular belief, holiness is not simply the absence of faults. Holiness consists rather in sharing and spreading a dynamic and towering love. Some of the Commandments may be written in negative terms, but they remain, thousands of years after they were handed to Moses, a very positive blueprint for making the world a better place through the constant expression of love of God and love of neighbor.

The Source of Spiritual Life

Christ was and is the source of our spiritual life. "When Christ *our life* appears," said St. Paul, "then you shall appear with him in glory" (Colossians 3:4). St. John echoed these words when he said: "God gave us eternal life and this life is in his Son" (1 John 5:11). Thus, Christ is the source of the life – the "living water" – that is channeled to us through the seven Sacraments. These Sacraments provide grace – a share in God's life – from the cradle to the grave. Their supernatural life parallels our natural life.

We come into natural existence through birth. *Baptism* is our spiritual birth. We grow in physical strength. *Confirmation* gives us the spiritual strength of the Holy Spirit. Our bodies need nourishment. The *Holy Eucharist* gives nourishment to our souls. Disease must be warded off and, once contracted, cured.

Penance/Reconciliation helps to ward off the disease of sin and to cure those who have fallen into sin. Sickness and the advance of old age require medical attention. The *Anointing of the Sick* brings us spiritual and sometimes physical healing. Certain people in our lives help us to grow emotionally. *Holy Orders* gives us priests to help us grow spiritually. We need other people to share our lives with us and to help train others to make this a better world. *Matrimony* raises marriage to the level of a sacrament and gives husbands and wives the grace and strength they need to bring new lives into the world and to educate and guide them to follow God's will.

"I came that they might have *life* and have it to the full," Jesus told the Pharisees (John 10:10). Pope John XXIII described how our Lord's plan has been fulfilled when he said: "The Catholic Church, from its earliest period down through the centuries, has always had seven, neither more nor fewer, Sacraments, received as a sacred legacy from Jesus Christ. She has never ceased to dispense these throughout the Catholic world for the nourishing and fostering of the supernatural *life* of the faithful" (*Near the Chair of Peter*).

You Have to Prime the Pump

In southern California there was a general store on the fringe of the Aramagosa Desert, and on display in the store was a piece of brown wrapping paper mounted between two sheets of glass. On the paper was a message written in pencil. The message had been found in an old tin can that had been wired to an old pump on a seldom used trail in the middle of the desert. Here is what was written:

"This pump is all right as of June 1932. I put a new washer into it but the washer dries out and the pump has to be primed. Under the rock I buried a bottle of water, out of the sun and cork end up. There's enough water in it to prime this pump, but not if you drink some first. Pour about one-fourth and let her soak to wet the leather. Then pour in the rest medium fast and pump like hell. You'll git water. The well never has run dry. Have faith. When you git watered up, fill the bottle and put it back like you found it for the next feller.

"P.S. Don't go drinkin' up the water first. Prime the pump with it and you'll git all you can hold. And next time you pray, remember that God is like this pump. He has to be primed. I've given my last dime away a dozen times to prime the pump of my prayers, and I've fed my last beans to a stranger while a-saying Amen. It never failed to get an answer. You got to git your heart fixed to give before you can be give to. Pete."

THE PURPOSE OF LIFE

To sanctify oneself
"Be perfect"

To help others
"Proclaim the good news to all
creation"

But neither can be accomplished without

THE BLUEPRINT

The Ten Commandments

I, the Lord, am your God.
You shall not have other gods
besides me.

You shall not take the name of
the Lord, your God, in vain.

Remember to keep holy the
sabbath day.

Honor your father and your
mother.

You shall not kill.

You shall not commit adultery.

You shall not steal.

You shall not bear false
witness against your neighbor.

You shall not covet your
neighbor's wife.

You shall not covet your
neighbor's goods.

THE STRENGTH

The Seven Sacraments

Baptism

Confirmation

Holy Eucharist

Penance

Anointing of the sick

Holy Orders

Matrimony

VATICAN COUNCIL II

"Everyone in the Church does not
proceed by the same path, nevertheless all are called to sanctity"
(Dogmatic Constitution on the
Church, n. 32).

"The Church has been divinely
sent to all nations that she might
be the 'universal sacrament of
salvation.'" (Decree on the Missionary Activity of the Church, n.1).

The fruits of the Sacraments and the Commandments do not just automatically change our life. We have to work at it. There is plenty of "living water" (John 4:10), but we have to do some priming ourselves. Sometimes we may even have to "pump like hell," as the old prospector put it. And the fact that is so often lost today is that we cannot be selfish with the gifts given to us. When sacraments like Baptism and Confirmation are rightly understood, then we cannot keep these graces between ourselves and God; we have a Christian social obligation to be our brother's and sister's keeper. We must work for "the next feller."

Following the Master's Plan

Our Lord put some of these lessons in another way as he stood by the well talking to the Samaritan woman. After asking her for a drink, Christ spoke these words: "If only you recognized God's gift, and who it is that is asking you for a drink, you would have asked him instead, and he would have given you living water" (John 4:10). The Commandments (and Christ on this occasion was prodding the woman to keep the Commandments) and the Sacraments as channels of grace are the source of the living water. They are the only source of life that really counts.

Mediocre Christianity results from self-satisfied Christians. Living the Commandments and utilizing the Sacraments to their fullest imply a certain dissatisfaction with the so-so life we are leading and a willingness to sacrifice generously for what we believe in. Thomas A. Edison once said: "Show me a thoroughly satisfied man and I will show you a failure." Too many Christians today are quite satisfied with themselves, and the deplorable moral and spiritual condition of our society reflects their smug attitude.

The Commandments and the Sacraments provide the blueprint for our lives. Follow that plan and you will be a different person. Perhaps the words of St. Paul best describe what will happen: "The life I live now is not my own; Christ is living in me. I still live my human life, but it is a life of faith in the Son of God, who loved me and gave himself for me" (Galatians 2:20).

Chapter 2

Law and Liberty

Conscience must be informed and moral judgment enlightened. A well-formed conscience is upright and truthful. It formulates its judgments according to reason, in conformity with the true good willed by the wisdom of the Creator. The education of conscience is indispensable for human beings who are subjected to negative influences and tempted by sin to prefer their own judgment and to reject authoritative teachings. – *Catechism of the Catholic Church*, n. 1783

A human act is one that proceeds from the deliberate use of our free will. It is an act that is deliberately and knowingly performed by one having the use of reason. Therefore, both intellect and will are in use. When a person studies with a classmate, he is performing a human act. When a group of citizens prepares a petition to send to the governor, they are performing human acts. When a gang of criminals robs a bank, they are performing a human act.

Every human act derives its morality from three elements: the object of the act itself, the purpose of the act, and the circumstances surrounding the act. Let us analyze each of these elements.

In order to judge the morality of a human act, we must first consider *the object of the act itself*. This is "the primary and decisive element for moral judgment," said Pope John Paul, because it "establishes whether it is capable of being ordered to the good and to the ultimate end, which is God" (*Veritatis Splendor*, n. 79).

Singing in a church choir would seem, on the face of it, to be morally good. Certainly it is good as far as the act itself is concerned. An evil purpose (seeking the opportunity to steal something valuable) or some other circumstance might make the singing evil, but the act itself is a good one. The unauthorized taking of a car is in itself a bad act, although it is possible to imagine circumstances when it would be morally allowable (to rush a dying person to the hospital).

When the police arrive at the scene of an alleged crime, they are forced to make an immediate judgment based on the act itself. If a boy had been walking down the street playing a harmonica, the victim of the crime would have a hard time persuading the police to arrest the boy. On the other hand, if two men were caught setting fire to a building, the act itself would be sufficient for an arrest. The men arrested could claim a good reason for setting the fire, but they would have to explain that later to a judge. In the legal order as in the moral order, we must first consider the object of the act itself in passing judgment on the moral goodness or badness of any action.

The purpose of a human act is the reason why the act is performed. A woman lies about a neighbor for the purpose of destroying the neighbor's reputation. A husband lies to his wife about problems at his job because he fears that telling her the truth will disturb her peace of mind. In each case, a lie was told, but obviously the guilt of each party is radically different. What makes the difference? The purpose of the person who told the lie.

It should be noted that the purpose will not always change the morality of an act because some acts are intrinsically wrong (evil by their nature). Take for instance the act of rape. A rapist may argue that he had a good purpose, such as the release of his tensions, but that cannot change the evil nature of the act itself. Rape is always wrong.

The circumstances of a human act are those factors, distinct from the act itself and from its purpose, which may change the morality of the act. Consider the case of a man who strikes another man, and later strikes his own mother. We immediately perceive a great difference in these two physically identical acts. As we do in the case of one woman who stabs her husband in a fit of anger, and another woman who stabs a man who assaulted her on the street. So any careful moral judgment must weigh the circumstances surrounding the act.

How to Judge the Morality of an Act

Various fundamental principles must be applied in judging the morality of a specific act. The following is a list of some of the more important of these principles. A more extensive discussion of them can be found in paragraphs 71-83 of *Veritatis Splendor* and in articles 1749-1761 of the *Catechism of the Catholic Church*.

1. *An act is morally good if the object of the act itself, the purpose, and the circumstances are substantially good.* We say "substantially" good because an act may have minor moral shortcomings and still be a truly good act. A teenage boy who obeys the speed laws because he is afraid his father might take the car away from him is performing a good act even though his motive is more selfish than noble.

2. *If an act itself is intrinsically evil (evil by its very nature), the act is never morally allowable regardless of purpose or circumstances.* St. Paul taught the existence of intrinsically evil acts when he stated: "Do not deceive yourselves: no fornicators, idolaters, or adulterers, no sexual perverts, thieves, misers, or drunkards, no slanderers or robbers will inherit God's kingdom" (1 Corinthians 6:9-10).

The Second Vatican Council also listed a number of acts that are always seriously wrong by reason of their object:

"Whatever is opposed to life itself, such as any type of murder, genocide, abortion, euthanasia, or willful self-destruction; whatever violates the integrity of the human person, such as mutilation, torments inflicted on body or mind, attempts to coerce the will itself; whatever insults human dignity, such as subhuman living conditions, arbitrary imprisonment, deportation, slavery, prostitution, the selling of women and children; as well as disgraceful working conditions, where men are treated as mere tools for profit, rather than as free and responsible persons; all these things and others of their like are infamies indeed. They poison human society, but they do more harm to those who practice them than those who suffer from the injury. Moreover, they are a supreme dishonor to the Creator" (*Pastoral Constitution on the Church in the Modern World*, n. 27).

3. *If the object of the act is itself morally good (or at least neutral), its morality will be judged by the purpose or the circumstances.*

Eating in itself is morally neutral. If a person is eating to keep herself healthy, she is doing something good. If she is eating to the point of gluttony, she is doing something morally wrong.

4. *Circumstances may create, mitigate, or aggravate sin.* They may change a neutral or indifferent act into one that is morally sinful. For instance, shooting a gun may be suicide or murder or both or nothing. To use the name of God or Jesus to express anger or surprise is sinful; to do so in front of children adds the sin of scandal. Circumstances may make a mortal (grave) sin out of a venial (slight) sin, or a venial sin out of a mortal sin. To steal a small amount of money is ordinarily a venial sin; to steal the same amount from a very poor person would be a serious sin.

5. *If all three moral elements (the object of the act itself, the purpose, and the circumstances) are good, the act is good. If any one element is evil, the act is evil.* If a reservoir is fed by three streams, and one of them is polluted, the reservoir is polluted.

Conditions That Lessen Guilt

Since free will and knowledge always play a part in moral guilt, anything that might interfere with free will and/or knowledge must be considered in making a prudent judgment concerning the morality of an action. There are a number of conditions that may lessen or even remove moral responsibility entirely: ignorance, fear, concupiscence, violence, habit, temperament, and nervous mental disorders.

Ignorance is lack of knowledge in a person capable of possessing such knowledge. In some cases we are responsible for knowledge; in other cases we are not. We must distinguish between two types of ignorance, vincible and invincible.

Vincible ignorance is that which can and should be dispelled. The person ought to know that an action is wrong, and failure to know this implies some culpability or fault on his part. Thus, if a person suspects that it may be wrong to eat meat on the Fridays of Lent, but neglects to call a priest or a friend to find out, then he commits a sin if he eats meat on those days. Or if a married couple thinks that practicing artificial contraception may be against the Church's teaching, but deliberately avoids acquiring the knowledge so that they won't have to observe the teaching, they are guilty of sin.

Invincible ignorance is that which cannot be dispelled. This situation may exist either because an individual is unable to obtain adequate information, even after a reasonable effort, or because he simply does not know that there is any problem – in other words, he is ignorant of his own ignorance. This person cannot be expected to take steps to enlighten himself because he is unaware that he is in need of any enlightenment. Thus, if a new convert to the Church was unaware of the obligation to attend Mass on holy days, as well as on Sundays, there would be no sin involved in missing Mass on a holy day.

We can sum up by saying that invincible ignorance eliminates the moral responsibility for a human act; vincible ignorance does not eliminate moral responsibility, but it may lessen it (cf. *Catechism of the Catholic Church*, nn. 1790-1793).

Fear is a disturbance of mind resulting from some present or imminent danger. Fear is an emotion that can cause us such anxiety that our use of reason is affected and we may perform an immoral act that we normally would not perform. For instance, if we stole something because someone threatened to beat us severely, our moral guilt would be greatly diminished. However, even overwhelming fear would not justify performing an action that is intrinsically evil, such as abortion or rape.

Concupiscence is the rebellion of the passions against reason. Or to put it another way, it is the tendency of human nature toward evil. It is the revolt of our physical faculties against the higher faculty of reason. St. Paul spoke of this internal conflict: "I cannot understand even my own actions. I do not do what I want to do but what I hate" (Romans 7:15).

The passions may be defined as the physical appetites of human beings reaching out toward their objects. Under this heading come anger, hope, love, joy, grief, desire, aversion, courage, and fear. The passions are not in themselves evil; parents may and often should exercise a just anger in order to discipline their children. But the passions are, however, in revolt against our nobler and better selves, and that revolt is called concupiscence (cf. *Catechism of the Catholic Church*, nn. 1762-1774).

Obviously, an evil action performed in the heat of passion can be quite different from an evil action that is carefully planned and calculated. This distinction is often recognized in our courts by the different penalties attached to murder in the first degree and second degree. So the recognition of concupiscence as a factor in determining guilt is well founded for it does have an influence on the morality of human acts.

What happens if an individual deliberately arouses his or her passions? For instance, suppose a young man or woman deliberately reads a sexually graphic book before going on a date, or deliberately chooses such a video for both parties to view while they are alone for the specific purpose of getting the other person "turned on." Obviously, this would increase the moral guilt of the individual who planned the evening. On the other hand, culpability is lessened if the passion aroused on a date is spontaneous.

It is clear that certain emotions, such as anger, discouragement, or grief, can so influence a person's state of mind that the use of reason and free will is lessened. This in turn lessens the voluntary nature of human acts and their degree of guilt. For example, a very depressed sick person who attempts suicide is less blameworthy because of their state of mind. But a person who voluntarily fosters concupiscence, say by deliberately working oneself into a rage in order to force someone else to do something, would be morally responsible for that act.

Violence is an external force applied by one person on another in order to compel that person to perform an action against his or her will. In cases where the victim gives complete resistance, the violence is classified as perfect violence; where the victim offers insufficient resistance, the violence is classified as imperfect violence. That which is done under "perfect violence" is entirely involuntary, and there is no moral reponsibility in such cases. That which is done under the influence of "imperfect violence" is less voluntary, and the moral responsibility is lessened but not taken away completely.

A habit is an inclination to perform some particular action. It is acquired by repetition and characterized by a decreased power of resistance and an increased ease of performance. Formed by frequent repetition of some action, the habits of cursing or drinking, of praying or being kind to others – all have moral implications, either good or bad. Habit does not destroy the voluntary nature of our actions, and we are at least partially responsible for evil acts done out of habit as long as the habit is allowed to continue. If we know the consequences of an act and do it repeatedly, we cannot escape moral responsibility for the act. But if we sincerely try to overcome the bad habit, for instance, by staying away from persons, places, or things which may cause us to sin, then our moral guilt may be diminished if we fall into the habit inadvertently.

Temperament is the sum total of those emotional and mental qualities which mark an individual. Temperament may be loosely defined as disposition, and our temperament can affect our will to the extent of somewhat lessening the completely voluntary nature of our actions. Four basic temperaments are generally recognized in human beings: phlegmatic, or not easily aroused; choleric, or having a low threshold for anger; sanguine, or optimistic and free from anxiety; and melancholic, or given to introspection or pessimism about the future. Individuals may have more than one of these temperaments, and they can affect the way in which we act.

Nervous mental disorders can affect the intellect and the will and may take away completely or lessen the voluntary nature of human acts. Sin and moral responsibility depend on the use of the intellect and will and, since nervous mental disorders affect the proper operation of these two faculties, moral guilt is diminished or eliminated to the extent to which these faculties are affected. In concrete individual cases, it is most difficult to determine moral responsibility. We must leave the final judgment in these situations in the hands of God.

Caution should be exercised, however, lest we be tempted to use mental problems as an unwarranted excuse for immoral actions. How many times these days do we hear the perpetrators of heinous crimes described as "sick" or "crazy," when it is more likely that they are just plain evil? It is not up to us to judge anyone's motives – God alone knows what is in our minds and hearts – but let's not be so quick to rule out evil as the root cause of much of the criminal activity afflicting our society.

Occasions of Sin

An occasion of sin is any person, place, or thing which may lead us into sin. An outside influence or circumstance which offers an individual an enticement to commit a sin, it can be a person (a friend or acquaintance), a place (a bar, a beach, an empty house), or a thing (a car, a video, a book or magazine). Occasions of sin vary in intensity and, for that reason, they are classified as either proximate or remote. *A proximate occasion of sin* is one which may easily lead a person into sin. If it would tempt any normal person under normal circumstances (a sexually explicit book or film), the occasion is known as an absolute proximate occasion. If on the other hand it would tempt only certain people (a bar for a drunkard), then it is called a relative proximate occasion of sin.

A *remote occasion of sin* is one which is less likely to lead a person into sin. Here again we find a division into absolute and relative. An absolutely remote occasion of sin is that in which sin for the average person is possible but not probable, as for example reading the daily newspaper. A relatively remote occasion of sin is that in which a particular individual or class of persons does not as a rule sin, although it might constitute a serious occasion for average people. Consider the effect a book on human reproduction might have on a physician, and the effect the same book might have on a young teenager.

Another category of occasions of sin is based on their necessity. It is not necessary for the average person to watch pornographic films, but it may be necessary for a law enforcement official to view them as part of an effort to prosecute those who produce and distribute them. It is not possible for the husband or wife of a nagging or difficult spouse to live with that person for years without getting angry or annoyed, but this is a necessary occasion of sin that cannot be avoided.

We are morally obliged to stay away from sin. *Therefore, we are obliged to avoid all voluntary proximate occasions of sin, unless we have a sufficient reason for not doing so.* If we find ourselves in a necessary proximate occasion, we must take steps to render that occasion remote, to minimize its effect on us. In the case of the difficult husband or wife, the other spouse must take steps to avoid getting angry, such as exercising strong will power, praying for God's help, and avoiding as much as possible those things that start the nagging and lead to loss of temper.

We have a slight obligation to avoid remote occasions of sin unless we have a sufficient reason for not doing so. Since there is only a slight danger of sinning, and the temptation can easily be resisted, one would be morally allowed to continue reading the daily newspaper, even though it carries ever more explicit stories and ever more suggestive advertising. Actually, we could not really go through life avoiding all remote occasions of sin. Any attempt to do so would throw us into a state of scrupulosity, which is an unhealthy condition.

The Natural Law

The natural law is that rule of right and wrong which our own reason can perceive. The natural law exists in us as an integral part of our nature. Just as the laws of chemical reaction are inherent in the nature of the elements, so certain moral laws are inherent in our nature. A young child who has done wrong – lied, used bad words, or disobeyed – feels uncomfortable, ashamed, or even frightened, even though he or she may never have heard of the moral law. A person in a remote corner of the world may never have heard of the Commandments, but there is a law written on our hearts that says murder, adultery, and stealing are wrong. No society where such actions are tolerated could long survive.

The Second Vatican Council spoke of the fundamental law of right and wrong imbedded in human nature in these words:

"In the depths of his conscience, man detects a law which he does not impose upon himself, but which holds him to obedience. Always summoning him to love good and avoid evil, the voice of conscience can when necessary speak to his heart more specifically: do this, shun that. For man has in his heart a law written by God. To obey it is the very dignity of man; according to it he will be judged" (*Pastoral Constitution on the Church in the Modern World,* n. 16).

In its *Instruction on Respect for Human Life in Its Origin and on the Dignity of Procreation,* the Sacred Congregation for the Doctrine of the Faith explained the natural law this way:

"The natural moral law expresses and lays down the purposes, rights, and duties which are based upon the bodily and spiritual nature of the human person. Therefore, this law cannot be thought of as simply a set of norms on the biological level; rather it must be defined as the rational order whereby man is called by the Creator to direct and regulate his life and actions and in particular to make use of his own body" (*Donum Vitae,* n. 3).

If everyone, for example, could take the property of others at any time without fault or blame, no one would have any security in their property. All effort, all planning would be useless. Initiative would be stifled. The entire world would be in chaos. In other words, reason indicates that stealing is wrong. Therefore, we say that stealing is against the natural law. The same can be said for murder, adultery, rape, lying, and a host of other evils.

Natural law is universal because, being based on human nature, it binds all of us. It is also unchangeable because human nature is the same at all times and in all places. Therefore, all acts contrary to the natural law, such as murder, theft, and direct abortion, will always remain immoral. No human authority, not even the Supreme Court, has the power to negate, alter, or abrogate any precept of the natural law.

The ten Commandments are basically a summary of the principles of the natural law. The only exception is the third commandment, "Remember to keep holy the Sabbath day," which is a divine positive law. Men and women, even before the ten Commandments were given to Moses on Mount Sinai, could tell right from wrong. But people drifted away from God, and he saw the need for putting the natural law before them in a striking way, making it stronger and more explicit.

Every possible infraction of the natural law is not listed in the ten Commandments. The Commandments indicate the fundamentals of the natural law. For example, "Honor your father and your mother" embraces by implication all the obligations superiors and inferiors have in their relations with each other. The Commandments are not an exhaustive list of every possible infringement of the natural law. They are a series of essential guideposts indicating the proper line of conduct in various important departments of life.

The Sermon on the Mount

The fullest and most complete formulation of the moral law is contained in the Sermon on the Mount, which Pope John Paul called "the *magna charta* of Gospel morality" (*Veritatis Splendor*, n. 15). The Holy Father said that "Jesus brings God's commandments to fulfillment, particularly the commandment of love of neighbor, by interiorizing their demands and by bringing out their fullest meaning."

He said that "Jesus shows that the commandments must not be understood as a minimum limit not to be gone beyond, but rather as a path involving a moral and spiritual journey towards perfection, at the heart of which is love (cf. Col. 3:14). Thus the commandment 'You shall not murder' becomes a call to an attentive love which protects and promotes the life of one's neighbor. The precept prohibiting adultery becomes an invitation to a pure way of looking at others, capable of respecting the spousal meaning of the body" (n. 15).

In the course of human history, we find practically no argument over the validity of the ten Commandments. They are so obviously expressive of the law of our nature that few have been so foolish and unreasonable as to suggest that they have nothing to do with correct human behavior.

The natural law is not meant to interfere with our liberty, but to guide us in the proper use of that liberty. A traffic light is placed at a busy intersection not to hinder drivers and pedestrians but to keep them from harm. They are free to ignore the light, but in doing so they endanger themselves. Similarly, we cannot ignore the law of nature without doing harm to ourselves and others. The ten Commandments are God's directions on how human beings can avoid harm to themselves and attain true happiness both in this life and in the life to come.

Positive Law

A positive law is a precept imposed by one in authority. In some instances this authority is God, as in the ceremonial laws of the Old Testament or the necessity of Baptism stated in the New Testament. When God is the author of a positive law, it is called "divine positive law." In other instances the authority is human, as in the case of taxes and the formalities of a will in civil law, or the obligations imposed by Church authority, such as the requirement to attend Mass on Sundays and holy days, to observe the laws of fast and abstinence, or to abide by the marriage laws of the Church. This sort of law is called "human law." Having been made by human authority, positive laws can be changed or revoked by that same authority.

What Is Conscience?

Conscience is a practical judgment concerning the moral goodness or evil of some course of action. Conscience is not a separate faculty, a special little voice within us, whispering suggestions regarding our conduct. "It is a judgment which applies to a concrete situation the rational conviction that one must love and do good and avoid evil" (*Veritatis Splendor*, n. 59). St. Bonaventure teaches that "conscience is like God's herald and messenger; it does not command things on its own authority, but commands them as coming from God's authority, like a herald when he proclaims the edict of the king. This is why conscience has binding force."

Since it is an operation of the human intellect, conscience is subject to the shortcomings of our intellect. In addition, the operation of conscience implies knowledge, reflection, and freedom. These factors can vary with each person and explain why different judgments may be made by different individuals concerning the morality of the same act. For instance, one who bases moral decisions on the advice columns in the newspaper will reach different conclusions from one who makes the teachings of the Church an essential part of the equation.

A true conscience is one which indicates correctly the goodness or badness of moral conduct. An erroneous conscience is one which falsely indicates that a good action is evil, or an evil action is good. Since conscience is nothing more than the operation of the intellect, it is apparent that conscience may be in error. This error of conscience may at times exist because of some fault on the part of the individual, say, a failure to search out the correct information; or there may be an erroneous conscience that is not the fault of the individual, say, one who honestly thought that he or she was doing the right thing, or at least something that was not seriously wrong.

If a person performs an act that is in itself a slight sin, while his judgment (conscience) tells him it is a serious sin, he has committed a serious sin. A boy who thinks it is a serious sin to steal a small amount of money, and yet deliberately does so anyway, is guilty of a serious sin. If a person commits what is objectively a serious sin, truly thinking it is not serious, that person is guilty of only a slight offense. A young girl, thinking that it was not seriously wrong to strike her mother, would be guilty of only a slight sin because her conscience was in error.

A certain conscience is one which dictates a course of action in clear terms without fear of error. A doubtful conscience is one which leaves a person undecided as to the proper course of action. Conscience may err on the side of *laxity*. Those with a lax conscience sometimes become persuaded that great sins are permissible (consider the number of people today who favor abortion). They find excuses for grave misconduct, often beginning by rationalizing minor faults and gradually dulling their conscience until it is incapable of giving them proper moral direction. Rarer than laxity of conscience, but a problem for some people nevertheless, is *scrupulosity*. This is when a person sees evil where there is none. Scrupulosity in this sense is nothing to be admired; it is a tremendous drag on the soul and is as much to be avoided as laxity.

When our conscience is honestly and correctly formed, we are obliged to follow it in any circumstances. Once we are convinced that we have an obligation to do or to avoid a certain action, we are duty bound to act upon our convictions. In the words of the Second Vatican Council:

"In all his activity a man is bound to follow his conscience faithfully, in order that he may come to God, for whom he was created. It follows that he is not to be forced to act in a manner contrary to his conscience. Nor, on the other hand, is he to be restrained from acting in accordance with his conscience, especially in matters religious" (*Declaration on Religious Freedom*, n. 3).

An individual must always act in accordance with a certain conscience. This is true even if the certain conscience is false. If one's conscience points out a particular action as definitely bad, even though objectively the act might be good, the act must be avoided. Conversely, if a person's conscience points out an act as good and to be done, even though objectively the act is evil, that individual must perform the act. On the other hand, *no one is allowed to act with a doubtful conscience.*

How to Form a Correct Conscience

Here are some principles for formation of a correct conscience (cf. *Catechism of the Catholic Church*, nn. 1776-1802):

1. *There must be a readiness on the part of the person to seek and accept instruction and advice.* It is most important, of course, to know the teaching of the Church on the matter being considered. The Second Vatican Council put it this way:

"In the formation of their consciences, the Christian faithful ought carefully to attend to the sacred and certain doctrine of the

Church. The Church is, by the will of Christ, the teacher of the truth. It is her duty to give utterance to, and authoritatively to teach, that Truth which is Christ himself, and also to declare and confirm by her authority those principles of the moral order which have their origin in human nature itself" (*Declaration on Religious Freedom*, n. 14).

Pope John Paul II emphasized this same point in his "World Day of Peace Message" on December 8, 1990: "To claim that one has a right to act according to conscience, but without at the same time acknowledging the duty to conform one's conscience to the truth and to the law which God himself has written on our hearts, in the end means nothing more than imposing one's limited personal opinion."

2. *If one is in doubt whether there is a law forbidding a particular action, or whether his action would be in these particular circumstances forbidden by the law, he should obtain advice from the most authoritative source available.*

3. *If a person is in doubt concerning the lawfulness of an action, she may follow an opinion that is well-founded.* This will usually mean an opinion from another person who is truly qualified to give advice. But it could at times be the reasoned conclusion of the person herself if she is truly an authority in the field. For example, a doctor may judge it morally proper to perform a particular emergency operation on the basis of her training, even though she does not have time to consult a specialist in medical ethics.

4. *The more serious the obligation, or the more serious the basis of the law in question, the more effort must be made to resolve the doubt and the more certainty one must have.* The natural law takes precedence over the divine positive law, and the divine positive law takes precedence over a human law. The greatest certainty is demanded concerning the validity of Baptism (since it involves eternal salvation) as opposed to a doubt whether one has a sufficient reason to act contrary to the law of the Church.

5. *If some individual or group teaches something contrary to what the Church teaches, one's conscience must be formed on the basis of the official Church teaching,* i.e., what is taught by the Pope and those bishops in communion with him, rather than the opinion of one or more theologians.

Conscience is the umpire that "calls the play" in the game of morality, and the decision of conscience is final. There is no appeal to a higher authority above a conscience that is sincerely and properly formed. But beware of self-delusion, especially in these days when all kinds of evils are being justified under the banner of following your conscience. We are bound to take all reasonable steps to inform ourselves adequately in matters of morality and sin, and to listen sincerely to competent authority. Otherwise we cannot say that we have properly formed our conscience.

In their 1976 pastoral letter on the moral life (*To Live in Christ Jesus*), the U.S. Catholic Bishops offered this important statement about conscience:

"We must have a rightly informed conscience and follow it. But our judgments are human and can be mistaken; we may be blinded by the power of sin in our lives or misled by the strength of our desires. 'Beloved, do not trust every spirit, but put the spirits to a test to see if they belong to God' (1 Jn. 4:1). Clearly, then, we must do everything in our power to see to it that our judgments of conscience are informed and in accord with the moral order of which God is creator. Common sense requires that conscientious people be open and humble, ready to learn from the experience and insight of others, willing to acknowledge prejudices and even change their judgments in light of better instruction."

Sin and Its Consequences

When we deliberately violate our conscience, we commit a sin. **A sin is any willful thought, word, deed, or omission contrary to the law of God.** It is not only an offense against God, but also an offense against the Church. Recalling the words of Vatican II, Pope John Paul II said in 1992 that "sin's essential nature is that of an offense against God. This is an important fact which includes the perverse act of the creature who knowingly and freely opposes the will of his Creator and Lord, violating the law of good and freely submitting to the yoke of evil."

He said that "we must say that it is also an act which offends the divine charity in that it is an infraction against the law of friendship and covenant which God has established for his people and every person in the blood of Christ. Therefore, it is an act of infidelity and, in practice, a rejection of his love" (*Penance in the Church*).

The Holy Father went on to remind us that "sin is also a wound inflicted upon the Church. In fact, every sin harms the holiness of the ecclesial community. Since all the faithful are in solidarity in the Christian community, there can never be a sin which does not have an effect on the whole community. If it is true that the good done by one person is a benefit and help to all the others, unfortunately it is equally true that the evil committed by one obstructs the perfection to which all are tending." He said that "reconciliation with God is also reconciliation with the Church, and in a certain sense with all of creation, whose harmony is violated by sin."

There are two kinds of actual sin – mortal sin and venial sin. **"Mortal sin is sin whose object is grave matter and which is also committed with full knowledge and deliberate consent"** (*Veritatis Splendor*, n. 70). It is a sin which breaks our relationship with God, such as abortion, apostasy, blasphemy, murder, adultery, fornication, rape, sodomy, racism, or stealing a large amount of money (cf. Matthew 15:19; Romans 1:18-30; 1 Corinthians 6:9-10; *Veritatis Splendor*, nn. 80, 81, 100; and the *Catechism of the Catholic Church*, nn. 1852-1853).

In order to commit a mortal sin, three conditions are necessary: (1) Whatever is done must be of a *serious* nature. (2) We must *realize* that it is serious. (3) We must give the *full consent* of our will to the sin, i.e., deliberately commit the offense. All three conditions must be present simultaneously for a mortal sin to have been committed. If one of them is missing – the matter was trivial, there was not sufficient reflection before we did it, or we did not engage in the thought, word, deed, or act of omission on purpose – then there is no mortal sin.

There is a tendency today to play down the possibility of mortal sin, to suggest that only a fundamental and complete break with God constitutes mortal sin. This is not the official teaching of the Church. The Church teaches that "mortal sin exists also when a person knowingly and willingly, for whatever reason, chooses something gravely disordered. In fact, such a choice already includes contempt for the divine law, a rejection of God's love for humanity and the whole of creation: the person turns away from God and loses charity. Thus the fundamental orientation can be radically changed by individual acts" (Pope John Paul II, *Reconciliation and Penance*, n. 17).

While mortal sin is a grave offense that separates us from God and puts our eternal salvation in jeopardy, **venial sin is a slight offense against God**. But it still weakens our relationship with the Creator, and weakens our resistance to mortal sin. Quoting from St. Thomas Aquinas on the distinction between the two types of actual sin, Pope John Paul said that "when, 'through sin, the soul commits a disorder that reaches the point of turning away from its ultimate end – God – to which it is bound by charity, then the sin is mortal; on the other hand, whenever the disorder does not reach the point of a turning away from God, the sin is venial.' For this reason venial sin does not deprive the sinner of sanctifying grace, friendship with God, charity, and therefore eternal happiness, whereas just such a deprivation is precisely the consequence of mortal sin" (*Reconciliation and Penance*, n. 17).

This same distinction can be found in Scripture too: "Anyone who sees his brother sinning, if the sin is not deadly, should petition God, and thus life will be given to the sinner. This is only for those whose sin is not deadly. There is such a thing as a deadly sin; I do not say that one should pray about that. True, all wrongdoing is sin, but not all sin is deadly" (1 John 5:16-17).

Since the sacrament of Penance/Reconciliation can restore life to one who is sorry for having committed a mortal sin, the deadly sin to which John is referring in this case is probably apostasy or final impenitence, where an individual has stubbornly rejected God's mercy and forgiveness right up to the end.

The Mercy of God

While there may be people among us who seem to live with no fear of the judgment of Almighty God, surely no one but a fool can look back on past sins and not feel the slightest anxiety as death approaches. If we honestly take stock of our sins, including those secret sins that are known to God alone, and at the same time contemplate the *justice* of God, we can be filled with anxiety. Such fear, such apprehension, is good for us, especially if it deters us from further transgressions against the love and law of God. As the Bible says, "the fear of the Lord is the beginning of knowledge" (Proverbs 1:7).

It is not well, however, to live always in fear and apprehension. God is not only infinitely just, he is also infinitely merciful. If we are to see God as he truly is, we must consider both his justice and his mercy. If we combine our fear of his justice with our confidence in his mercy, we will live a balanced spiritual life. Pope Paul VI reminded us of the charity and tolerance of Christ: "Having come not to judge the world but to save it, he was uncompromisingly stern towards sin, but patient and rich in mercy toward sinners" *(Humanae Vitae,* n. 29).

It is the teaching of the Church that a person who dies in unrepented mortal sin will go to everlasting punishment, and a healthy fear of such a terrible outcome is a good thing. While we should avoid sin primarily out of love for God, it is true that fear of eternal separation from God in hell can also be a powerful deterrent to sin. Nevertheless, we must keep in mind that between sin and its punishment comes the mercy of God.

As Jesus told us, God is like the good shepherd who leaves the ninety-nine faithful sheep to go search for the one that is lost: "And when he finds it, he puts it on his shoulders in jubilation. Once arrived home, he invites friends and neighbors in and says to them, 'Rejoice with me because I have found my lost sheep.' I tell you, there will likewise be more joy in heaven over one repentant sinner than over ninety-nine righteous people who have no need to repent" (Luke 15:3-7).

In the Old Testament, God says, "Though your sins be like scarlet, they may become white as snow; though they be crimson red, they may become white as wool" (Isaiah 1:18). God is like a fisherman who tries every sort of device to entice fish into his net, and is more pleased to catch big fish than small ones. Let us never forget that souls are in hell not because they have committed sins, but because they have not *repented* of the sins they committed.

Another shining example of the mercy of God occurred when Jesus was dining at the house of Simon the Pharisee and a woman of low reputation entered the dining hall uninvited during the meal. This poor sinner went straight to the feet of Jesus, fell to her knees, and cried. Her tears fell on our Lord's feet, and she wiped them dry with her hair. She also kissed his feet and anointed them with a precious ointment she had brought with her.

Simon and his friends were shocked that Christ would allow such a woman to touch him. But Jesus explained that "her many sins are forgiven because of her great love. Little is forgiven the one whose love is small." He then told the woman, "Your sins are forgiven. Your faith has been your salvation. Now go in peace" (Luke 7:36-50).

What a beautiful thing is the mercy of God! It is tender, it is loving, it is prompt, it is generous. And that mercy is ready to be poured out at all times. How are we to open the floodgates of the mercy of God? As the repentant woman did long ago: by seeking forgiveness at the feet of Christ, by taking full advantage of the sacrament of forgiveness, which we call Penance or Reconciliation, given to us by our Lord himself on that first Easter Sunday night (John 20:22-23).

Chapter 3

The Strange Gods of Today

The first commandment summons man to believe in God, to hope in him, and to love him above all else. – *Catechism of the Catholic Church*, n. 2134

Is God really being served today? Or is the first commandment being widely ignored by Christians and non-Christians alike? "I, the Lord, am your God. You shall not have other gods besides me." Many people, when asked how that commandment can be violated, would promptly reply, "The first commandment forbids us to worship idols." But what about the millions who give little or no thought to their *positive obligation* to worship God, and who just drift through life with no religious practice? Those who say that they believe in God, but who live as if God did not exist?

Or what about those who belong to some religion, but only practice it when they feel like it? What about the superstitious people who put their trust and faith in some object or arrangement of planetary bodies instead of putting their faith in God? What about the Christian who picks and chooses his or her beliefs and moral principles, casting aside those teachings of Christ that are difficult to keep? Are not all of these people running their lives contrary to the spirit of the first commandment, which says that we should always put God first?

Christ's Reminder to the World

At the beginning of Christ's last three years on earth, he had set aside time for forty days of prayer and fasting, in union with his heavenly Father, before beginning the mission that would end with his death and resurrection in Jerusalem. He spent that time in a lonely mountainous region, not far from Jericho, on what is known today as the Hill of Temptation. It was there that Satan confronted the hungry and weakened Jesus and three times tried to tempt our Lord to abandon his mission.

After being twice frustrated, Satan appealed to the instinct of pride and the desire for worldly gain – a pitfall for many in our own time. He showed Christ all the kingdoms of the world, with their glory and riches, and said: "All these will I bestow on you if you prostrate yourself in homage before me" (Matthew 4:9). But Jesus, in both a rebuke to the devil and a stark reminder to the world today, replied: "Away with you, Satan! Scripture has it: 'You shall do homage to the Lord, your God; him alone shall you adore' " (Matthew 4:10).

Christ said no more, but in those few words are summed up the essence of Christianity in contrast to the spirit of paganism and secularism. That standard of Christ is violated by the avaricious person who neglects God while spending time accumulating money, by the lustful person who ignores God while pursuing sexual pleasure, by the power-crazed person who rejects God while seeking control over the lives of others.

In each of the Commandments there is both a positive and a negative aspect. "I, the Lord, am your God. You shall not have other gods besides me" reminds us of certain things that we must do, as well as pointing out certain things that we are forbidden to do. We are obliged by the first commandment to offer to God the worship due to him alone, through acts of faith, hope, and charity and through adoration and prayer. By faith we give assent to all that God has revealed to the world; by hope we trust in the goodness of God to help us; by charity we love God first of all, and then all others because that is his wish.

The Virtue of Faith

There are three main things involved in our obligation to practice the virtue of faith. First, we must take the proper steps to find out what God has revealed, what truths he has made known to the world. Second, once we have come to know these truths, we must give assent to them. Third, we must profess and defend our faith staunchly and openly when necessary. This obligation was clearly stated by Christ himself: "Go into the whole world and proclaim the good news to all creation. The man who believes in it and accepts baptism will be saved; the man who refuses to believe in it will be condemned" (Mark 16:15-16). We ought therefore to value the gift of faith, to guard it with the greatest care, and to ask God to strengthen it.

Faith is a gift – a gift that can be cultivated but, if neglected, can also be lost. A person may strengthen the foundation of faith by frequently expressing belief in God's revealed truths, not just taking them for granted, and by building up knowledge of religion in every way possible. Faith is built up by living a good life, and is torn down by breaking God's laws. You cannot separate faith (what we must believe) from morals (what we must do); if the one is neglected, the other invariably will suffer. Many a person's loss of faith had its beginning in moral lapses.

Faith is the acceptance of supernatural truths on the authority of God himself, who would never deceive us. Or in the words of Pope John Paul: "Faith is a lived knowledge of Christ, a living remembrance of his commandments, and a truth to be lived out" (*Veritatis Splendor*, n. 88). Even when we do not understand these truths fully (the Trinity, for example), we accept them on the word of God, who is Supreme Truth. We must learn to see the hand of God in our lives. Christ meant us to do more with the truths revealed to us than merely to accept them. He wants them to influence our lives for the better and in that way bring us eventually to eternal happiness in heaven.

Having the gift of faith does not mean that we will understand all the teachings of our religion. Our role is one of children in relation to our heavenly Father – to accept and believe even if we do not completely comprehend. Faith is the acceptance of God as our Teacher, and we can't have a better teacher than him. The truths he wants us to believe and put into practice are found in the Bible and in the Church founded by Christ. The reward for a life of faith is to enjoy everlasting happiness with the Giver of that faith (cf. *Catechism of the Catholic Church*, nn. 1814-1816),

Sins Against Faith

We must not only worship God, but we must worship him in

the way he wants. If God established a Church to carry on his work in the world, we must look for that Church today, and when we find it, follow its directions. A Catholic who has come to the conclusion that the Catholic Church is the true Church of Christ is no longer free to pick and choose from that Church's teachings, or to separate from that Church, or to become a member of any other Church. In the words of Vatican II:

"Whosoever, therefore, knowing that the Catholic Church was made necessary by God through Jesus Christ, would refuse to enter her or to remain in her could not be saved" (*Dogmatic Constitution on the Church*, n. 14).

Apostasy is the rejection of the entire Christian Faith by a baptized person. It usually implies the sin of pride, the refusal to submit to the authority entrusted to the Church by Christ.

Heresy is the obstinate denial of one or more truths of divine revelation. It is sinful to refuse to accept the truths that God has revealed to us. It is sinful to believe some truths and to reject others that have been made known to us through the Bible or the Catholic Church. It is sinful to be a "cafeteria Catholic," i.e, a person who picks and chooses which doctrines to accept and which ones to ignore or reject. We must accept and put into practice all the teachings of the Church, not just those we agree with or find easy to follow.

To those who claim that they can dissent from the teachings of the Catholic Church, and still remain Catholics in good standing, Pope John Paul II, in a visit to Los Angeles on September 16, 1987, issued this warning: "This is a grave error that challenges the teaching office of the bishops of the United States and elsewhere .... Dissent from Church doctrine remains what it is, dissent; as such it may not be proposed or received on an equal footing with the Church's authentic teaching."

The Holy Father repeated this warning in *Veritatis Splendor*:

"Dissent, in the form of carefully orchestrated protests and polemics carried on in the media, is opposed to ecclesial communion and to a correct understanding of the hierarchical constitution of the People of God. Opposition to the teaching of the Church's pastors cannot be seen as a legitimate expression either of Christian freedom or of the diversity of the Spirit's gifts. When this happens, the Church's pastors have the duty to act in conformity with their apostolic mission, insisting that the right of the faithful to receive Catholic doctrine in its purity and integrity must always be respected" (n. 113).

Indifferentism is the false theory that it really doesn't matter what religion you belong to, that all religions are equally good and true. This theory has been refuted in Chapter 3 of *Catholicism and Reason*, a companion volume in this series, and we can summarize that chapter briefly.

We believe that Christ is God and that he established the one true Church ("on this rock I will build my Church" – Matthew 16:18), not many churches. If Christ established one Church to carry on his work in the world, isn't it illogical to say that all churches are equally good and true, that Christ does not care what church you belong to? Furthermore, different churches teach different and even contradictory things – Jesus is God, Jesus is not God; hell exists, hell does not exist; abortion, divorce, and homosexual behavior are wrong, abortion, divorce, and homosexual behavior are right.

Obviously, all of these beliefs cannot be true, anymore than one can say that two plus two equals four and two plus two equals five. Though good and sincere people may think some of these things are true, that cannot change the objective fact that some of these beliefs are false and contrary to what the Church founded by Christ teaches. Therefore, it does make a difference which church a person chooses to join.

Since all religions are not equally true, a Catholic is not allowed to become a member of a non-Catholic denomination and remain a Catholic in good standing. To do so would be a denial in practice of the principles a Catholic professes to hold. Christ was not indifferent. He was willing to die rather than change or compromise one part of his teachings. He laid down a program for the world on how to get to heaven and chose death on the cross rather than change one of the truths he taught. The first Christians followed this example of their Founder, even to the point of dying for Christ and his teachings instead of rejecting the blueprint given by the Son of God.

To suggest that it matters little what we believe or how we live, or that one church's beliefs are just as reliable as those of any other church, is to say that our Lord didn't know what he was doing and doesn't care very much what we believe or do. But we know from Scripture that Christ had very definite doctrines and standards and that he defended them with his life. One cannot be indifferent to religious truths and still claim to be a loyal follower of Jesus.

All around us there are radio and television waves in the air, sent out by thousands of transmitters and satellites. We cannot see them, we cannot hear them, but we know that without them we would not be able to hear voices and see images carried from the far corners of the earth. Without a radio or TV we can hear and see nothing. Faith is like a radio or TV in that it is the receiving apparatus of our soul.

Christ is constantly speaking to the world, and it is through faith that we receive the divine communications. At the turn of a switch we can silence our radio or TV, and when the batteries or electronic parts grow weak, our reception is weakened. Faith, too, can be weakened or lost, silencing the voice of Christ in our soul, unless we keep this gift in good working order by remaining in close contact with the Divine Communicator.

The Virtue of Hope

By hope we mean a trust and confidence in God that he will provide us with all the means we need to attain our salvation. History is filled with people who kept hoping for the best in spite of what seemed to be overwhelming odds. Abraham Lincoln, for instance, saw business ventures fail twice, and he ran unsuccessfully for political office nine times before he was elected President in 1860. Helen Keller, blind and deaf from infancy, never lost hope and eventually graduated from Radcliffe College with honors and went on to become a famous author and lecturer.

There is an old axiom that virtue steers a middle course, and so it is with hope, which stands in the middle between despair and presumption. **Despair is doubt that God will save us.** It is deliberately failing in our duty to trust God to do his part in our journey toward salvation. **Presumption is expecting that God will save us without us doing our part.** It is the foolish attitude that God will take care of us no matter what we do and no matter if we expend any effort or not.

Standing between these two extremes is hope, which expresses complete confidence in God, come what may, and which realizes that God will not save us without our cooperation. The working out of our salvation is a partnership between God and ourselves. We can be sure that he will not fail in his part of the bargain, so we had better make sure to keep our part too because on this virtue depends much of our happiness here and all of our happiness hereafter (cf. *Catechism of the Catholic Church*, nn. 1817-1821).

Fr. James Keller, M.M., the founder of the Christophers, once gave this summary of hope:

> Hope looks for the good in people instead of harping on the worst.
> Hope opens doors where despair closes them.
> Hope discovers what can be done instead of grumbling about what cannot.
> Hope draws its power from a deep trust in God and the basic goodness of human nature.
> Hope "lights a candle" instead of "cursing the darkness."
> Hope regards problems, small or large, as opportunities.
> Hope cherishes no illusions, nor does it yield to cynicism.
> Hope sets big goals and is not frustrated by repeated difficulties or setbacks.
> Hope pushes ahead when it would be easy to quit.
> Hope puts up with modest gains, realizing that "the longest journey starts with one step."
> Hope accepts misunderstanding as the price for serving the greater good of others.
> Hope is a good loser because it has the divine assurance of final victory.

"Hope is a gift of the Holy Spirit," said Pope John Paul in a general audience on May 27, 1992. He added that "even in the face of the difficulties of this life and the painful experiences of misconduct and failure in human history, hope is the source of Christian optimism. Certainly the Church cannot close her eyes to the many kinds of evil in the world. Nevertheless, she knows how to rely on Christ's victorious presence and she inspires her long and patient activity with this certainty, ever mindful of what her Founder declared in his farewell speech to the Apostles:

'I have told you this so that you might have peace in me. In the world you will have trouble, but take courage. I have conquered the world' (John 16:33)."

The Virtue of Charity

Charity is a word which means love – not sentimental or emotional love, but rather a love that is measured by deeds. Love is part of our human nature. Our task is to steer this love into the proper channels. Some turn their love to sin, and so we might say that sin is love gone wrong. We can see this in some of the capital sins. Pride is a false love of self; covetousness is a false love of material possessions; lust is a false love of sexual pleasure; gluttony is a false love of eating and drinking; sloth is a false love of ease. The challenge before us is to channel our love unselfishly toward God and toward our neighbor (cf. *Catechism of the Catholic Church*, nn. 1822-1829).

In the words of Pope John Paul II at a general audience on June 3, 1992: "Charity requires a willingness to serve one's neighbor. In the Church throughout history there have always been numerous people who have dedicated themselves to this service. We can say that no religious society has ever inspired as many works of charity as the Church has: service to the sick, the disabled, service to young people in schools, to people struck by natural disasters and other misfortunes, support for all kinds of poor and needy."

Love of God can influence every action of ours and give a new meaning to all that we do. Years ago in some places there were prisoners who traveled in groups called "chain gangs" because they were bound with chains. They could be seen along highways breaking stones with sledgehammers, bending over their monotonous task from morning to night, devoid of any spark of interest, ambition, or enthusiasm.

Compare their situation with that of a sculptor standing before a huge block of marble, hammer and chisel in hand, chipping away enthusiastically from morning to night. What is the difference? It is the end or purpose which the wielder of the hammer has in view – the aimless breaking up of stones or the creation of a beautiful work of art. Our work, whatever it may be, can take on a whole new meaning when motivated by love of God. That is what we mean by cultivating a spirit of charity.

That spirit of charity can be broken by sins against the first commandment, such as hatred for God or for other people. And this is true whether it involves individuals, groups of people, or even nations. "God is love, and he who abides in love abides in God, and God in him," said St. John .... "We for our part love because he first loved us. If anyone says, 'My love is fixed on God,' yet hates his brother, he is a liar. One who has no love for the brother he has seen cannot love the God he has not seen. The commandment we have from him is this: whoever loves God must also love his brother" (1 John 4:16-20).

Sins Against the First Commandment

Sacrilege is the contemptuous treatment or abuse of any sacred person, place, or thing. For example, a person who violently strikes a priest or religious person, or who commits a sin of unchastity with someone who has taken a vow of chastity, is guilty of the sin of sacrilege. A person who vandalizes a church, who murders someone or commits some act of debauchery in a church is guilty of sacrilege. A person who steals sacred vessels or uses them for sinful purposes, who receives the Eucharist while in the state of grave sin, or who shows grave irreverence for the Eucharist is guilty of sacrilege.

St. Paul criticized the irreverent treatment of the Eucharist by the Corinthians, saying that "whoever eats the bread or drinks the cup of the Lord unworthily sins against the body and blood of the Lord" (1 Corinthians 11:27). He said that the sickness and death of many Corinthians was a punishment for their irreverence to "the body and blood of the Lord" (1 Corinthians 11:30).

Superstition is giving to a creature or an object some power that belongs to God alone. The superstitious person who believes in good-luck charms, dreams, fortune tellers, horoscopes, etc., is engaging in false worship and failing to give to God the worship that is due to him alone. There is nothing new about superstition. It originated in paganism and was widespread hundreds of years before Christ came to earth. Its sinfulness was mentioned by God himself early in the Old Testament: "Let there not be found among you ... a fortune teller, soothsayer, charmer, diviner, or caster of spells, nor one who consults ghosts and spirits or seeks oracles from the dead. Anyone who does such things is an abomination to the Lord" (Deuteronomy 18:10-12).

Many Catholics have been caught up in New Age activities and have attended workshops on the enneagram, which purports to fit people into nine personality types: perfectionist, caregiver, achiever, artist, observer, team player, optimist, competitor, and peacemaker. But there are scientific, social, and theological problems with the enneagram, as well as many non-Christian elements in the enneagram system. For some good reasons to stay away from those promoting the enneagram and other New Age activities, see Fr. Mitch Pacwa's book *Catholics and the New Age*, particularly chapter five ("Occult Roots of the Enneagram").

Spiritualism is the belief that we can contact deceased relatives and others in the spirit world. It is the belief that the dead can communicate with the living through such means as tapping, seances, and trances. This process is usually manifested through a person called a medium. The origins of modern spiritualism date from 1848 when the parents of two young girls, Margaret and Kate Fox, heard strange tapping noises coming from the childrens' room in their isolated farmhouse in Hydesville, New York. John Fox and his wife were frightened by the noises and told neighbors about these "rappings."

Someone suggested that perhaps a dead person was trying to communicate with the living. The neighbors asked the "spirit" if a murder had ever been committed in the house, and they suggested a coded answer, one rap for "yes" and two raps for "no." When an affirmative answer came back, the spectators were certain that some dead person was trying to contact the living. Within weeks, an enterprising older sister organized what she called "The Society of Spiritualists," and Hydesville became famous overnight. The news traveled rapidly, both in the United States and Europe, a number of people saw an easy way to make some fast money, and spiritualism began to spread. Soon Margaret and Kate were touring the major cities in America as celebrities.

The story of their lives is amazing, but the most interesting part of the story is the end. After almost forty years as a spiritualist medium, Margaret converted to the Catholic Church. She also gave a signed confession to the press in 1888, revealing that the first rappings were produced by an apple on a string, and the later rappings by an ability the girls had to snap their toes the way ordinary people snap their fingers. Her confession of fraud may at first have seemed funny, but it was in reality a heart-rending document, filled with remorse and sorrow.

Harry Houdini, the brilliant magician, spent the best part of his life investigating and exposing false mediums. What angered Houdini was that these tricksters, sometimes under the cloak of religion, deceived not just anybody but particularly innocent old people who had been plunged into grief by the death of a loved one. Even very intelligent persons can be deceived because they are vulnerable and *want* to believe that they are communicating with someone they loved in life. Deceiving someone in this fashion is truly a terrible sin.

There is no doubt that God could allow the dead to contact the living. In some very extraordinary cases, he apparently has done so, such as when the Blessed Mother has appeared in places like Lourdes and Fatima. But the Blessed Virgin is no ordinary person, and has a very particular role to play in the salvation of souls. On the other hand, there is no evidence that God permits such things to happen in the ordinary course of events, even for serious reasons. In fact, there is clear evidence against it.

Recall the time that Jesus told the story about the rich man and the beggar named Lazarus, who died and was carried to the "bosom of Abraham." The rich man eventually wound up in hell and asked Abraham to send Lazarus "to my father's house where I have five brothers. Let him be a warning to them so that they may not end in this place of torment. Abraham answered, 'They have Moses and the prophets. Let them hear them'" (Luke 16:27-29).

If God would not allow spiritualism for the purpose of saving souls, it is hardly likely that he would allow it for lesser reasons. Also, if spiritualism is a good and practical idea, why did Christ not recommend it? It is apparent that physical contact between the dead and the living is not part of God's ordinary plan. He wants us to wait until we join our loved ones in the next world. So the next time you hear of such contacts with the spirit world, know that they are not the work of God, but are either the work of the devil or of some trickster relying on fraud, hypnosis, or self-deception. This is the reason why Catholics should never take part in seances or other manifestations of the false religion of spiritualism.

Obsession by the Devil

Human beings have two principal parts, body and soul. In our body we resemble the animals; in our soul we resemble God and the angels. We are here on earth temporarily. We are on trial to see whether we will be worthy of God's reward or his punishment. Our trial comes from three directions: the world, the flesh, and the devil. We are tempted by the world, that is, by the persons and things around us; we are tempted by the flesh, that is, by our own passions and concupiscence; and we are tempted by the devil, that is, by those fallen angels of God who themselves failed their own trial and became sworn enemies of God. By far the most clever, the most baffling, the most mysterious temptations we face come from Satan, the prince of devils, and from his disciples.

The devils hate God, but they can do nothing directly against him. So they vent their fury against us, who are made in the image and likeness of God. The great theologian, St. Thomas Aquinas, once said that "the knowledge that a creature of earth will occupy his place in heaven causes a devil more pain than the flames of hell." Thus, the devil tries to lead us away from God and heaven. It was the devil who led Adam and Eve to sin; it was the devil who led Judas to betray our Lord; and it is the devil who tries to lead us into sin.

At an audience on November 15, 1972, Pope Paul VI delivered a strong warning about the devil and his evil influence in the world. The Holy Father described the devil as "a living, spiritual being, perverted and perverting. A terrible reality. Mysterious and frightening .... He is the enemy number one, the tempter par excellence. So we know that this dark and disturbing spirit really exists, and that he still acts with treacherous cunning; he is the secret enemy that sows errors and misfortunes in human history."

The devil's great object is to ruin the Church, which he knows is the means of destroying his power on earth. We must therefore follow the advice of St. Peter and "stay sober and alert. Your opponent the devil is prowling like a roaring lion looking for someone to devour. Resist him, solid in your faith, realizing that the brotherhood of believers is undergoing the same sufferings throughout the world" (1 Peter 5:8-9).

It is important to remember that the devil can do no real harm to anyone who keeps the Commandments of God and avoids sin. He can give us a bad time, but he cannot force us to lose our soul. He cannot drag us into hell. Only we can turn ourselves against God. Only we can put ourselves in hell. A dog that is tied up can do no harm to those who stay beyond the reach of his chain. The devil is like a chained dog. He can work on our memory and imagination, but he has no power over our will. He can *persuade* us to do evil, but he cannot *compel* us to do so. God sometimes allows saintly people to be tested severely by the devil, with terrible temptations against purity and sometimes even physical assaults.

The devil assailed Job in the Old Testament, he tempted Jesus in the New Testament, and he went after such saints as Catherine of Siena, who told him, "Do what you can; if God allows it, I accept it"; Anthony the Hermit, who remarked sarcastically, "You must be very feeble since you have brought such a crowd of devils to tempt me"; and John Vianney, the holy parish priest of Ars in France, who was plagued off and on for thirty years with noises and voices and physical attacks. When a priest friend said, "You must get very frightened," the Cure of Ars responded, "I'm used to it."

Possession by the Devil

A stranger phenomenon than *obsession* by the devil is *possession* by this evil spirit. In the time of our Lord, many people were possessed by demons, and Jesus expelled them on many occasions. In our own times, there are increasing reports of diabolical possession, not only in pagan lands where there are virtually no prayers, blessings, holy water, Masses, or sacraments, but even in our own country where the unwise and the unwitting join in rituals to worship the devil.

Sometimes persons, even children, become possessed by a demon or a group of demons for no apparent reason. Once the Church has determined through diligent investigation that the person is truly possessed by an evil spirit, and is not merely the victim of some nervous disorder or mental condition, it will send in an exorcist, a holy priest who is highly trained in dealing with the diabolical forces of evil.

Some signs of possession are speaking unknown languages, revealing hidden things about others, exhibiting strength all out of proportion to one's age and circumstances, shouting filthy and blasphemous remarks, and reacting feverishly and furiously to the prayers of exorcism and holy objects. The official ritual of the Church gives instructions and prayers to deal with diabolical possession, but the procedure can only be carried out by one who is an expert on possession and who has the degree of holiness necessary to engage in a long and difficult struggle with the powers of hell.

While there is reason to watch out for the devil, there is no reason for great fear. "The power of Satan is not infinite," Pope John Paul II said on August 20, 1986. "He is only a creature – powerful, in that he is a pure spirit, but nevertheless always a creature ... subordinated to the will and dominion of God."

The ordinary means provided by the Church to ward off the devil include the Sign of the Cross, holy water, the use of relics, and earnest prayer. There is the Our Father ("deliver us from evil") and the prayer to St. Michael, which goes like this: "St. Michael, the archangel, defend us in the battle. Be our protection against the malice and snares of the devil. Rebuke him, O God, we humbly beseech you, and do you, O prince of the heavenly hosts, by the divine power, drive into hell Satan and the other evil spirits who wander through the world seeking the ruin of souls. Amen."

Saints and Relics

Some people have a very confused understanding of the role of saints and relics in the Catholic Church. Some people believe that Catholics adore or worship these people and objects, which of course is not true. Catholics adore and worship only God; they venerate or pay special honor to the Blessed Mother and the saints, and to objects or places associated with them, because of the special role they have played in the life of the Church. Since we single out certain persons in the history of our country who have led outstanding lives by erecting statues in their honor and naming streets and institutions after them, is there any reason why we cannot honor in similar fashion those persons, places, and things that bring us closer to God?

The saints are those in heaven who came through the difficulties of this life victoriously and are now chosen friends of God. They were men and women, boys and girls, who came from all walks of life and all occupations and circumstances. Their one common trait was their extraordinary love for God and others while dealing with the same problems, failures, and frustrations that we face. That is why they can serve as role models for us as we try to imitate their lives of holiness and fidelity to God. That is why we take their names at Baptism and Confirmation, so that we will have friends in heaven to look after us, to intercede with God for us, to add their prayers to ours before the throne of God. Because we are all members of the Communion of Saints – the blessed in heaven, the souls in purgatory, and those of us on earth struggling to get to heaven – we have an interest in the well-being of each other and we pray and care for each other.

"The Church," said Pope John Paul, "proposes the example of numerous saints who bore witness to and defended moral truth even to the point of enduring martyrdom, or who preferred death to a single mortal sin. In raising them to the honor of the altar, the Church canonized their witness and declared the truth of their judgment, according to which the love of God entails the obligation to respect his commandments, even in the most dire of circumstances, and the refusal to betray those commandments, even for the sake of saving one's own life" (*Veritatis Splendor*, n. 91).

Of all the angels and saints, the highest and closest to God is the Blessed Virgin Mary, the Mother of God, the woman chosen from all women who ever lived to bring the Savior into the world. If we were seeking a favor from a person, we could go directly to the person; or we could ask a mutual friend to put in a good word for us; or better still, if we knew the person's mother, we might ask her to speak on our behalf. We never hesitate to take this approach in our daily lives, so why hesitate in approaching God in the same way. The saints are close friends of Jesus, and Mary is his mother. Wouldn't we be foolish not to ask their help from time to time? Their intercession can be very valuable for us.

That is why we have statues and pictures of Jesus, Mary, and the saints. It is not that Catholics worship these objects; rather they remind us of the persons whom they represent, and they help us keep our mind on God while we are praying. We would never think of accusing a person who carries a picture of a loved one in a wallet, or someone who has a photograph of deceased parents on the mantelpiece, of worshiping those pictures. They serve to keep those whom we love uppermost in our mind. So, too, statues and pictures of our Lord and the saints assist us in our devotion, focus our attention on what we are doing, and help to prevent distractions.

Relics are the remains of the bodies of the saints or objects connected with them or with Christ while they were here on earth. Some people consider it odd to venerate the relics of saints, but there is nothing odd about a practice that goes back many thousands of years. Followers of Buddha, Confucius, and Mohammed have long venerated the relics of those ancient religious leaders, and people in our own time treasure the belongings of loved family members and friends, as well as of historical figures. There are memorabilia of American Presidents stored in museums across the country, and every year thousands of Americans visit the "Tomb of the Unknown Soldier" at the national cemetery in Arlington, Virginia, to pay tribute to an anonymous soldier who gave his life in World War I. It is this same spirit that motivates Catholics to venerate the relics of holy people.

At times God chooses to work a miracle through the relic of a saint, and that has been true from the time of the Apostles to our own day. For those who think that there is no justification in Scripture for the Catholic veneration of relics, we call their attention to the Acts of the Apostles. Speaking of the "extraordinary miracles" that God worked through the hands of Paul, St. Luke writes: "When handkerchiefs or cloths which had touched his skin were applied to the sick, their diseases were cured and evil spirits departed from them" (Acts 19:12). The Catholic Church does not declare that relics have any magical healing power, only that they are sometimes the occasion for God to bring about a miraculous cure.

God Alone Must Be Adored

While we venerate and honor the angels and saints, we reserve the special worship of adoration for God alone. We owe God both interior and exterior worship since we are composed of body and soul. The cultivation of faith, hope, and charity, adoration and prayer is an expression of our interior worship of God. But we can also worship him in an external, visible way – by prayerfully taking part in the Holy Sacrifice of the Mass; by touching our right knee to the floor (genuflecting) when we enter or leave church, or when we pass in front of the tabernacle where Jesus is present in the Blessed Sacrament; by stopping in church to make a visit during the day; by making the Stations of the Cross; by kneeling when we pray; and in many other ways.

Prayer is a particularly valuable way of worshiping God. It is our way of communicating with God, of engaging in a conversation with him, of opening up our minds and hearts to him. Prayer has four purposes: (1) *adoration*, whereby we praise and glorify God and acknowledge our dependence on him; (2) *thanksgiving*, whereby we thank God for his many wonderful gifts to us; (3) *petition*, whereby we ask God for pardon and forgiveness of sins, as well as for help with our needs and the needs of other people; and (4) *reparation*, whereby we offer up our prayers, works, joys, and sufferings for our own sins and the sins of the world.

Jesus was a man of prayer. He persevered in prayer, especially before all the important events in his life. How can we be any different? We must pray constantly, humbly, confidently, and realistically, realizing that although God answers every prayer, he sometimes does not give us what we want, perhaps because what we seek may not be in our best interests or in the interests of the person for whom we are praying. Yet we should never cease praying, but should follow the example of the Lord in the Garden of Gethsemani, where "he prayed with all the greater intensity," while saying to his Father, "not my will but yours be done" (Luke 22:42-44).

The importance of prayer was emphasized by Pope John Paul II at a general audience on September 9, 1992: "Prayer particularly belongs to the Christian religion, in which it occupies a central position. Jesus urges us to 'pray always without becoming weary' (Luke 18:1). Christians know that for them prayer is as essential as breathing, and once they have tasted the sweetness of intimate conversation with God, they do not hesitate to immerse themselves in it with trusting abandonment."

The fourth and final section of the *Catechism of the Catholic Church* (nn. 2558-2865) is devoted to "Christian Prayer," and there are many valuable insights to be gained by a careful reading of that part of the *Catechism*.

In the face of the rising tide of paganism and secularism threatening us today, evidenced by the increasing number of people who live as if God did not exist, we need to renew our relationship with God, to recognize him as our greatest benefactor, the One who created us and keeps us in existence every moment of every day, and to make him known and loved by all with whom we live and work and socialize. We must remind them of their duty to "do homage to the Lord your God; him alone shall you adore" (Matthew 4:10).

Chapter 4

The Name That Was Never Spoken

The second commandment *prescribes respect for the Lord's name*.
Like the first commandment, it belongs to the virtue of religion
and more particularly it governs our use of speech in sacred matters. – *Catechism of the Catholic Church*, n. 2142

Two authors of this book have spent some in the Holy Land. One
visit took us to the large level area where once stood the great
Jewish temple of old, built by the Jews at God's express command.
As we entered the temple area, we saw a sign bearing this inscription in Hebrew, English, and French: "How awesome is this place;
this is none but the house of G-d and this is gate of heaven." In
each language, the full spelling of the name of God was omitted.
This omission is an indication of the tremendous reverence devout
Jews have for God's name. From the most ancient times, long before the coming of Christ, they would never utter God's holy name,
but passed over it in silence. They took seriously the second commandment given by God to Moses on Mount Sinai.

What's in a Name?

Many years ago, Shakespeare had a character in one of his plays
ask this question: "What's in a name?" The answer implied was,

"Nothing." And of course it is true that what you *are* is more important than your name. Nevertheless, God has indicated that names are important.

In the Bible, we come across situations where God chose certain people to do some special work and gave them a new name which had special significance. For example, when God chose *Abram* to be the father of his chosen people, he changed his name to *Abraham*, which means "the father of a multitude of people." And when Jesus chose *Simon* to be the leader of his Church, he changed his name to *Peter*, which means "rock," since Peter was to be the rock or foundation upon which the Church of Christ would be built.

The name of God himself also has special meaning. When God appeared in the burning bush and Moses asked him what his name was, God responded with the Hebrew word "Yahweh," which means "I am who am." It is the most perfect name that can be given to God because it describes as nearly as possible in human language the nature of God. The name Yahweh has always been held so sacred by the orthodox Jew that it is never pronounced. That great name is sacred to Christians, too.

But to Christians the most beloved name of all is the name of Jesus Christ. The name "Jesus" simply means "Savior," and is therefore a very descriptive title. The name "Christ" means "the anointed one." Our Lord is the anointed Son of God, the Messiah, the chosen One who is our great High Priest. St. Paul tells us that there is no other name by which we are saved but by the name of Jesus. He also says that "at Jesus' name every knee must bend in the heavens, on the earth, and under the earth, and every tongue proclaim to the glory of God the Father: JESUS CHRIST IS LORD!" (Philippians 2:10-11).

Another beloved name is the beautiful name of Mary, a name that has been invoked lovingly by Christians all through the centuries. It is not certain how the name of Mary originated, but possibly it dates back to the time of Moses when the Jews were living in Egypt. The Hebrew name for Mary is "Miriam," which was the name of Moses' sister. It seems to have come from two Egyptian words: "Meri" – a Egyptian prefix meaning "beloved of," and "Yam" – meaning "God." Yam was the Egyptian way of saying "Yahweh," the name that God gave himself when he was speaking to Moses. Therefore, Meri-Yam or Miriam or Mary means "beloved of God," a most appropriate title for our Blessed Lady, who was indeed beloved of God.

Misusing Holy Names

Some years ago there was an admirable Catholic man who was the principal of a Catholic school in New Jersey. We will call him "Joe." He was a giant of a man, with a deep and powerful voice, and his love for God was just as deep and powerful as his voice. One day while he was having his hair cut in a barber shop, another customer came in and sat in the chair next to Joe. The stranger started to use some bad language, but Joe did not say anything. Then the man began to abuse the name of Jesus. Joe jumped out of his chair, the white cloth flying in the air, shook his fist in the face of the offender, and roared, "That's my friend you're talking about."

How many times in the course of a day do we hear people, even those who call themselves followers of Christ, using the holy name of Jesus to express anger, surprise, disgust, or some other emotion? Is there any other figure in history whose name is used in this fashion? Have you ever heard anyone shout "Julius Caesar!" at another person? Or show disgust by saying, "Oh, for Napoleon's sake!"? Why is it only the name of the holiest Person who ever lived, the One who gave up his life for us on the cross, that is so badly misused?

Isaac Newton, the famous astronomer, had a deep regard for the name of God. He used to take his hat off and bow whenever the name was spoken in his presence. St. Ignatius, the Bishop of Antioch, also had a great reverence for the name of Jesus. There is a story that Ignatius was the little child whom Jesus one day placed in front of a group of listeners and said, "Unless you change and become like little children, you will not enter the kingdom of God" (Matthew 18:3). Whether the story is true or not, it is true that Ignatius, shortly before his death, said that the name of Jesus "shall never leave my lips or be effaced from my heart." Such a praiseworthy attitude is a far cry from the abuse of that holy name that is so widespread today.

We know of a woman who makes the Sign of the Cross every time she hears someone misuse the name of Jesus. She doesn't say a word to the offender, but simply blesses herself. People are puzzled at first, she says, but then they realize what she is trying to tell them. After a few weeks, the woman said, the number of times her friends and co-workers abused the name of Jesus had decreased dramatically. All because of her simple gesture. Perhaps more of us who love the name of Jesus should do the same.

Sins Against the Second Commandment

There are a number of ways in which we can violate the second commandment. **Blasphemy is insulting or abusive language that expresses contempt for God either directly or indirectly through his saints, through those consecrated to his service, or through holy objects.** An angry person who shouts that God is unjust or does not care about people may not be guilty of a mortal sin of blasphemy because he does not realize what he is saying. But the person who knowingly and deliberately attacks God, who denies God's goodness and love, who ridicules religious people or sacred things, is indeed guilty of blasphemy. That sin reaches the peak of infidelity since it totally repudiates our obligation to love and honor God. It cuts off our friendship with God and, if unforgiven, places us on the road to hell.

Cursing means to call down evil on someone or something. It is a grave offense against justice and charity since it is asking God to damn someone for all eternity. Many of those who say, "God damn you," do not even understand what they are saying, but they are still guilty of a venial sin for showing disrespect for God. If, however, a person truly was asking God to damn someone to hell, then it would be a mortal sin. And those who misuse God's name in this way can also be guilty of scandal.

Profanity means using the name of God or Jesus to express anger, fear, surprise, impatience, or without proper reverence. This careless or flippant misuse of God's or Jesus' name is ordinarily a venial sin, but the true believer in God, and the sincere follower of Jesus, will avoid this kind of carelessness since it undermines respect for the Father and the Son.

The power of the name of Jesus was illustrated by Peter and John who, shortly after the ascension of our Lord into heaven, passed by a man who had been crippled from birth as they walked into the temple in Jerusalem. The man kept himself alive by begging alms from temple visitors, and he asked the two Apostles for some money. Peter looked at him and said: "I have neither silver nor gold, but what I have I give you! In the name of Jesus Christ, the Nazorean, walk!" (Acts 3:6). Cured through the invocation of the name of Christ, the man jumped up, began to walk around, and "went into the temple with them – walking, jumping about, and praising God."

How can we then take that wonderful and powerful name, or the name of God, and drag it down to the depths of sinful conversation? How can so-called good Catholics use expressions like "O my God" or "For Christ's sake" as a regular part of their vocabulary? If you find yourself doing that, then it is time to correct this sinful habit.

Oaths and Vows

The second commandment also involves calling upon the name of God to attest to the truth of what we are saying or to the sincerity of a promise we are making. **An oath is the calling upon God to witness to the truth of a statement.** Thus, a person in court swears on a Bible to "tell the truth, the whole truth, and nothing but the truth. So help me, God." Or a person accepting public office promises on the Bible to perform faithfully the duties of that office.

It would be better if we did not have to take oaths, if we could, as Jesus urged, "say 'Yes' when you mean 'Yes' and 'No' when you mean 'No' " (Matthew 5:37). But even Jesus himself swore an oath during his trial before Caiaphas when the high priest ordered him "to tell us under oath before the living God whether you are the Messiah, the Son of God" (Matthew 26:63-64). Our Lord answered in the affirmative and was sentenced to death for blasphemy, for claiming to be God.

Oaths are religious acts that are necessary because of original sin. We do not always speak the truth, and others cannot always trust what we say. "Men swear by someone greater than themselves," said St. Paul. "An oath gives firmness to a promise and puts an end to all argument" (Hebrews 6:16). But no one should take an oath without serious thought and good reason because we are asking God to put his official seal on what we say. St. Augustine compared an oath to a medicine that is taken only on the advice of a competent physician and for a sound reason.

Perjury is taking a false oath or lying under oath. It shows great dishonor to God because it calls upon the Creator, the Author of all truth, to witness to a lie. It is not only a grave sin, but it is also a crime because it undermines our legal system and destroys the trust people have in each other. Think of the chaos in a society where one could not believe even those who swear to God that they are telling the truth.

A vow is a free and deliberate promise made to God to do something that is good and pleasing to God. Vows are usually associated with members of religious orders, who promise to live lives devoted to poverty, chastity, and obedience. By these vows, individuals dedicate themselves to God in order to serve him better. They consecrate to God not only all they do, but their whole being. No person should make a vow without serious thought and reliable advice. For as Scripture reminds us: "You had better not make a vow than make it and not fulfill it" (Ecclesiastes 5:4).

Watch Your Language!

George Washington, one of the greatest generals in American history, had a great respect for the name of God. In 1776, he issued this order against profanity among his soldiers:

"The General is sorry to be informed that the foolish and wicked practice of profane cursing and swearing, a vice hitherto little known in our American Army, is growing into fashion. He hopes that the officers will, by example as well as influence, endeavor to check it and that both they and the men will reflect that we can little hope of the blessing of heaven on our army if we insult it by our impiety and folly. Added to this, it is a vice so mean and low without any temptation that every man of sense and character detests and despises it."

What would George Washington think of the profanity and vulgarity that is so pervasive today not only in the military but even in society at large? It is contrary to the law of God and to common decency, as well as a poor way of expressing ourselves, but it has become commonplace even on prime-time television. "The mouth speaks whatever fills the mind," said Jesus (Matthew 12:34). And James called the tongue "a restless evil, full of deadly poison. We use it to say, 'Praised be the Lord and Father'; then we use it to curse men, though they are made in the likeness of God. Blessing and curse come out of the same mouth. This ought not to be, my brothers!" (James 3:8-10).

It is up to followers of Christ to cultivate by example and effort the honor due to God and his name by the faculty of speech that he has given to us. Blaspheming, cursing, taking God's name in vain, swearing false oaths, betraying vows, or engaging in profanity and vulgarity are sinful habits that degrade ourselves and those around us. In our day, we need to strive for the high ideals suggested by James the Apostle and George Washington and to restore adherence to the second commandment of God.

One way of doing this would be to recite every day the pledge that was made famous by the Holy Name Society:

Blessed be God.

Blessed be his Holy Name.

Blessed be Jesus Christ, true God and true man.

Blessed be the Name of Jesus.

I believe, O Jesus, that you are the Christ, the Son of the living God.

I proclaim my love for the Vicar of Christ on earth.

I believe all the sacred truths which the holy Catholic Church believes and teaches.

I promise to give good example by the regular practice of my Faith.

In honor of his Divine Name, I pledge myself against perjury, blasphemy, profanity, and obscene speech.

I pledge my loyalty to the flag of my country and to the God-given principles of freedom, justice, and happiness for which it stands.

I pledge my support to all lawful authority, both civil and religious.

I pledge my active support and prayers for the fulfillment of human rights for all my brothers and sisters in Christ, regardless of race, creed, or color.

I dedicate myself to the honor of the Sacred Name of Jesus Christ and beg that he will keep me faithful to these pledges until death.

Chapter 5

A Time to Worship, A Time to Rest

The Sunday celebration of the Lord's Day and his Eucharist is at the heart of the Church's life. – *Catechism of the Catholic Church*, n. 2177

We read in the Bible that "there is an appointed time for everything, and a time for every affair under the heavens" (Ecclesiastes 3:1). That means that there is a time to work and a time to rest. God indicates the importance of keeping work and rest in proper proportion by allowing us to work six days and requiring us to rest on the seventh: "Six days you may labor and do all your work, but the seventh day is the Sabbath of the Lord, your God. No work may be done then either by you, or your son or daughter, or your male or female slave, or your beast, or by the alien who lives with you. In six days the Lord made the heavens and the earth, the sea and all that is in them; but on the seventh day he rested. That is why the Lord has blessed the Sabbath day and made it holy" (Exodus 20:9-11).

God went even further and commanded us to dedicate this special day of rest to him by keeping it holy. The Sabbath day is to be set apart for rest and prayer lest we give God second place in our lives, or last place, or no place at all. Modern life is filled with anxieties, with pressures, with fast-paced living. Our daily routine and our daily worries can give rise to a twofold danger: We tend to forget the God who made us, and we become too caught up in a whirlwind of work and other activities. To protect against this twofold temptation, our Creator gave us a twofold law: Every seventh day is to be a day of prayer and worship, and every seventh day is to be a day of rest and relaxation.

Since God created us and keeps us in existence every moment of our lives, all our time belongs not to us but to him. Through the third commandment he asks that we merely set aside one day out of seven and dedicate it to him. We are made up of body as well as soul, so we must worship God with our whole being, with some outward adoration. Society itself must honor God, and that is why there should be a public observance of the Lord's Day.

From Saturday to Sunday

Before the time of Christ, the Jews were commanded to set aside the seventh day of the week – Saturday – as their Sabbath. This obligation of giving one day a week to God did not cease with the beginning of Christianity. But the day was changed from the seventh day of the week to the first day – Sunday – by the Apostles, who had been given the authority to make such decisions by our Lord himself (Matthew 16:19).

Under the guidance of the Holy Spirit, the Apostles changed the Sabbath from Saturday to Sunday because that was the day on which Jesus rose from the dead. It was also the day on which the Apostles received the power to forgive sins (John 20:23), and on which the Holy Spirit descended upon the Apostles on the first Pentecost (Acts 2:1-4), the birthday of the Church, and gave them the wisdom, understanding, and courage to go out and spread the Gospel message.

Prior to the Second Vatican Council (1962-1965), Catholics worshiped God at Mass only on Sunday. But the Council instituted an important change by permitting the celebration of a vigil or anticipated Mass on Saturday evening that would fulfill the Sunday obligation. This was particularly helpful for those who had a legitimate reason to work on Sunday, such as doctors, nurses, police officers, firefighters, and those in public transportation. So Catholics may now participate in the Holy Sacrifice of the Mass either on Sunday or on Saturday, the ancient Sabbath day of the Jewish people. This is a wonderful symbol of our spiritual closeness to the Jews, from whom came Jesus and his mother.

What We Must Do on Sunday

The Lord's Day is a day to attend Mass. Because the Mass is the greatest of all prayers, and the central act of worship for a Catholic, we should never neglect to participate in the Eucharist on the Lord's Day. The Catholic Bishops of the United States have said that "it is both a privilege and a serious duty of the individual Catholic, as well as the Catholic faith community, to assemble on Sunday in order to recall the Lord Jesus and his acts, hear the Word of God, and offer the sacrifice of his Body and Blood in the Eucharistic celebration" (*Sharing the Light of Faith*, n. 105a). This obligation is so serious, in fact, that to miss Mass deliberately without a good reason (illness, great difficulty in getting to church, or such urgent duties as caring for a sick person) is a grave sin.

The origin, purpose, and nature of the Mass was well summarized by the Second Vatican Council in its *Constitution on the Sacred Liturgy*:

"At the Last Supper, on the night when he was betrayed, our Savior instituted the Eucharistic Sacrifice of his Body and Blood. He did this in order to perpetuate the sacrifice of the cross throughout the centuries until he should come again, and so to entrust to his beloved spouse, the Church, a memorial of his death and resurrection: a sacrament of love, a sign of unity, a bond of charity, a paschal banquet in which Christ is consumed, the mind is filled with grace, and a pledge of future glory is given to us" (n. 47).

Because of what the Mass is, the Council went on to say, "Christ's faithful, when present at this mystery of faith, should not be there as strangers or silent spectators. On the contrary, through a proper appreciation of the rites and prayers they should participate knowingly, devoutly, and actively. They should be instructed by God's word and be refreshed at the table of the Lord's Body; they should give thanks to God; by offering the Immaculate Victim, not only through the hands of the priest, but also with him, they should learn to offer themselves too. Through Christ the Mediator, they should be drawn day by day into ever closer union with God and with each other, so that finally God may be all in all" (n. 48).

The Mass was instituted by Christ himself at the Last Supper, and he told the Apostles, and us, to "do this as a remembrance of me" (Luke 22:19). That is why we should attend Mass, not because it is an obligation, but because Jesus, on the night before he died for our sins, asked us to do this in memory of him. God gives us 168 hours every week. Is it asking too much for us to give him back one of those hours by participating enthusiastically in this Eucharistic banquet that is celebrated throughout the world from the rising of the sun to its setting (Malachi 1:11)?

We were not able to be at the Last Supper on Holy Thursday or at Calvary on Good Friday, but by going to Mass in our parish church every week, or even every day, we can be part of those great events in salvation history as they are renewed and perpetuated in our own time. Christ filled a great reservoir of grace by his death on the cross, but we cannot benefit from that limitless reservoir unless we tap into it by faithful attendance at Mass. How spiritually foolish are those who are so blinded by the things of the world that they turn their backs on this great gift that God has given to us!

The Lord's Day is a day of prayer. On Sunday we should be particularly careful about our prayer life. It is a good day to check up on how conscientious we are about praying. Do we say morning prayers on rising each day, including the Morning Offering in which we offer up our prayers, works, joys, and sufferings of that day? Do we ask God's blessing before meals, and express our thanks to him after meals? Do we pray during the day, on the way to and from school or work or recreation? When we read or hear of someone's death, or of some catastrophe, do we think to ask God to be merciful or helpful to those involved? Do we carry a rosary with us, and do we pray the rosary? Do we say our night prayers , perhaps reviewing what we might have done wrong that day and asking God for forgiveness by reciting an Act of Contrition?

The Lord's Day is a day to think about our relationship with God. We should spend some time reading from the Bible, the word of God (you will be surprised how fascinating it is, and how helpful it can be in your life). There are other books about God and Jesus, about the saints and the things of God, that make interesting and enjoyable reading. Why not turn the television off for a while and do some spiritual reading that will help you to know God better and to love him more so that you will be able to serve him better?

The Lord's Day is a day to spend time with our families and to be considerate of others. In our busy society today, with people constantly running to jobs, meetings, sports events, and other activities, the times when families are all together at the same time have unfortunately become increasingly rare. So it's important to set aside time, perhaps at Sunday dinner, for family members to share each other's company and to talk over what's going on in their lives.

It's also important, if you have done your Sunday praying or reading, or even if you don't intend to do either, at least to have the decency to refrain from creating so much noise and disturbance that nobody else can say a prayer or think about God. Keep the radio or TV or cassette player at a reasonable volume so that other members of the family, or neighbors half a block away, can enjoy some peace and quiet on Sunday. If it's absolutely essential that you mow the lawn on Sunday, don't start the mower at eight o'clock in the morning and wake up everyone on your street. Be considerate of others.

The Lord's Day is a day of rest. On Sunday, we are supposed to get away from the work or school routine of the week and enjoy some rest and relaxation before we start all over again on Monday morning. This is mentally, physically, and spiritually healthy. We must remember that Sunday is not our day, but the Lord's Day. To ignore God and to use the day only for our own benefit is to neglect one of our most serious obligations. It is to put ourselves first instead of God.

In the words of Pope John XXIII: "It is the right of God, and within his power, to order that man put aside a day each week for proper and due worship of the divinity. He should direct his mind to heavenly things, setting aside daily business. He should explore the depths of his conscience in order to know how necessary and inviolable are his relations with God" (*Mater et Magistra*, n. 249).

What We Must Not Do on Sunday

In that same encyclical letter, which was issued in 1961, Pope John noted, "with deep sorrow," the many people who even then were treating Sunday as just another day of the week. What would the Holy Father think today if he could witness the almost total disregard of the Lord's command to observe Sunday as a day of prayer and rest? As a result of this disregard for the third commandment, Sundays have become the most profitable business days of the week for merchants. What those who like to go to shopping malls on Sunday overlook, however, is that the employees of those malls are being exploited and do not have the opportunity for rest and recreation themselves.

The third commandment and Church law forbid work on Sunday that is unnecessary and that requires strenuous physical activity. The only exceptions are those tasks that are necessary for the good of society or the well-being of the family. Airlines and other public transportation must continue to operate, public safety must be maintained, power plants and communications facilities must be in good working order. And certain household tasks are permitted provided that they are necessary.

This would include cooking and laundry, mowing the lawn or working in the garden, and even painting the house if that is the only chance a homeowner has to spruce up a house because the increasing demands of supporting a family in difficult economic times often require people to work more than one job and to be employed on nights and weekends.

Persons who would like to rest on Sunday, but who must work to support their families or to maintain their jobs, are excused from the Sabbath rest. If your employer insists that you work on Sunday, you don't have much choice if you want to hold on to your job. Of course, if Catholics and others would stop patronizing department stores and other workplaces on Sunday, merchants would stay closed on the Lord's Day.

Jesus said that "the Sabbath was made for man, not man for the Sabbath" (Mark 2:27). Thus, the Church takes the middle road of not outlawing all activity and pleasure on Sunday and, on the other hand, of not considering Sunday as only a day of rest and enjoyment. Recreation is never forbidden on Sunday. The day is meant as a day of rest as well as a day of worship. The Catholic Church never supported laws that outlawed all amusements and pleasures, but the Church reminds all Catholics that the first purpose of Sunday is the worship of God. Anything else, including legitimate recreation, belongs in second place. To reverse the order of things by making Sunday primarily for recreation and pleasure, to the neglect of the duties of prayer and worship, would be sinful.

Recall that God said to the Jews, "Six days there are for doing work, but the seventh day is the Sabbath of complete rest, sacred to the Lord. Anyone who does work on the Sabbath day shall be put to death" (Exodus 31:15). Obviously observance of the Sabbath is no trifling matter. God is our Creator and our Benefactor *par excellence*. He could demand much more of us than he does. Let us at least give him wholeheartedly the honor he requires – attendance at Mass and rest from work on Sunday – and also do whatever is in our power to encourage and convince others to do the same.

Chapter 6

By What Authority?

According to the fourth commandment, God has willed that, after him, we should honor our parents and those whom he has vested with authority for our good. – *Catechism of the Catholic Church*, n. 2248

Arago, the famous astronomer, was one day delivering a lecture at a college in France on the laws of nature that govern the universe. "Next week a solar eclipse is to take place," he said at the end of the lecture. "The moon will enter into conjunction with the sun and intercept its rays. On that day, at that hour, at that minute, at that second, three stars will obey not our prediction but God's law. Only men will not obey ...."

Arago's point was that the inanimate world acts invariably according to the laws of nature and nature's God, while the animal world acts according to laws of instinct. But in creating human beings, God left us free to obey or disobey his laws. What the fourth commandment does is to remind us of our duty of respect and obedience toward those who exercise authority in the name of God – parents, church authorities, secular or civil authorities; in other words, anyone who holds a rightful place as a superior.

"Honor your father and your mother" is an expression of one of the most fundamental obligations we have under the heading of respect and obedience. It serves as a reminder that we have that obligation not only to parents but to all other representatives of God on earth. And in God's plan, there are not only obligations on the part of inferiors toward superiors but also corresponding duties on the part of those in authority.

Every person owes his or her parents obedience in all that is not sinful. Parents for their part have the duty to give good example to their children, and are obliged to provide for the spiritual and temporal welfare of those entrusted to their care. All of us must respect and obey ecclesiastical superiors, and bishops, priests, and others holding authority in the Church must conscientiously guide, govern, and instruct those under them and guard their spiritual welfare.

The citizens of a country have obligations toward civil and temporal authorities, duties that come under the virtue of patriotism. Civil authorities must rule justly and see that the natural rights of all are protected. So, too, employees must fulfill their obligations reasonably, conscientiously, and justly, while their employers must pay a just wage, provide suitable working conditions, and treat employees as brothers and sisters who have God as their common Father.

The Example of Christ

Everyone on earth has a duty of obedience to some authority, and those in rightful authority must remember that they hold that authority not in their own name but in the name of God, the Source of all authority. "You would have no power over me whatever," Jesus told Pontius Pilate, the Roman ruler in Jerusalem, "unless it were given you from above" (John 19:11). Christ was completely obedient to his Father, even to the point of dying on the cross. In the Garden of Gethsemani, our Lord resisted the temptation to abandon his mission of salvation, saying to his Father, "Not my will but yours be done" (Luke 22:42).

That marvelous spirit of obedience was first evidenced when Jesus, at the age of twelve, had traveled with Mary and Joseph to Jerusalem for the feast of the Passover. At the end of the feast, they began their homeward journey thinking that Jesus was with a group of friends. But realizing after a day's travel that the Boy was not with friends, Mary and Joseph returned hastily to the city to search for him. On the third day, they found him "in the temple sitting in the midst of the teachers, listening to them and asking them questions" (Luke 2:46).

When his parents saw him, Mary asked: "Son, why have you done this to us? You see that your father and I have been searching for you in sorrow." Jesus replied: "Did you not know I had to be in my Father's house" (Luke 2:48-49)? These words indicate that our Lord, even at the age of twelve, was conscious of his future mission. But we know nothing more of his life from that time until he began his public ministry at the age of thirty, except that "he went down with them then, and came to Nazareth, and was obedient to them" (Luke 2:51).

What better role model could we have? Here was the Creator of heaven and earth paying the obligation of obedience to two of his creatures. We would like to know more about the hidden life of Jesus during those thirty years, but we are left with what is perhaps the most important bit of information about those years: He was obedient to them.

If a person were to die young or with little or no apparent accomplishment in life, that life would still be of great value if we could say of that person, he or she was obedient – obedient to the will of God and to all lawful superiors. This value might not be recognized by the world, but it would be pleasing to Christ, who gave the world a singular example of obedience. And his obedience did not cease at Nazareth, but continued until the end of his life, when in fulfillment of the will of his Father, he obediently accepted even death, death on a cross!

Children and Parents

Of all those whom we are obliged to love, respect, and obey, our parents certainly hold first place. After God, we owe to them our existence and our upbringing. They are God's representatives and our greatest benefactors. Every person ought to love his or her parents, promote their happiness, and help them in their material and spiritual needs. We ought to respect our parents, to speak and act toward them in a way that shows we recognize the special place they hold in God's plan. We ought to obey them cheerfully and take correction in the right spirit.

Kind feelings are not enough. Real love is measured not by word or feeling so much as by doing. Obedience means fulfilling all their wishes and commands (as long as they are not sinful). In the words of St. Paul: "Children, obey your parents in the Lord, for that is what is expected of you. 'Honor your father and your mother' is the first commandment to carry a promise with it – 'that it may go well with you, and that you may have long life on the earth' " (Ephesians 6:1-3).

On the other hand, parents have the duty of providing for their children, caring for them, helping them to get to heaven. Of course, if a parent orders a child to do something sinful, such as stealing, selling drugs, or engaging in sexual acts, there is no requirement to obey on the child's part. This time it is St. Peter who gives us our guidance: "Better for us to obey God than men!" (Acts 5:29). And when it comes to the choice of a vocation or state in life, parents have no right to determine that. This choice belongs to each individual, although parents should certainly be available for advice and counsel.

As the Second Vatican Council recalled, "parents must be acknowledged as the first and foremost educators of their children. Their role as educators is so decisive that scarcely anything can compensate for their failure in it. For it devolves on parents to create a family atmosphere so animated with love and reverence for God and men that a well-rounded personal and social development will be fostered among the children. Hence, the family is the first school of those social virtues which every society needs" (*Declaration on Christian Education*, n. 3).

In brief, parents must strive to make a house where people live into a home where people live in love (cf. *Catechism of the Catholic Church*, n. 2223).

Parents and Children

In one of his letters to Timothy, St. Paul said that "if anyone does not provide for his own relatives and especially for members of his immediate family, he has denied the faith; he is worse than an unbeliever" (1 Timothy 5:8). Though this warning was issued many centuries ago, it is just as applicable to family life today. Not a day goes by that we do not read or hear of crime among adults and young people, and one of the major factors behind this wave of crime is the breakdown of family life and the disregard of fundamental values.

In his masterful treatment of "The Role of the Christian Family in the Modern World," Pope John Paul II said that some disturbing signs of this breakdown include "serious misconceptions regarding the relationship of authority between parents and children; the concrete difficulties that the family itself experiences in the transmission of values; the growing number of divorces; the scourge of abortion; the ever more frequent recourse to sterilization; the appearance of a truly contraceptive mentality" (*Familiaris Consortio*, n. 6).

Parents and guardians of families must resume their proper

roles and raise the children entrusted to them by God in the manner in which God desires. Only when family life is strong again will there be a decrease in criminal activity in society.

What are some of the ordinary responsibilities toward children that some parents are neglecting? Well, for one thing, they are failing to give good example in their own spiritual life – no prayer, no attendance at Mass, no reception of Holy Communion, no recourse to the sacrament of Penance. How many times when we tell children in Catholic schools and parish religious education programs about the importance of weekly Mass do they respond by saying that their parents do not go to church? Some children truly want to go to Mass, but Mom or Dad can't be bothered to take them. They want their children to receive First Communion and Confirmation, but they do little to nurture the faith in their sons and daughters.

Mothers, fathers, and guardians must remember that the teaching of religion and morality begins not in school or in religious education classes, but in the home. As soon as children begin to talk and understand things, prayers should be taught to them, stories about Jesus, Mary, and the saints should be read to them, and the principles of right and wrong should be instilled in them. The mind of a young child is like a sponge; it is able to absorb a lot of information through repetition. Make sure that the information being absorbed is sound information.

This is particularly true when it comes to the matter of human sexuality. Education for chastity is absolutely essential for children, and parents must give them what Pope John Paul called "a clear and delicate sex education" (*Familiaris Consortio*, n. 37). The Holy Father said in the same document that "sex education, which is a basic right and duty of parents, must always be carried out under their attentive guidance, whether at home or in educational centers chosen and controlled by them."

He also said that "the Church is firmly opposed to an often widespread form of imparting sex information dissociated from moral principles. That would merely be an introduction to the experience of pleasure and a stimulus leading to the loss of serenity – while still in the years of innocence – by opening the way to vice." (Parents can also find sound information and advice in the Pontifical Council for the Family's important document entitled *The Truth and Meaning of Human Sexuality*.)

Those responsible for children should pray for them and with them. "Only by praying together with their children," said Pope

John Paul, "can a father and mother – exercising their royal priesthood – penetrate the innermost depths of their children's hearts and leave an impression that the future events in their lives will not be able to efface" (*Familiaris Consortio*, n. 60).

Raising children has never been an easy task, but if more time were spent praying, and less time worrying, much more good would be accomplished. Parents should put their worries in the hands of God and ask for his help with the children he has entrusted to them. They should follow the example of St. Monica, the mother of St. Augustine, who prayed for many years that her wayward son would abandon his sinful life. Her prayers were answered as Augustine not only returned to God, but went on to become a great saint.

Second, some parents are neglecting to give their children good example. Parents cannot expect children to do the right thing – to pray, to go to church, to frequent the Sacraments, to refrain from misusing the name of God and Jesus, to be fair in their dealings with others, to tell the truth, to drive safely, to use alcohol moderately when they are legally old enough to drink, to stay away from obscene reading materials and videos – unless they set a good example for their children in all of these areas. The worst thing a parent can do is to tell a child to do one thing while the parent does precisely the opposite. The obligation of good example cannot be overemphasized. Parents are called to holiness, and the example of a holy life can have a profound effect on the lives of children.

Third, parents and guardians are duty bound to find out what their boys and girls are reading and what they are watching on television, who their companions are, and what they do and where they go outside the home. The temptations put in front of young people today are truly mind-boggling, and parents who do little or nothing to prepare their sons and daughters to resist these temptations are guilty of a serious sin of omission. Those who seem to care little what happens to their children, as long as there is peace and quiet in the home, will have to answer to God for their neglect. Many children are reaching out for help, and parents and guardians must respond willingly and promptly to these cries for advice and assistance.

Parental Examination of Conscience

In addition to providing food, clothing, shelter, education, and other necessities of life for their children, parents ought to examine their consciences from time to time to see how well they are fulfilling their God-given responsibilities. Attention to these duties will affect the happiness of parents and children not only in this world, but also in the world to come. Parents and guardians might ask themselves these very practical questions:

– Have I had my children baptized within weeks after birth, or have I negligently waited for months or even years?

– Have I taught my children their prayers, encouraged them to invoke the aid of the Blessed Virgin and the saints, and said the family rosary with them?

– Have I provided for the religious instruction of my children, either in a Catholic school or in a parish religious education program, and helped them prepare for the sacraments of Penance, Holy Eucharist, and Confirmation?

– Have I ignored, or perhaps even contributed to, the sinful tendencies of my children by allowing them access to such occasions of sin as bad companions, bad magazines, bad television, and bad films?

– Have I given my children the good example of a life lived in accordance with the teachings of Jesus and his Church?

– Have I taught my children by word and deed to live by the Golden Rule: "Treat others as you would have them treat you" (Matthew 7:12)?

– Have I failed to encourage my children to follow that vocation or state in life to which they appear to have been called by God?

Roles in the Family

Any efforts to solve the problems facing society today must begin with strengthening the family, which is "the first and vital cell of society" (Vatican II, *Decree on the Apostolate of the Laity*, n. 11). And strong families are those where each member recognizes and carries out a particular role. The family is not a democracy, where decisions are arrived at by vote of the majority. Of course there should be discussion of important matters, but the ultimate authority rests with the parents. God has given them the responsibility for the well-being of the family, and they must exercise that responsibility wisely and firmly, even if sometimes a decision may not sit well with children. As time goes on, and children demonstrate maturity, reliability, honesty, and prudence, parents can relax the rules and give children more responsibility for their own life. It is all part of the process of growing up and preparing for life on our own.

Echoing the Second Vatican Council, the *Catechism of the Catholic Church* called the family "a domestic Church" (n. 2204) because that is where the Faith is first preached to the child by word and example and that is where children are encouraged in their choice of a vocation in life, particularly a religious vocation. As members of that domestic Church, said Pope John Paul, "all members of the family, each according to his or her own gift, have the grace and responsibility of building, day by day, the communion of persons, making the family 'a school of deeper humanity': this happens where there is care and love for the little ones, the sick, the aged; where there is mutual service every day; where there is a sharing of goods, of joys, and of sorrows" (*Familiaris Consortio*, n. 21).

The Holy Father went on to say that "a great spirit of sacrifice" is required to preserve and perfect family communion because "there is no family that does not know how selfishness, discord, tension, and conflict violently attack and at times mortally wound its own communion." The way to overcome the many and varied forms of division in family life, he said, is through "participation in the sacrament of Reconciliation and in the banquet of the one Body of Christ" (*Ibid.*).

The truly Christian family is a beautiful and noble thing. It is like that great redwood tree in California that has been growing for thousands of years. Towering hundreds of feet into the sky, the tree is called the "Grizzly Giant." People look like ants at its base. Around the tree there is a fence and a sign that reads: "Do not injure this noble tree." There is even a park ranger there to protect this God-given treasure.

The Christian family is also a towering institution of beauty and strength that was created by Almighty God. The fence which protects the family is love and respect and obedience, and God constantly issues this warning: "Do not injure this noble family." If parents and children work together as a team, fully understanding and faithfully living their responsibilities, then we will have the strong families we need to Christianize our society.

The Holiest Family of All

No better example of family life can be found than that of the Holy Family at Nazareth, and particularly Joseph's unquestioned and immediate obedience to the will of God. We first hear of St.

Joseph in the Gospel of Matthew, where we learn that after he and Mary were espoused, but before they lived together (the Jewish custom of the time was for a man and woman to live apart for one year after their marriage), Joseph discovered that Mary was pregnant. He was very upset and confused because he knew that he was innocent and that Mary was a woman of great purity and holiness. But God sent an angel to explain to Joseph that Mary was miraculously pregnant through the power of the Holy Spirit and the Child she was carrying was the Savior of the world promised by God. The angel told Joseph to "have no fear about taking Mary as your wife" (Matthew 1:20), and Joseph "did as the angel of the Lord had directed him and received her into his home as his wife" (Matthew 1:24).

We read in the Gospel of Luke that the Emperor Caesar Augustus had decreed that a census of the world be taken and that everyone go to his home town. "And so Joseph went from the town of Nazareth in Galilee to Judea, to David's town of Bethlehem – because he was of the house and lineage of David – to register with Mary, his espoused wife, who was with child" (Luke 2:4-5). After Jesus was born in Bethlehem, Joseph, obeying the law of Moses, "brought him up to Jerusalem so that he could be presented to the Lord" in the temple (Luke 2:22).

Mary and Joseph returned to Bethlehem, but received another message from an angel that King Herod wanted to kill Jesus. "Joseph got up and took the child and his mother and left that night for Egypt. He stayed there until the death of Herod" (Matthew 2:14-15). After Herod's death, an angel appeared again to Joseph and told him to go back to Israel. "He got up, took the child and his mother, and returned to the land of Israel. He heard, however, that Archaelus had succeeded his father Herod as king of Judea, and he was afraid to go back there. Instead, because of a warning received in a dream, Joseph went to the region of Galilee. There he settled in a town called Nazareth" (Matthew 2:21-23).

St. Joseph is the perfect example of what it means to be obedient to the will of God. His attitude was quite different from many people in our own time, who do only what they feel like doing instead of what God wants them to do. How much more peaceful would our families, and our society, be if more people would practice the virtue of obedience to God and to all lawful authority. And this means not just *doing* what is commanded, but being *ready and willing* to do what is commanded. St. Augustine calls obedience the greatest of virtues because it is the parent and source of the other virtues. Even the Son of God gave us the example of obedience by making himself subject to two human beings, Mary and Joseph.

The Holy Family at Nazareth "is therefore the prototype and example for all Christian families," said Pope John Paul. "It was unique in the world. Its life was passed in anonymity and silence in a little town in Palestine. It underwent trials of poverty, persecution, and exile. It glorified God in an incomparably exalted and pure way. And it will not fail to help Christian families – indeed, all the families in the world – to be faithful to their day-to-day duties, to bear the cares and tribulations of life, to be open and generous to the needs of others, and to fulfill with joy the plan of God in their regard" (*Familiaris Consortio*, n. 86).

Spiritual and Secular Authorities

The fourth commandment also covers obligations outside the home and family. God has set up two authorities to act in his name and as his representatives in the world: spiritual authorities who are to care for souls, and secular authorities who are to care for the peace, order, and material well-being of people. The highest spiritual authority was given by Jesus to our Holy Father, the Pope, who is Christ's vicar or chief representative on earth. Remember our Lord's words: "Whatever you declare bound on earth shall be bound in heaven; whatever you declare loosed on earth shall be loosed in heaven" (Matthew 16:19). Catholics are very fortunate to have a reliable spiritual spiritual authority to whom they can turn for counsel on religious and moral matters.

The same obligation we have to obey the Pope in spiritual matters, we also have to bishops and priests who are faithful to the teachings of the Holy Father. Disobedience, contempt, and disrespect toward them are sinful. These spiritual authorities, of course, have a serious obligation to devote their life and energies to guiding and guarding the spiritual welfare of those in their care. The duties of those on both sides were succinctly stated by St. Paul: "Obey your leaders and submit to them, for they keep watch over you as men who must render an account" (Hebrews 13:17).

As citizens of a country, we also have an obligation to show respect and obedience to lawful civil authority, whether on the national, state, or local level. We have a duty to obey just laws, not merely to avoid the penalty for breaking them, but because those in authority hold their authority from God. Recall the words of

Christ to Pilate: "You would have no power over me whatever unless it were given you from above" (John 19:11). However, if unjust commands are given, or unjust laws are passed, a follower of Christ must resist them because it is "better for us to obey God than men" (Acts 5:29).

Our duties as citizens can be summed up in the virtue of patriotism, whereby we are obliged to love our country and to defend it in a just cause. We owe reverence and respect to all lawful authority. We must share the burdens of government by paying just taxes, recalling that Jesus himself paid taxes (Matthew 17:24-27) and that our Lord told the Pharisees: "Give to Caesar what is Caesar's, but give to God what is God's" (Matthew 22:21).

We must take an active interest in our community and our country, studying the issues, voting intelligently for the best candidates for public office, regardless of their political party or affiliation, and working to make our community and country truly "one nation, under God, with liberty and justice for all."

St. Paul summarized well the obedience that we owe to those in authority:

"Let everyone obey the authorities that are over him, for there is no authority except from God, and all authority that exists is established by God. As a consequence, the man who opposes authority rebels against the ordinance of God; those who resist thus shall draw condemnation down upon themselves. Rulers cause no fear when a man does what is right but only when his conduct is evil. Do you wish to be free from the fear of authority? Do what is right and you will gain its approval, for the ruler is God's servant to work for your good. Only if you do wrong ought you to be afraid. It is not without purpose that the ruler carries the sword; he is God's servant, to inflict his avenging wrath upon the wrongdoer. You must obey, then, not only to escape punishment but also for conscience' sake" (Romans 13:1-5).

Much is expected also of those who hold public office. They must gain the proper knowledge so that they can exercise their authority in a competent and fair manner. They must have moral integrity, which means following the principles of Christ in whatever position one holds and not swaying with the tide of public opinion or acting in response to pressure groups. One cannot be privately or personally opposed to certain evils, such as abortion, and support those evils publicly without causing scandal and giving bad example. In the words of the Sacred Congregation for the Doctrine of the Faith's *Declaration on Procured Abortion*:

"A Christian can never conform to a law which is in itself immoral, and such is the case of a law which would admit in principle the licitness of abortion. Nor can a Christian take part in a propaganda campaign in favor of such a law, or vote for it. Moreover, he may not collaborate in its application" (n. 22).

"No Catholic," the U.S. Bishops have said, "can responsibly take a 'pro-choice' stand when the 'choice' in question involves the taking of innocent human life." For some sound advice on this matter, see *The Obligations of Catholics and the Rights of Unborn Children*, a pastoral letter issued by Bishop John Myers of Peoria, Illinois.

It is sinful to accept bribes or to take graft to obtain an office or to vote a certain way. Those in positions of public responsibility are obliged to rule justly, enforce law and order fairly and impartially, and in every way provide for the common good of all citizens.

The principles that should apply in the political sphere, said Pope John Paul, include "truthfulness in the relations between those governing and those governed, openness in public administration, impartiality in the service of the body politic, respect for the rights of political adversaries, safeguarding the rights of the accused against summary trials and convictions, the just and honest use of public funds, the rejection of equivocal or illicit means in order to gain, preserve, or increase power at any cost" (*Veritatis Splendor*, n. 101).

The Pontiff warned that "when these principles are not observed, the very basis of political coexistence is weakened and the life of society itself is gradually jeopardized, threatened, and doomed to decay .... As history demonstrates, a democracy without values easily turns into open or thinly disguised totalitarianism."

Being a public official has never been an easy task, and it is particularly difficult in our own time. That is why we should pray often for our leaders at all levels of government. In the words of St. Paul: "I urge that petitions, prayers, intercessions, and thanksgiving be offered for all men, especially for kings and those in authority, that we may be able to lead undisturbed and tranquil lives in perfect piety and dignity" (1 Timothy 2:1-2).

Chapter 7

Do No Person Harm

Human life, as a gift of God, is sacred and inviolable .... Society as a whole must respect, defend, and promote the dignity of every human person, at every moment and in every condition of that person's life. – *Evangelium Vitae*, n. 81

Every one of the Commandments includes much more in God's sight than the mere statement might imply at first. While each commandment gives a concise rule of morality, it also covers a wide range of human actions. The fifth commandment, for instance, simply states that "You shall not kill," but it is also a summation of our duties concerning the bodily and spiritual welfare of our neighbors and ourselves. The person who considers himself righteous because he has never killed anyone may in fact have violated the fifth commandment in other ways. Recall the words of our Lord:

"You have heard the commandment imposed on your forefathers, 'You shall not commit murder; every murderer shall be liable to judgment.' What I say to you is everyone who grows angry with his brother shall be liable to judgment; any man who uses abusive language toward his brother shall be answerable to the Sanhedrin, and if he holds him in contempt he risks the fires of Gehenna" (Matthew 5:21-22).

So the fifth commandment not only forbids taking the life of an innocent person, but it also forbids taking our own life, jeopardizing our life and health through abuse of alcohol and drugs, damaging our bodies through mutilation or sterilization, harming another's spiritual well-being through anger and hatred, and killing the life of God in another person's soul through scandal, that is, by leading a person into sin.

Each of us has received the gift of life, but we are not the masters of that life; God is. He has made us stewards or guardians of life, and he expects us to take care of this wonderful gift. But there is such a "conspiracy against life" (*Evangelium Vitae*, n. 17) today – abortion, infanticide, euthanasia, war, sterilization, racism, bigotry, anger, and hatred – that many have forgotten about the dignity of the body, which is the dwelling place of the soul.

In the administration of the Sacraments, there are ceremonies performed on the body of the recipient, such as anointings with oil and tracing the Sign of the Cross on the forehead. These are reminders of the dignity and worth of our bodies. They were made by God and, like everything made by the Creator, they are good (Genesis 1:31). Jesus put his stamp of approval on the body by taking on human form himself, and our bodies have been further sanctified by the indwelling of the Holy Spirit.

In the words of St. Paul: "You must know that your body is a temple of the Holy Spirit, who is within – the Spirit you have received from God. You are not your own. You have been purchased, and at a price! So glorify God in your body" (1 Corinthians 6:19-20).

Since our bodies are not our own, we have the obligation to take care of them by eating properly, getting enough rest and exercise, and avoiding those things that would harm our bodies or ruin our health. God will one day demand an accounting of how we used the bodies he gave us as the vehicle to help our souls along the road to heaven. Thus, we must preserve and protect our bodies so that they will be a help and not a hindrance to our eternal salvation.

For this reason, it is wrong to harm our bodies by mutilating them or by direct sterilization. Obviously, it would not be wrong to amputate a diseased arm or leg if this were necessary for the good of the entire body, but in general we are to take good care of our bodies. Therefore, it is also a grave sin for a man or woman to have themselves sterilized in order to prevent pregnancy.

Indirect sterilization, where a woman, for example, has a cancerous womb removed to save her life, is morally permissible. But such sterilizing procedures as tubal ligation for the woman or vasectomy for the man have long been condemned by the Church (see Pope Paul VI in *Humanae Vitae*, n. 14, and Pope John Paul II in *Familiaris Consortio*, n. 6).

Murder and Suicide

The willful taking of the life of an innocent person is always a grave evil. A person who is unjustly attacked by an aggressor has the right to protect his life, even to the point of taking the life of the aggressor in self-defense if there is no other alternative. A soldier has the right to take the life of an enemy in defense of his country, or in defense of some other country whose freedoms are under attack, provided that the conditions for a just war are fulfilled. Those conditions, according to the *Catechism of the Catholic Church* (n. 2309), are:

– the damage inflicted by the aggressor on the nation or community of nations must be lasting, grave, and certain;
– all other means of putting an end to it must have been shown to be impractical or ineffective;
– there must be serious prospects of success;
– the use of arms must not produce evils and disorders graver than the evil to be eliminated. The power of modern means of destruction weighs very heavily in evaulating this condition.

Society also has the right to defend itself through the use of capital punishment or the death penalty against persons who have committed grievous crimes. This right is based on Scripture and the teaching of the Church. For example, St. Paul says that "it is not without purpose that the ruler carries the sword; he is God's servant, to inflict his avenging wrath upon the wrongdoer" (Romans 13:4). This right was affirmed by the Council of Trent in the 16th century, by Pope Pius XII in 1952, and by the *Catechism of the Catholic Church* (n. 2266).

"Even when it is a question of the execution of a man condemned to death, the state does not dispose of the individual's right to live," Pius XII said. "Rather, it is reserved to the public authority to deprive the criminal of the benefit of life, when already, by his crime, he has deprived himself of the right to live."

In recent years, however, Popes and the Catholic bishops of the United States, without denying the compatibility of capital punishment with Catholic teaching, have come out against the death penalty for a variety of reasons. They have said that capital punishment is not a deterrent to crime, that it could lead to the execution of an innocent person, that it prevents the possible conversion of a criminal, that it is most commonly inflicted on blacks and persons of low economic status, and that it leads to the further erosion of the respect for life in our society.

Those who favor the death penalty argue that it definitely deters the criminal executed from committing any more crimes, that one would have to abolish all laws to avoid completely the punishment of innocent persons, that a criminal is more likely to repent when faced with death rather than life in prison, that many crimes are committed by blacks and persons of low economic status, frequently against those in the same environment, and that respect for life might be improved if those guilty of horrendous crimes were swiftly and permanently punished.

In summary, there is a long Catholic tradition in favor of capital punishment, but a reluctance today to inflict it on anyone. The governing principle was stated in the *Catechism of the Catholic Church*:

"If bloodless means are sufficient to defend human lives against an aggressor and to protect public order and the safety of persons, public authority should limit itself to such means because they better correspond to the concrete conditions of the common good and are more in conformity to the dignity of the human person" (n. 2267).

But apart from self-defense, a just war, or capital punishment fairly administered, taking a human life under any circumstances is a serious sin.

Since we are not the masters of our own life, suicide is also a gravely immoral matter, whether self-inflicted or with the assistance of a physician. "To concur with the intention of another person to commit suicide and to help in carrying it out through so-called 'assisted suicide' means to cooperate in and at times to be the actual perpetrator of an injustice which can never be excused even it is requested," said Pope John Paul (*Evangelium Vitae*, n. 66).

The Holy Father said that "true 'compassion' leads to sharing another's pain; it does not kill the person whose suffering we cannot bear. Moreover, the act of euthanasia appears all the more perverse if it is carried out by those like relatives, who are supposed to treat a family member with patience and love, or by those such as doctors, who by virtue of their specific profession are supposed to care for the sick person even in the most painful terminal stages" (*Ibid.*).

Whether it is a mortal sin for the suicide victim depends, as always, on whether there was sufficient knowledge or reflection by the person and whether the act was carried out with full consent of the will. In the past, the Church denied a funeral Mass to a suicide victim on the grounds that the act was a violation of the fifth commandment and that it also constituted a sin of despair in that it signified rejection of the merciful forgiveness of God.

Today the Church celebrates a Mass for those who have taken their own lives on the grounds that we cannot know with certainty the state of the victim's mind when the suicide took place. Killing oneself is so contrary to human nature that there is the presumption that the person was not mentally capable of the sufficient reflection and full consent of the will necessary to commit a mortal sin. In other words, the Church gives the victim the benefit of the doubt and leaves the judgment of that tormented soul to God. The funeral Mass is offered both for the salvation of the deceased and for the consolation of family members and friends (cf. *Catechism of the Catholic Church*, nn. 2280-2283).

Abortion and Euthanasia

The sanctity of human life is being violated on a wide scale today by the twin scourges of abortion and euthanasia, which attack human life at both ends of the spectrum. **Abortion is the deliberate killing of the unborn child in the womb, while euthanasia is the deliberate killing of the old and the sick.** The reasons offered to justify the killing of the born and the unborn usually come down to one thing: the child in the womb, the handicapped infant, or the sick or dying senior citizen are perceived to be a financial or social burden to someone, a burden that interferes with one's career or lifestyle. Those caught up in this culture of death would rather choose to eliminate the burden by abortion or euthanasia than to find ways to solve whatever problems might be posed by an unwanted pregnancy or a terminal illness.

The Catholic Church has always condemned these evils, calling abortion an "unspeakable crime" (Vatican II, *Pastoral Constitution on the Church in the Modern World*, n. 51) and denouncing euthanasia as one of several grave wrongs "opposed to life itself" (*Pastoral Constitution on the Church in the Modern World*, n. 27). The reasons for these condemnations were spelled out in greater detail by the Vatican's Sacred Congregation for the Doctrine of the Faith in its *Declaration on Procured Abortion* and in its *Declaration on Euthanasia*, by the *Catechism of the Catholic Church* (nn. 2270-2279), and by Pope John Paul in *Evangelium Vitae* (nn. 58-65).

All of these documents are must reading for Catholics who wish to combat these evils intelligently and who wish to defend the right to life of the least of our brothers and sisters. (For a fuller treatment of abortion and euthanasia, see Chapter 7 of *Catholicism and Society*, a companion volume in this series.)

Drunkenness and Drug Abuse

The fifth commandment forbids the abuse of alcohol or narcotic drugs because of the harm they can cause to the body and the mind. The key word is "abuse." The moderate use of alcohol, or the use of drugs under the supervision of a physician, is not wrong. It is only when we use these substances to excess, or when we use them without a good and sufficient reason, that we commit a sin. Human beings are distinguished from animals by the use of reason and by free control of our actions. Alcohol and drug abuse reduce a person to the level of an animal because they take away or diminish our ability to reason and to make free and wise choices (cf. *Catechism of the Catholic Church*, nn. 2290-2291).

Not only is the abuse of these substances a sin, but it can lead us to commit other serious sins. The woman who gets drunk at a party runs the risk of sexual promiscuity, which could lead to pregnancy and even to abortion. The man who gets behind the wheel of a car after taking drugs runs the risk of causing an accident and even killing himself or some innocent party. These tragedies are the result of intemperance – of following the philosophy of "eat, drink, and be merry, for tomorrow we die" – and millions of people have shattered their own lives, or the lives of others, by abusing alcohol or drugs.

Do you have a problem with liquor or narcotics? Ask yourself these questions?

– Have I ever said I could stop drinking or taking drugs anytime I want to – and then continued abusing them?

– Have I ever decided to stop drinking or taking drugs for a week or two, only to find that my resolve lasted only a day or two?

– Do I get mad when people ask me about my drinking or drug abuse?

– Do I ever drink or take drugs in the morning?

– Do alcohol or drugs ever cause me trouble at home, in school, or on the job?

– Have I missed school or work because of alcohol or drugs?

– Do I sometimes have blackouts or partial loss of memory?

– Have I ever switched from one kind of liquor or drug in the hope that it would keep me from getting drunk or too high?

– Have I ever felt that my life would be much better if I stopped drinking or taking drugs?

If you answered yes to one of these questions, you may have a problem. If you answered yes to three or more questions, you definitely have a problem. There are people and agencies who can help you, but only if you want to help yourself.

We all know the future that awaits a person addicted to these substances. You become more an animal than a human being. You are a slave to an evil habit. You may become a thief or a prostitute to finance your habit. You may neglect your duties, ruin your family, lose your friends, contract a disease like AIDS, bring children into the world who are already addicts, face arrest for crimes committed, drag others down with you by selling them drugs or encouraging them to drink, condemn yourself to an early death, abandon God and your religion, and, worst of all, lose your soul.

The only way to prevent these terrible things from happening is never to take that first drink of alcohol or that first illegal drug. Or if you do drink, do so always in moderation. Throughout the Bible you will find the clear distinction between the use and the abuse of alcohol. For instance, Proverbs 20:1 says that "wine is arrogant, strong drink is riotous; none who goes astray for it is wise," while Proverbs 31:6-7 says, "Give drink to one who is perishing, and wine to the sorely depressed; when they drink, they will forget their misery, and think no more of their burdens."

In the New Testament, St. Paul told the Ephesians to "avoid getting drunk on wine; that leads to debauchery" (Ephesians 5:18). But he also told Timothy, "Take a little wine for the good of your stomach, and because of your frequent illnesses" (1 Timothy 5:23).

Hatred and Anger

Also falling under the fifth commandment's umbrella of respect for the bodily well-being of ourselves and others is the obligation to respect the mental and spiritual side of our neighbors. If we call God "our Father," then that makes us all brothers and sisters. "You have heard the commandment, 'An eye for an eye and a tooth for a tooth...' " Jesus said in the Sermon on Mount. "My command to you is: love your enemies, pray for your persecutors. This will prove that you are sons of the heavenly Father, for his sun rises on the bad and the good, he rains on the just and the unjust. If you love those who love you, what merit is there in that? Do not tax collectors do as much" (Matthew 5:38-46)?

Our Lord emphasized that one can stop far short of murder and still seriously violate the fifth commandment. It is sinful to wish evil on one's neighbor, to hate him or to be jealous of her. There is a relationship between the spirit and motive underlying hatred and the spirit and motive that prompts one to murder. "Anyone who hates his brother is a murderer," warned St. John (1 John 3:15). And Christ himself, after saying that "every murderer shall be liable to judgment," added that "everyone who grows angry with his brother shall be liable to judgment" (Matthew 5:21-22).

We must be careful not to mistake our likes and dislikes for a spirit of hatred. We have a natural preference for some people, and a natural distaste for others. But we must "love one another" (John 13:34) even if we do not like some people very much. This means that we want good for all people, even our enemies. We can hate the sin without hating the sinner. We can pray for others that they will turn away from their annoying or even sinful ways, but we may never wish anyone evil since we are all children of the same Father and beneficiaries of the death of his Son on the cross.

This attitude of love also precludes seeking revenge for injuries done to us. Recall the words of St. Paul: "Never repay injury with injury. See that your conduct is honorable in the eyes of all. If possible, live peacefully with everyone. Beloved, do not avenge yourselves; leave that to God's wrath, for it is written: 'Vengeance is mine, I will repay,' says the Lord'" (Romans 12:17-19).

Envy and Jealousy

Envy and jealousy of the good fortune and success of others are as old as the human race. Cain slew his brother Abel because God had "looked with favor on Abel and his offering" (Genesis 4:4). St. Paul was the target of Demetrius the silversmith, whose business of making idols fell off after Paul came to Ephesus. Calling together other silver craftsmen, Demetrius said: "Men, you know that our prosperity depends on this work. But as you can see and hear for yourselves, not only at Ephesus but throughout most of the province of Asia, this Paul has persuaded great numbers of people to change their religion. He tells them that man-made gods are no gods at all. The danger grows, not only that our trade will be discredited, but even that the temple of the great goddess Artemis will count for nothing" (Acts 19:25-27).

Similar cases of envy and jealousy could be multiplied many times over today. The person who is disturbed because an acquaintance receives an honor in some business or organization, the man who is irked when a fellow-worker is promoted, the woman who is annoyed by the wealth or influence of a neighbor, the teenager who is not as popular as some members of the class. The result of these situations is often hatred, envy, jealousy, and at times even nasty and malicious attacks on the character of those who have been singled out for acclaim.

Sometimes these feelings lead to an unjust anger that takes control of a person, causing them to seethe inside and eventually to get so riled up that all perspective is lost. The ironic thing about unjust anger is that it usually causes more harm to the person who is angry than to the one who is the target of the anger. Have you ever found out that someone was still furious with you for something you had done months ago and had forgotten all about? That person's anger had no effect on you, but it made them bitter as they kept stewing about whatever you had done to them and perhaps even built up a grudge against you.

While there may be times when anger is justified, as when Jesus drove the moneychangers out of the temple in Jerusalem because they had turned his Father's house "into a den of thieves" (Matthew 21:13), or when a parent or teacher must deal with serious wrongdoing by a child, there is no place in the heart of a follower of Christ for unjust and all-consuming anger. "If you forgive the faults of others, your heavenly Father will forgive you yours," Jesus said. "If you do not forgive others, neither will your Father forgive you" (Matthew 6:14-15).

St. Francis de Sales gave some good advice when he was asked how he kept so calm in the face of hostility and difficulty. "I have made an agreement with my tongue never to say a word while my heart is excited," he said. When you feel anger arising in you, do as the Apostles did in the boat when the sudden storm came up on the Sea of Galilee: go to the Lord for help and ask him, "Lord, save us" (Matthew 8:25). Bear in mind that this is the same Lord who said of those who had nailed him to a cross and were mocking and jeering him: "Father, forgive them; they do not know what they are doing" (Luke 23:34).

Scandal

If it is a sin and a crime to hurt a person's body, it is a much worse thing to harm one's soul. This is what scandal does. **Scandal means inviting or influencing another person, by word or example, to commit a sin.** It is the work of the devil because it attempts to undo the work of Christ. It was the sin that Jesus had in mind when he warned the world that "it would be better for anyone who leads astray one of these little ones who believe in me, to be drowned by a millstone around his neck, in the depths of the sea" (Matthew 18:6).

Our Lord went on to say that "terrible things will come on the world through scandal! It is inevitable that scandal should occur. Nonetheless, woe to that man through whom scandal comes! If your hand or your foot is your undoing, cut it off and throw it from you! Better to enter life maimed or crippled than be thrown with two hands or two feet into endless fire. If your eye is your downfall, gouge it out and cast it from you! Better to enter life with one eye than be thrown with both into fiery Gehenna" (Matthew 18:7-9).

Jesus was not advocating that we mutilate our bodies. He was using hyperbole or exaggerated speech to emphasize the horrible evil of scandal. He was saying that one would be better off spiritually to lose organs or limbs as long as we get to heaven than to engage in sinful actions with a physically sound body and wind up in hell.

Scandal is not just spreading gossip about others. It can mean ridiculing belief in God and religion, using the name of God and Jesus to express anger or disgust, staying in bed on Sunday morning rather than taking the children to Mass, bragging about cheating in school or on one's income tax, using foul and obscene language in front of children, staggering home drunk in the middle of the night, or trying to persuade another to lie, steal, hate, vandalize, use alcohol or drugs, read or view sexually explicit books and films, and engage in sexual acts. The person who talks another into committing a sin is guilty of two sins – the sin itself and the sin of scandal.

"If you persuade your neighbor to sin, you are his murderer," said St. Augustine, because killing the life of God in the soul is worse than killing the life of the body. God expects us to love and honor him, but scandal causes others to turn their backs on God. It is impossible for us to know the far-reaching effects of our good or bad actions. But of one thing we can be sure: the good or bad that we do seldom stops with us. Like the stone tossed into a pond, it not only makes a splash at the time, but it also send ripples to the distant shore.

There are sincere non-Catholics who would like to enter the Catholic Church, but who are put off by the scandalous actions of members of the Church, by people who call themselves Catholics but who seldom act in the way that Catholics are supposed to act. But there are also faithful Catholics who are wonderful and inspiring examples of what a follower of Christ is supposed to be. All of us are called to be worthy apostles and witnesses of Christ.

So wherever you go, whatever you do, avoid giving scandal to others. You would not push a person in front of a car; you would not put out your foot to trip someone; you would not put an obstacle in front of someone in the dark. So why would you want to trip up another person spiritually? If we are truly our brother's and sister's keeper, then we had better make sure to keep them on the road to heaven, not on the path to hell (cf. *Catechism of the Catholic Church*, nn. 2284-2287).

The Importance of Good Example

In the early days of Christianity, there was in Egypt a non-Christian soldier named Pachomius. He was quartered for a time with a Christian family, who treated him with true Christian kindness and gave him such good example that he entered the Catholic Church and became St. Pachomius. Such is the power of good example! Just as bad example is harmful to the souls of those with whom we come into contact, especially children, so good example is helpful to others. St. Paul put it well when he said, "We must consider how to rouse each other to love and good deeds" (Hebrews 10:24). We must let our light shine before all, Jesus said, "so that they may see goodness in your acts and give praise to your heavenly Father" (Matthew 5:16).

But in our efforts to lead a good Christian life, we must be humble and not proud. We should not perform good works in order to impress other people, but because it is the right thing to do. The proud person claims all the credit for his accomplishments, while the humble person gives credit to God for any talents and abilities he possesses. Our Lord wants us to do good things in public so that others will see us and be drawn to God.

The advice given by St. Peter two thousand years ago is just as relevant today: "Though the pagans may slander you as trouble-makers, conduct yourselves blamelessly among them. By observing your good works they may give glory to God on the day of visitation" (1 Peter 2:12).

We can show love for our neighbor by responding generously to his or her bodily needs. One of the best summaries of what that means can be found in the corporal works of mercy. We must feed the hungry, give drink to the thirsty, clothe the naked, visit the sick, shelter the homeless, visit the imprisoned, and bury the dead. When we perform these acts of love for the least of our brothers and sisters, we perform them for Jesus himself, who will say to us at the end of the world: "Come! You have my Father's blessing! Inherit the kingdom prepared for you from the creation of the world" (Matthew 25:34).

Chapter 8

Sex Has Its Rules

All the baptized are called to chastity. The Christian has 'put on Christ,' the model for all chastity. All Christ's faithful are called to lead a chaste life in keeping with their particular states of life.
– *Catechism of the Catholic Church*, n. 2348

Former world heavyweight boxing champion Gene Tunney was once invited to be the guest of a group of businessmen in a midwestern city. Following the banquet there was a floor show that soon became immoral. Tunney, a man with strong beliefs in Christian modesty, stood up, turned to those at the head table, and said: "Gentlemen, I don't care for this type of exhibition. I find it indecent and offensive. You'll have to excuse me." And with that, one of the great figures in the world of boxing walked from the room. Others followed him and the show was a failure.

During his career, newspapers carried stories of Gene Tunney's great victories in the ring. Government records give evidence of his heroism on the battlefield with the U.S. Marines. But one of the greatest but least publicized victories he ever won was the moral victory on that night in the Midwest when he walked out on an indecent show. How many modern-day athletic heroes and heroines would have the moral courage to do what Tunney did? Probably not very many since we live in a world that attacks our purity in a thousand ways, and even some well-intentioned people have become complacent about the tide of immorality, pornography, and lack of reverence for sex that threatens to inundate our country and our communities.

There certainly were temptations against the sixth and ninth commandments in Gene Tunney's time, but those temptations pale by comparison to what our families and our children are exposed to today. Once upon a time, a person had to go to a theater or a nightclub to see films or performances that featured sexual immorality; now those films and performances come into our homes via television on a daily basis. Once upon a time, a person had to go to a disreputable part of a large city to obtain pornographic books and magazines; now this filth is available at the local supermarket or convenience store.

Once upon a time, parents could expect to have the values instilled at home reinforced in the classroom; now schools have become places where the name of God cannot be mentioned, but where explicit sexual information can be imparted without moral guidance, where condoms can be passed out to teenagers, and where pregnant girls can be shipped out for an abortion during the school day without either the knowledge or consent of their parents.

Sin Has Its Consequences

Violations of the sixth and ninth commandments, and a widespread rejection of God's plan for sex, are all around us. The sexual sins of adultery, fornication, masturbation, homosexual behavior, and lustful thoughts are put in a favorable light, and even glorified, in the movies and on television, in newspapers, books, magazines, music, and so-called works of art. Chastity and purity, if not ignored, are ridiculed and attacked as anachronisms of a bygone era.

But there are serious consequences when the divine plan is ignored. Every one of the ten Commandments was meant for our good, and disaster strikes when we disregard God's blueprint. Just as a driver who ignores the instruction booklet that comes with a new car will eventually ruin the car, so those who deliberately ignore the Creator's instructions handed on to us through the Bible and the Catholic Church founded by Jesus himself will eventually ruin their lives.

The terrible results of rejecting the sixth and ninth commandments are all too plain to see: the breakdown of family life, sexual abuse of children, more than a million teenage pregnancies each year, millions of abortions, an epidemic of sexually transmitted diseases, the scourge of AIDS, and other social problems. All of these consequences could be avoided simply by following the Creator's plan for sex. God did not give us the sixth and ninth commandments to keep us from enjoying ourselves, as some would have you believe, but rather to guide us in the proper use of his marvelous gift of sex so that we can get to heaven. That is why it is important for us to know the details of this divine plan.

Sex: A Noble Gift of God

There is widespread discussion today about sex. But along with the valuable insights gained from this discussion, unfortunately there are also many false ideas in circulation, and many people are confused. Followers of Christ must help to clear up this confusion by stating and restating what God had in mind when he gave us this beautiful, noble, and special gift. We know that God created Adam and Eve directly, and he could have created each one of us in the same way. Instead, he gave us a share in the creation of new life. We are co-creators with God; he creates the soul and husband and wife create the body. God is the third partner in marriage and, without him, no marriage can last.

To help us share in the creation of new life, God gave us sexual powers. He gave us sexual urges so that men and women would be attracted to each other and want to marry. He made the act of creating new life, which we call sexual intercourse or marital intercourse, a pleasurable experience in order to reward married couples for taking on the difficult task of bringing children into the world and raising them. Therefore, in the plan of God, sexual acts are only to be used in marriage. Sex is good and holy when used by married couples as God intended; it is wrong and sinful when used by people who are not married at all or who are not married to each other. Sexual pleasure belongs in marriage; it is wrong and sinful to seek sexual pleasure before marriage or outside of marriage.

In summary, we may say that sexual intercourse has two purposes in the plan of God:

1. **It is to be life-giving.** Since sex brings children into the world, it is restricted to marriage because only married couples can provide the stable, loving environment which a child needs to grow and develop properly. Therefore, any actions taken before, during, or after intercourse which would prevent the conception and development of a new life are a violation of God's plan and are grave sins. These immoral actions include sterilization, artificial methods of contraception, and abortion. Thus, the Catholic Church teaches today, as it has taught in the past and will teach in the future, that "each and every marriage act must remain open to the transmission of life" (*Humanae Vitae*, n. 11).

The use of contraceptive drugs and devices – the pill, condoms, diaphragms, intrauterine devices, etc. – is always and everywhere evil and sinful. Their use can never be condoned or justified as a morally acceptable means of controlling births or limiting the size of a family. To those who wish to practice responsible parenthood, who have "serious motives" to space out the births of their children, Pope Paul, and his successors, have said that they may resort to Natural Family Planning. This means abstaining from marital relations during those days when a woman is fertile and capable of conceiving a child.

Natural Family Planning is safer than chemical means of controlling births (the pill and spermicides) and more effective than mechanical means (condoms, diaphragms, IUDs). It also requires the cooperation of both spouses, as opposed to artificial methods which put all of the burden on one partner. This mutual involvement of husband and wife, which demands real communication and cooperation between them, has over time proved to enhance the respect, increase the affection, and deepen the love which they feel for one another.

Surveys have also shown virtually no divorces among couples practicing NFP, while couples practicing artificial contraception have very high rates of divorce. (For a fuller discussion of these issues, see Chapter 7 of *Catholicism and Society*, a companion volume in this series.)

To those couples caught up in the contraceptive mentality, or who are struggling to follow the Church's teaching on the proper regulation of births, Pope Paul offered this compassionate advice: "Let them implore divine assistance by persevering prayer; above all, let them draw from the source of grace and charity in the Eucharist. And if sin should still keep its hold over them, let them not be discouraged, but rather have recourse with humble perseverance to the mercy of God, which is poured forth in the sacrament of Penance" (*Humanae Vitae*, n. 25).

2. **It is to be love-giving.** Sexual intercourse in marriage is the deepest expression of love between a man and a woman. It is the total giving of oneself to another person. It is mutual sharing and trust. Therefore, if sex is used selfishly, if it is used only for one person's enjoyment or pleasure, if one person is treated as an object to be used rather than as a person to be loved, then it is a violation of God's plan and a serious sin.

This means that if one spouse physically or emotionally abuses the other during intercourse, or if a drunken partner demands sex from the other partner, then the love-giving aspect of sex has been disregarded.

When couples "respect the inseparable connection between the unitive [love-giving] and procreative [life-giving] meanings of human sexuality," Pope John Paul II said, "they are acting as 'ministers' of God's plan and they 'benefit from' their sexuality according to the original dynamism of 'total' self-giving, without manipulation or alteration" (*Familiaris Consortio*, n. 32).

Sins Against Chastity

Chastity means using our sexual powers according to God's plan. We violate that plan when we seek or obtain sexual pleasure before marriage or outside of marriage. "Acts of fornication" and "adulterous conduct" are evils that spring "from the deep recesses of the heart," Jesus said (Mark 7:21-22). He was echoed by St. Paul: "Do not deceive yourselves: no fornicators, idolaters, or adulterers, no sexual perverts ... will inherit God's kingdom .... Shun lewd conduct. Every other sin a man commits is outside his body, but the fornicator sins against his own body. You must know that your body is a temple of the Holy Spirit" (1 Corinthians 6:9, 18-19).

Since sexual intercourse and sexual pleasure belong only in marriage, the following actions have always been taught as grave sins: **Adultery** – sexual intercourse between a married man and a woman who is not his wife, or between a married woman and a man who is not her husband. **Fornication** – sexual intercourse between two unmarried people. **Homosexuality** – sexual acts between people of the same sex. **Masturbation** – self-abuse or stimulation of one's own genitals to achieve sexual pleasure.

The Catholic Church has long taught that each of these actions is gravely immoral matter. See, for instance, the *Catechism of the Catholic Church* (nn. 2351-2359, 2380-2381), the Sacred Congregation for the Doctrine of the Faith's *Declaration on Certain Problems of Sexual Ethics*, the encyclical *Veritatis Splendor*, the Pontifical Council for the Family's document *The Truth and Meaning of Human Sexuality*, and the U.S. Catholic Bishops' *Basic Teachings for Catholic Religious Education*.

In the latter document, the Bishops said: "In a sex-saturated society, the follower of Christ must be different. For the Christian there can be no premarital sex, fornication, adultery, or other acts of impurity or scandal to others. He must remain chaste, repelling lustful desires and temptations, self-abuse, pornography, and indecent entertainment of every description" (n. 19).

Since there is such a widespread effort today to portray homosexual behavior as a respectable lifestyle that should be considered on a par with heterosexual behavior, it should be noted that homosexual behavior has been condemned in Scripture as gravely depraved (Romans 1:26-27 and Jude 7). The Church teaches that "homosexual acts are intrinsically disordered and may never be approved in any way anywhere" (*Declaration on Certain Problems of Sexual Ethics*, n. 8).

At the same time, the Church insists on distinguishing between homosexual orientation, which is not sinful, and homosexual behavior, which is sinful. Writing to the Catholic Bishops of the United States in the summer of 1992, the Sacred Congregation for the Doctrine of the Faith deplored "violent malice in speech or in action" against homosexuals. It went on to say, however, that the homosexual condition is disordered and that "there are areas in which it is not unjust discrimination to take sexual orientation into account, for example, in the placement of children for adoption or foster care, in employment of teachers or athletic coaches, and in military recruitment" (*Some Considerations Concerning the Response to Legislative Proposals on the Non-Discrimination of Homosexual Persons*, nos. 7, 11).

In this area, as in all matters of sexuality, we also have to distinguish between the sin and the sinner. Objectively speaking, all of these actions are gravely sinful. But whether they are mortal sins for the persons committing them depends on whether those persons possessed sufficient knowledge and understanding that what they were about to do was gravely sinful and whether they deliberately performed the actions anyway, giving them the full consent of their will. Individual lapses are not always mortal sins. Guilt can be reduced when reflection or consent are decreased by ignorance, passion, or other factors.

As the Bible states, we are all sinners. We are weak, we face many temptations, and we can fall. Nobody is immune from the consequences of original sin, which has darkened our minds so that we do not always see evil clearly and weakened our wills so that we do not always do the right thing. St. Paul described well the clash between good and evil that affects all of us: "I cannot even understand my own actions. I do not do what I want to do but what I hate .... What happens is that I do, not the good I will to do, but the evil I do not intend" (Romans 7:15, 20).

The important thing to remember is that if we do fall into sin, we should rush into the arms of our Lord, express our sorrow, and obtain his forgiveness. Even if we should fall again and again, we must keep on trying, and never get discouraged. No matter how terrible our sins, they can be washed away in the vast ocean of God's mercy. The sacrament of Reconciliation, given to us by Jesus on that first Easter Sunday night, is a never-failing channel of divine mercy and forgiveness. The Holy Spirit will, in the words of St. Paul, inspire in us a "fresh, spiritual way of thinking" that will help us to become a new person "created in God's image, whose justice and holiness are born of truth" (Ephesians 4:23-24).

Towards those around us who seem steeped in sin, we must not show self-righteous condemnation, but compassion and help. We should not emphasize the indignity of their deeds, but rather the dignity of their persons and the sublimity of their destiny. We must love the sinner while hating the sin and try, with prayer, charity, and good example, to lead them to repentance and renewal of virtue.

In the area of sex, as in all phases of life, we must strive to be faithful followers of Christ. After death we will not be judged by the world, but by Christ himself. We must therefore follow his principles and the guidance of his Church. We must not imitate those whose understanding is darkened, but must "live as children of light" (Ephesians 5:8). Millions have lived lives of heroic virtue before us and, with God's powerful and never-ceasing help, so can we. We must glorify God not only in our minds and hearts, but also in our bodies because we "have been purchased, and at a price" (1 Corinthians 20). Our struggle in this life will be crowned by great happiness in the next life as we spend all eternity in union with God.

A Saint for Our Times

On June 25, 1950, millions of Americans saw headlines in their newspapers reporting that Maria Goretti had been canonized. The media carried the details of an eleven-year-old Italian girl who had been raised to sainthood because she had died in defense of her purity early in this century. On the day of her canonization at St. Peter's in Rome, half a million people were present for the ceremonies, including Maria's 86-year-old mother and 62-year-old brother. Never before in the history of the Catholic Church had a mother seen her child being declared a saint.

At the time of her martyrdom in 1902, Maria lived with her father and mother and brothers and sisters on a farm near Anzio in Italy. They shared the house with John Serenelli and his 19-year-old son Alexander, who had grown up as an undisciplined youth. On more than one occasion, Alexander had tried to get Maria to forget her high moral ideals, but he was repulsed. So he obtained a knife, chose a time when he knew Maria would be alone, and went to her room in the hope of terrorizing her into submitting to him.

Maria was sewing in her room when Alexander entered, brandishing the knife and demanding that she have sex with him. Maria refused, so he dragged her across the room by the hair, stabbed her fourteen times, and ran from the room thinking that she was dead. Maria was found still alive by her mother and, during the 24 hours before she died, the young girl told her mother what had happened because she would not compromise her purity. She also forgave her attacker and Alexander, who was deeply sorry for the evil he had done and had completely reformed his life after seeing Maria in a vision, was present at the canonization in 1950.

God always gives the world saints to fill the needs of a particular time in the history of the Church. In this century, when the world is in such dire need of shining examples of chastity, he has given us Maria Goretti, the modern martyr of sexual purity. Let us pray every day to her to inspire the young people of today to follow her example of a virtuous life.

Occasions of Sin

The only sure way of remaining chaste in today's sex-saturated society is to avoid all occasions of sin, i.e., to stay away from those persons, places, or things that might lead us into sin. Just as the person who charges recklessly into physical danger will probably be injured, so too the person who needlessly puts himself or herself in an occasion of sin is likely to suffer spiritual harm. How many sexual sins, how many sexually transmitted diseases, how many pregnancies, how many abortions, how many ruined lives could have been avoided simply by not foolishly exposing ourselves to occasions of sin? A person would not expose himself unnecessarily to the danger of contracting a deadly disease, so why expose himself to the danger of deadly sin by frequenting the occasions of impurity?

If traveling with certain companions often leads you into sin, you must stay away from those companions. If being alone in an intimate setting with a member of the opposite sex usually leads to sins against purity, you must avoid being alone with that person. If visiting certain places – theaters, secluded beaches and parks, or houses where adults are not present – puts you in danger of sin, you must stay away from those places. If reading pornographic books and magazines and watching sexually explicit movies or videos give rise to impure thoughts and desires, you must change your reading and viewing habits.

There are those who contend that they can read or watch pornography without being affected by it, but they are kidding themselves. The biggest audience for pornography is young men between the ages of fourteen and eighteen, who during those very years are shaping their attitudes toward women. And what does porn say about women and sex?

It says that what God intended to be beautiful and private and exclusively for married couples can be sick, public, and for anyone who wishes to engage in the most perverted and even cruel sexual acts. Women are abused and degraded and treated as sex objects in this medium, and the most bizarre acts are made to seem legitimate and normal because the actresses are shown smiling and seemingly enjoying themselves.

Pornography can be addictive and those caught up in it become increasingly desensitized to acts and scenes that might once have revolted them. They seek more and more graphic materials and may after several years even consider acting out what they have seen.

Ted Bundy, the serial killer whose addiction to hard-core pornography fueled his sexual fantasies and inspired his murderous rampage, said: "You reach that jumping off point when you begin to wonder if actually doing it would give you that which is beyond just reading about it or looking at it." The day before his execution in Florida, Bundy said that porn users "are not some kind of inherent monsters. We are your sons and we are your husbands. We grew up in regular families. Pornography can snatch a kid out of any home today."

The pornography industry is controlled by organized crime, and it brings into their coffers about $10 billion a year. So when you buy or rent these sleazy materials, you not only jeopardize your spiritual life but you also contribute to organized crime. If you wish to see how evil this industry really is, and if you have a strong stomach, you should read the *Final Report of the Attorney General's*

Commission on Pornography. The commission, which held hearings in six American cities and heard testimony from more than 1,000 persons, concluded that pornography is addictive, that it progressively corrupts its addicts, and that it desensitizes men's attitudes towards women.

Brenda MacKillop, a former Playboy bunny, told the commission that *"Playboy* is more than a pornographic magazine with pictures of naked women. It is a philosophy that enticed me to throw aside my Judeo-Christian ethic of no premarital sex and no adultery and to practice recreational sex with no commitments." To those who cite free-speech considerations, Andrea Dworkin told the commission that pornography is not a free-speech issue; it is "a civil rights issue for women ... because it turns women into subhuman creatures. Pornography is a civil rights issue for women because it is a systematic exploitation of a group of people because of a condition of birth. Pornography creates bigotry, hostility, and aggression toward all women, without exception."

But even those who will never achieve the depths of a Ted Bundy must stay away from pornography because it presents a false picture of sex. It also gives us impure thoughts and desires that can lead to impure actions. What normal teenage boy and girl watching a sexually explicit movie can fail to be sexually aroused by what they see on the screen?

Sexual thoughts and desires are not unusual in a society which uses sex to sell everything from automobiles to zucchini. But we violate the ninth commandment only if we deliberately encourage and keep those thoughts and desires in our minds and take pleasure from them. No matter how much we are troubled by sexual images and ideas, they are not sinful unless we decide to sit back and enjoy them.

When impure thoughts arise, we must resist them firmly and fight them vigorously; we must think about something else, do something different to clear our minds. We must pray to God and to the Blessed Virgin Mary to help us get rid of these thoughts. We must take advantage of the sacraments of Penance and the Holy Eucharist to make us strong enough to say no to these thoughts.

It is not enough to say that we have never committed adultery or fornication; we must also avoid impure thoughts and desires, recalling the words of Jesus: "You have heard the commandment, 'You shall not commit adultery.' What I say to you is: anyone who looks lustfully at a woman has already committed adultery with her in his thoughts" (Matthew 5:27-28).

The "Chastity Lady"

Molly Kelly is the widowed mother of eight children (her husband was killed in a sledding accident when their oldest child was twelve). She is known as the "Chastity Lady" because she travels around the country speaking to 100,000 teenagers a year on the subject of "Teens and Chastity" (her highly entertaining and spiritually solid talks are available on video). Her message is a simple one: chastity is sexual self-control, and teenagers can say no to sexual immorality if they want to.

Mrs. Kelly chastises her own generation of adults for telling kids to say no to drugs, but at the same time insisting that they should be given condoms and other contraceptives because they are incapable of saying no to sex. She says that the multi-billion-dollar contraceptive industry is intent on giving young people "the tools to do things that cause problems that you wouldn't have if you didn't use these tools in the first place." These contraceptives, she says, not only have a significant failure rate in preventing such physical consequences as disease and pregnancy, but those who push them never talk about the emotional and psychological consequences of premarital sex.

Sex is a beautiful, powerful, and controllable gift, says Molly Kelly, one that should be unwrapped only in marriage because of the fidelity, trust, and permanency of the marriage state. She tells her teenage audiences that she has a high regard for their generation's sensitivity towards others and their ability to act in a sexually reponsible manner. She urges them to follow the upward path of chastity instead of the downward road of unchastity, saying that "chastity is the only solution placing sexual intercourse in marriage where it belongs. It's 100 percent effective, it costs nothing, it has no harmful side effects, and it puts you in control of your own life."

Molly Kelly also brings words of encouragement to those who have already engaged in sexual activity. She advocates what she calls "secondary virginity" and says that a person does not always have to have sex just because they have had it once. "You have been taught to say no since you were a child," she says, adding that "everybody can change their behavior with help."

This is the same message that Pope John Paul brought to the young people of Uganda early in 1993. He urged them not to be "deceived by the empty words of those who ridicule chastity or your capacity for self-control. The strength of your future married love depends on the strength of your present commitment to learning true love, a chastity which includes refraining from all sexual relations outside of marriage. The sexual restraint of chastity is the only safe and virtuous way to put an end to the tragic plague of AIDS which has claimed so many young victims. Helped by God's grace in the sacraments of Penance and the Eucharist, be strong and of good courage. The Pope urges you to commit yourselves to this spiritual revolution of purity of body and heart. Let Christ's redemption bear fruit in you! The contemporary world needs this kind of revolution."

Purity Is Security

Despite all the propaganda to engage in sex early and often, it is possible and normal to be pure, to keep our passions in check, to live according to God's plan. Millions of people are leading chaste lives, and you can too. Purity is possible provided (1) we want to be pure, (2) we take the necessary steps, and (3) we form Christian attitudes toward sex. Assuming that a person understands the pitfalls of sexual immorality and wants to be pure, one of the first steps is obtaining a sound and balanced view of sex, one that includes many of the principles we have already covered in this chapter.

The Catholic Church expects parents to give their children, as they advance in years, a "positive and prudent sexual education" (Vatican II, *Declaration on Christian Education*, n. 1). Pope John Paul elaborated on this instruction by calling on parents "to give their children a clear and delicate sex education." He said that "sex education, which is a basic right and duty of parents, must always be carried out under their attentive guidance, whether at home or in educational centers chosen and controlled by them."

Referring to many of the sex education programs being presented in schools today, the Holy Father said that "the Church is firmly opposed to an often widespread form of imparting sex information disassociated from moral principles. That would merely be an introduction to the experience of pleasure and a stimulus leading to the loss of serenity – while still in the years of innocence – by opening the way to vice" (*Familiaris Consortio*, n. 37).

Parents must protect their children from these programs that bear no resemblance to the divine plan and which steer children as young as first graders in the wrong direction. Parents can also instill sexual values through the example of their own holy married lives and by shielding their offspring from the harmful influence of indecent entertainment, pornography, bad companions, alcohol, and drugs. (For more sound advice in this area, see the Pontifical Council for the Family's document *The Truth and Meaning of Human Sexuality*, especially sections 65-75).

Another important step is to cultivate the virtue of modesty, which has to do with matters that could lead to sexual arousal, such as conversation, touches, dances, music, reading and viewing materials, and mode of dress. Modesty can be compared with the drawbridge that protects a castle. If the person in charge of the drawbridge is careless, intruders could invade and capture the castle.

If a person is not careful how they talk, touch other people, and dance; what they listen to or watch; and how they dress, they will find their purity threatened and even destroyed by themselves or by others. If a person talks, acts, or dresses in order to get himself or herself, or someone else, sexually excited, these actions are wrong and sinful. Being our brother's or sister's keeper means not saying or doing anything that would lead them into sin.

Molly Kelly says that we communicate with other people through three kinds of language: verbal language, body language, and clothes language. Saying no to sex verbally while dancing provocatively or dressing in revealing clothes sends a confusing message. She says that our entire self has to say no, and we have to say no in a convincing manner.

That no should be expressed at the beginning of a date, and not when sexual excitement has reached its peak and the couple is parked in a car in some remote place. The moral ground rules should be established early in a relationship, while both parties are thinking clearly, instead of trying to put the brakes on the powerful locomotive that is sexual desire after the point of no return has been crossed.

Another important step in keeping chaste is daily prayer and frequent recourse to the sacraments of Penance and the Holy Eucharist. Practicing sexual self-control is virtually impossible on our own, but with the help of God and the Blessed Mother, the model of purity, we can achieve this goal. We must also do good works, read the Bible and the lives of the saints, practice penance and self-denial (if we never deny ourselves anything, if we never make sacrifices, we will find it awfully hard to say no to sexual temptations), avoid occasions of sin, and take a healthy interest in such things as sports, hobbies, and jobs.

St. Paul tells us that "God keeps his promise. He will not let you be tested beyond your strength. Along with the test he will give you a way out of it so that you may be able to endure it" (1 Corinthians 10:13). Temptations will come, particularly through the devil, but no one can make us sin. God is there to help us if only we ask for his help. If we do fall into sin, it is not God's fault; it is our fault for saying yes to the temptation.

Finally, we must develop Christian attitudes toward sex. This means that we must respect our bodies as temples of the Holy Spirit; we must recognize that original sin has left us with an inclination toward evil that can be overcome only with God's assistance; we must accept and develop our own male or female personalities; we must respect and honor members of the opposite sex, never using or abusing another person for our own enjoyment and always treating others as we would like them to treat us (Matthew 7:12); we must remember that sex is holy and sacred if used in the way God intended and strive to make sex a passport to heaven and not a ticket to hell; and we must develop a healthy outlook on marriage and prepare for this wonderful vocation by learning to love, to share, and to live unselfishly with others.

Chapter 9

Justice For All

The seventh commandment forbids unjustly taking or keeping the goods of one's neighbor and wronging him in any way with respect to his goods .... The tenth commandment ... forbids coveting the goods of another, as the root of theft, robbery, and fraud, which the seventh commandment forbids. – *Catechism of the Catholic Church*, nn. 2401, 2534

Christ spent several years of his life teaching the world his doctrine. Many of his teachings were different from those of the religious leaders of his time, and he inspired many reforms in the life and thought of the world of his day. He was laying down a plan of life for Christianity that would be different from the way people had lived up until then. The old standard, for instance, was "an eye for an eye and a tooth for a tooth" – to return evil for evil. If someone injured you, you were expected to seek revenge and injure that person in return. Then Jesus came onto the scene and said, "Love your enemies, pray for your persecutors" (Matthew 5:44).

Many people before the time of Christ had as their goal in life to get as much enjoyment as possible, to get as much worldly wealth and pleasure as possible. But our Lord offered a different standard: "Whoever wishes to be my follower must deny his very self, take up his cross each day, and follow in my steps" (Luke 9:23). He then went on to state another basic principle of Christianity, one that ought to serve as a warning to those whose only goal in life is the accumulation of material goods: "What profit does he show who gains the whole world and destroys himself in the process?" (Luke 9:25).

All of us may agree with that principle at least in theory, but how many of us violate it in our daily actions? How many of us are much too concerned with piling up material wealth, and too little concerned with helping those in need? How many of us are so intent on getting all the money and things of this world we can that we ignore the commandments forbidding us to steal or to covet our neighbor's goods? Oh, many of us will say, "I would not think of breaking into someone's house and stealing something, or robbing a bank, or dipping into the treasury of the organization to which I belong." And that is probably true for a lot of people, but there are other ways of violating the seventh and tenth commandments, of grasping for worldly goods, to the detriment of our souls.

There is the employer, for instance, who pays less than a fair wage to those who work for him so that he can make as much money as possible. There is the employee who does as little work as possible even though he knows in his heart that he has an obligation before God to perform a day's work for a day's pay. There are those who take materials, tools, office equipment, and other things from their place of employment on the grounds that the company "will never miss them."

There are those who are careless with or do damage to another's property without making up for it. There are those who borrow items and never return them, who run up huge debts with no intention of repaying them, who take bribes and kickbacks to obtain jobs or contracts, who file phony insurance claims, exaggerated expense accounts, and falsified tax returns. All of these actions constitute stealing. They are violations of the virtue of justice and of the commandment that forbids us to take what does not belong to us.

We think of Judas primarily as the man who betrayed Jesus for thirty pieces of silver. But long before that happened, Judas was stealing money from the Apostles. Recall the time when Mary, the sister of Lazarus, anointed the feet of Jesus with precious ointment. Judas protested what he considered to be a waste of the ointment, saying that it could have been sold for three hundred silver pieces, "and the money have been given to the poor." But John the Apostle saw through Judas and tells us that "he did not say this out of concern for the poor, but because he was a thief. He held the purse, and used to help himself to what was deposited there" (John 12:1-8).

Judas' evil habit of stealing money from the Apostles eventually led him to the much greater sin of selling his Savior for money.

And that is what theft can do, lead us from "small" sins to bigger sins. The man who robs a bank did not start his career of stealing on such a large scale; his thievery probably began with taking money from his mother's purse, or from those in school with him, and progressed from petty theft to grand theft. It is important then that we heed the warning of St. Paul that no thieves or robbers "will inherit God's kingdom" (1 Corinthians 6:10).

The Seventh and Tenth Commandments

No one likes to be called a thief. Yet stealing is one of the most common sins. Perhaps there are two reasons for that: first, because of the covetousness of human nature; we want what others have. "The love of money is the root of all evil," said Paul. "Some men in their passion for it have strayed from the faith, and have come to grief amid great pain" (1 Timothy 6:10). Note that Paul didn't say that *money* is the root of all evil, but rather that *love of money* is the problem. The second reason why stealing is so common is because there are so many opportunities to take things that do not belong to us, especially small things.

The seventh and tenth commandments remind us that it is God who has supreme dominion over the world and its goods. We have been granted the use of those goods, and will be required to give an account of how we used them (Luke 16:2). We are to be stewards or trustees of the money and earthly possessions that God has made available to us, and we carry out our responsibilities properly if we use these things to satisfy our own legitimate needs and those of others who are less fortunate than we are. Every person has a right to keep something of what has been earned by work or talent, but there is also the obligation to share with others, and not just from our surplus but even from our essentials if someone else is in greater need than we are.

"All that we have received from God – life itself as well as material goods – does not belong to us but is given to us for our use," said Pope John Paul II. "Generosity in giving must always be enlightened and inspired by faith: then we will truly be more blessed in giving than in receiving" (*Redemptoris Missio*, n. 81).

The Holy Father also urged that we show special concern for the poor. He said that "this love of preference for the poor, and the decisions which it inspires in us, cannot but embrace the immense multitudes of the hungry, the needy, the homeless, those without medical care, and, above all, those without hope of a better future.

It is impossible not to take account of the existence of these realities. To ignore them would mean becoming like the 'rich man' who pretended not to know the beggar Lazarus lying at his gate" (*On Social Concern*, n. 42).

The *Catechism of the Catholic Church*, said Pope John Paul, presents "a series of kinds of behavior and actions contrary to human dignity: theft, deliberate retention of goods lent or objects lost, business fraud (cf. Dt. 25:13-16), unjust wages (cf. Dt. 24:14-15), forcing up prices by trading on the ignorance or hardship of another (cf. Am. 8:4-6), the misappropriation and private use of the corporate property of an enterprise, work badly done, tax fraud, forgery of checks and invoices, excessive expenses, waste, etc.

"It continues: 'The seventh commandment prohibits actions or enterprises which for any reason – selfish or ideological, commercial or totalitarian – lead to the enslavement of human beings, disregard for their personal dignity, buying or selling or exchanging them like merchandise. Reducing persons by violence to use-value or a source of profit is a sin against their dignity as persons and their fundamental rights'" (*Veritatis Splendor*, n. 100).

Ill-Gotten Treasures

There is a story of a certain king who wished to construct a building in a field not far from his palace. The woman who owned the field adjoining the king's property did not wish to sell it because it had belonged to her family for many generations. But the king ignored her wishes. He did, however, accede to a request she made, that she be allowed to take a basket of dirt from the field. When the large basket was filled, the woman asked the king to lift it for her. He tried, but it was too heavy to pick up. "If you find this one basket of earth too heavy to lift," the woman said to the king, "how are you going to bear the burden of the whole piece of land for eternity?" The remark so struck the monarch that he gave the woman back her land.

Sometimes we can be so intent on obtaining money or some desired thing that we ignore God's admonition against stealing. We think only of the material gain involved and not of the spiritual loss that may follow. What temporary profit can be worth the loss of our soul for all eternity? "Ill-gotten treasures profit nothing but virtue saves from death" (Proverbs 10:2), the Bible tells us. Wise words, but how many fail to follow them in their daily lives? We must try to cultivate the realization that whenever a person takes something that belongs to someone else, there is no real gain involved. Though on the surface the taker may seem to have benefited, the temporal gain cannot be balanced by the spiritual loss.

We also need to remind ourselves and others of the proper place of money and material wealth in the plan of God. "Do not lay up for yourselves an earthly treasure," Jesus said. "Moths and rust corrode; thieves break in and steal. Make it your practice instead to store up heavenly treasure, which neither moths nor rust corrode nor thieves break in and steal. Remember, where your treasure is, there your heart is also" (Matthew 6:19-21). Our Lord also emphasized that "no man can serve two masters. He will either hate one and love the other or be attentive to one and despise the other. You cannot give yourself to God and money" (Matthew 6:24).

There is a danger in seeking to accumulate riches, Jesus warned, saying that "I assure you, only with difficulty will a rich man enter into the kingdom of God" (Matthew 19:23). He told his listeners a parable about "a rich man who had a good harvest. 'What shall I do?' he asked himself. 'I have no place to store my harvest. I know!' he said. 'I will pull down my grain bins and build larger ones. All my grain and my goods will go there. Then I will say to myself: You have blessings in reserve for years to come. Relax! Eat heartily, drink well. Enjoy yourself!' But God said to him, 'You fool! This very night your life shall be required of you. To whom shall all this piled-up wealth of yours go?' That is the way it works with the man who grows rich for himself instead of growing rich in the sight of God" (Luke 12:16-21).

The Importance of Honesty

While there are many honest people in the world, honesty is nevertheless a declining virtue. We must admit that, or we are not even being honest with ourselves. Consider some of the practical applications of the seventh commandment's prohibition against stealing.

First of all, we must pay our just debts. It is a sin, therefore, not to pay back what we have borrowed, or not to pay the plumber or the painter, or anyone else with whom we have dealings. Sometimes people have the money to pay their bills, but they choose to spend it on pleasure instead. To do so is sinful.

Many people waste time at work, thereby committing the sin of not giving an honest day's work for a day's pay. Employers must pay their help a just wage, enough for an individual to provide a decent standard of living for himself and his family, and employees must avoid habitual tardiness, "goofing off" on the job, taking items home, and leaving work early.

Manufacturers or suppliers of products must not cheat customers by selling goods that are inferior. Persons in business must not sell defective products, nor charge unfair prices. A person selling a house must let the buyer know of any problems with the structure, such as a leaky roof or water in the cellar. All of these things involve being honest with others, treating them as we would like to be treated.

Those holding public office, whether by election or appointment, are forbidden to take bribes or payoffs for contracts or jobs. They must also be conscious of their obligation to act as trustworthy administrators of public funds. To squander or divert these funds to unapproved uses is sinful. It amounts to stealing from the taxpayers.

We are also forbidden to damage another's property, whether it's breaking a neighbor's window, carving initials in a school desk, tearing pages out of a library book, denting someone's car in a parking lot and then driving away without reporting it, and many other infractions that occur every day. Some of these may seem like "little" things, but remember the words of Jesus: "If you can trust a man in little things, you can also trust him in greater; while anyone unjust in a slight matter is also unjust in greater" (Luke 16:10).

It is not only a sin to cheat customers by selling them inferior goods or by not performing the work we agreed to perform, it is also wrong to cheat in the games we play or to cheat in school. Getting the test ahead of time, or copying the answers from our sleeve or from someone else's paper is always a sin. We may get away with it in the classroom and come up with a passing mark, but we are really only cheating ourselves.

How would you like to go to a doctor who cheated his way through medical school, or be defended in court by a lawyer who cheated her way through law school, or fly in a plane with a pilot who cheated on the flying exam? When we present ourselves as being qualified to do something we are not really qualified to do because we cheated our way through the qualifying process, we put in jeopardy not only ourselves but also those who depend on us.

Sin and Restitution

Some violations of the seventh and tenth commandments are mortal sins and some are venial sins. The sin is large or small in proportion to the amount involved and the harm done to another person. To steal a large amount of money is obviously a serious sin, while stealing a small amount is usually a venial sin. But taking a small amount of money from a poor person could be a grave sin since it is in effect the same thing as stealing a lot of money from a wealthy person or a properous company. But we have no right to take even the smallest thing that does not belong to us. That is still a violation of God's law, and remember that stealing small amounts can eventually lead to stealing large amounts.

In order to gain God's forgiveness for any violation of the seventh commandment, we must be sorry for what we have stolen, we must intend not to commit that sin in the future, and we must make restitution, that is, we must restore or pay for whatever was taken or damaged, and we must return whatever was loaned to us in the same condition in which we received it. Even if what was given to us was stolen by someone else, we have the obligation to return it to its rightful owner after taking reasonable steps to determine who the rightful owner is.

We can return the stolen goods – or their value – to the person, store, or hotel anonymously if we would rather not do so personally or publicly, as long as proper restitution is made. If it is so long after the fact that perhaps the place from which the items were stolen is no longer in business, or if it is truly impossible to find out the real owner of stolen goods, we can make restititution by contributing the approximate value of the goods to charity. But the bottom line is that we must make up for the injustice we committed.

One day when Jesus was visiting the city of Jericho, he entered the house of Zaccheus, a wealthy tax collector. Many of those following Christ were scandalized because "he has gone to a sinner's house as a guest." It is true that Zaccheus was a sinner, that he had cheated people in his job as a collector of taxes. But his encounter with Jesus changed his life. He admitted that he had done wrong and promised to restore whatever he had stolen: " 'I give half my belongings, Lord, to the poor. If I have defrauded anyone in the least, I pay him back fourfold.' Jesus said to him: 'Today, salvation has come to this house' " (Luke 19:7-9).

Seventh and Tenth
Commandments Forbid:

THEFT (unjustly taking another's possessions)
BRIBES (wrongfully accepting payments for jobs or contracts)
DEPRIVING an employee of just wages
STEALING from an employer or **NEGLECTING** one's work
DAMAGING or **UNJUSTLY KEEPING** something borrowed
CHEATING (unjustly gaining something by deceit)
AVARICE or **COVETOUSNESS** (excessive desire for material wealth)
ENVY (sadness at the good fortune of another)

Seventh and Tenth
Commandments Require:

TO GIVE every person those goods to which he or she has a right
TO BE HONEST in dealing with everyone in all matters
TO RESTORE anything we have unjustly taken or damaged
TO BE CONTENT with what God in his providence has given us and not to be desirous or envious of what others have

The Need for Justice

If we give a person what we owe them, we have been just. If we have a habit of giving others what is owed to them, we have acquired the virtue of justice, of giving to others what is due to them. Justice is not only concerned with money, but with anything we might owe anyone, such as work for which we are paid or the obligation to provide for our family.

The virtue of justice also has to do with punishment we owe for having broken the law. A court is a tribunal of justice. The symbol of justice – the blindfolded figure balancing the scales – that we often see in front of courthouses is a great symbol because it illustrates that the scales must be kept in balance, and justice must be impartial, or societies collapse and anarchy results.

St. Joseph, the foster father of Jesus, is described in the Bible as an upright or just man (Matthew 1:19). This means that he gave everyone what was due to them. To God, he gave worship in word and deed; to those in authority, he gave obedience; to his family, he gave love and support; to his equals, he showed fraternal charity; to his subordinates, he meted out rewards and punishments. We should all emulate the justice of Joseph.

God is also just. He rewards the good that we do, and punishes the evil. God's justice is not in conflict with his mercy or goodness. While he is all-loving, merciful, and forgiving, he is also all-just. His mercy and forgiveness, along with his just punishments, are described throughout the Scriptures – from the rewards given to Noah and Abraham and the punishment given to Cain in the Old Testament to the reward given to the repentant thief on the cross and the punishment meted out to Judas in the New Testament.

But not all of God's justice is administered in this life. Some will not get the reward they deserve until they get to heaven, or the punishment they have earned until they get to hell. Things will eventually be straightened out; some here, some hereafter. But they will be straightened out. The good thing about God's system of justice is that he knows all the circumstances in the case. He knows our intentions, our mental limitations, our talents or lack of talents. We can never be perfectly accurate in deciding what punishment fits a certain crime, but God, who knows all things, will make the punishment fit the crime. We judge other people from outward appearances, but God judges the heart.

Justice and Peace

Suppose you live in a country where criminals are given just punishment for their crimes. You can walk along the street in peace. But suppose you live in a country where criminals are not punished. Then you walk along the street in fear. You are not at peace because peace is the fruit of justice. Where there is no justice, there can be no peace. For a nation to be at peace, criminals must receive just punishment for their crimes, and must be obliged to make restitution to those individuals they have harmed, and to society in general. Also, every citizen must be treated fairly. There must be "liberty and justice for all," as we say in the Pledge of Allegiance to the American flag.

Since justice respects the rights of everyone, it makes for honesty in our dealings with others. It curbs the deceitful, checks the ruthlessness of the powerful, protects the poor and helpless, and thus establishes an orderly society. Without justice, as many millions in other lands can ruefully attest, there is anarchy, oppression, warfare, and the triumph of evil. When the virtue of justice is linked with the virtue of charity, then all people benefit because they receive not only what is due to them in strict justice, but also what love of neighbor prompts generous and charitable people to do.

Justice is also linked with peace. "Justice will bring about peace," said the prophet (Isaiah 32:17). The Popes in the twentieth century have on many occasions focused on the role of justice in securing peace. The motto of Pope Pius XII was *Opus iustitiae pax*, "peace as the fruit of justice." Or listen to the words of Pope John XXIII:

"There is an immense task incumbent on all men of good will, namely the task of restoring the relations of the human family in truth, in justice, in love, and in freedom: the relations between individual human beings; between citizens and their respective political communities; between political communities themselves; between individuals, families, intermediate associations, and political communities on the one hand, and the world community on the other. This is a most exalted task, for it is the task of bringing about true peace in the order established by God" (*Pacem in Terris*, n. 162).

Pope John Paul II said that "the goal of peace, so desired by everyone, will certainly be achieved through the putting into effect of social and international justice, but also through the practice of the virtues which favor togetherness, and which teach us to live in unity, so as to build in unity, by giving and receiving, a new society and a better world" (*On Social Concern*, n. 39).

And the *Catechism of the Catholic Church* says that "peace is not merely the absence of war, and it is not limited to maintaining a balance of powers between adversaries. Peace cannot be obtained on earth without safeguarding the goods of persons, free communication among men, respect for the dignity of persons and peoples, and the assiduous practice of fraternity. Peace is 'the tranquility of order.' Peace is the work of justice and the effect of charity" (n. 2304).

Chapter 10

Always Speak the Truth

The eighth commandment forbids misrepresenting the truth in our relations with others. This moral prescription flows from the vocation of the holy people to bear witness to their God who is the truth and wills the truth. – *Catechism of the Catholic Church*, n. 2464

A young man lay on an operating table in a New York hospital. Because he was suffering from cancer, several doctors and nurses stood in readiness for the surgery that would remove his tongue. The surgeon asked if there was anything he would like to say before the anesthesia was administered. Speaking very slowly and softly, the man said: "I want my last words to be, 'Praised be the sacred name of Jesus.' "

What a wonderful example to the world, but one can't help but wonder how many people in that situation would think of praising the name of the Lord. So many today use the names of God and Jesus, not in praise and glory, but to express surprise, fear, disgust, anger, and a host of other emotions. So many people use the same tongue on which they receive Jesus in Holy Communion to blaspheme, curse, scream profanities, and spread lies and gossip to their own spiritual detriment and to the harm of other people and their reputations. What a contradiction!

The tongue is a small and seemingly trivial organ of our human body, but its powers for good and evil are incalculable. One uncharitable remark, one scandalous utterance, can act as a tiny match which touches off a forest fire. One malicious lie, one whispered bit of gossip, can ruin the good name of another person. Though the person may have spent many years acquiring that good name, all that effort can be wiped out in one day. And even if the lie is later demonstrated to be false, many people will remember only the falsehood. The truth will never travel as far as the lie, particularly if the lie appeared in the newspapers or on radio or television. How many good people do we know of personally who have been unfairly maligned in the media, whether it's the local press or the national networks?

No wonder that the Bible compares the tongue to a "sharp sword" (Psalm 57:5), reminding us that we ought to be as careful with our faculty of speech as a person dueling with a sword. Using that sharp instrument carelessly can have disastrous consequences. It is no more possible to call back the false or hurtful words that we have spoken than it is to stop a bullet once we have pulled the trigger of a gun. It was our Lord himself who warned us: "I assure you, on judgment day people will be held accountable for every unguarded word they speak. By your words you will be acquitted, and by your words you will be condemned" (Matthew 12:36-37).

Does that make you stop and think? Have you ever heard people say that they don't go to Confession because they never really commit any sins? They are probably thinking of the major sins, like murder, adultery, stealing a lot of money, and so forth. But what about speaking "unguarded words"? Are we not all guilty of this at least some of the time? And if we are, then Jesus said that we will be held accountable, and may even be condemned, for this sinful practice. So we had better watch our tongues carefully!

One of the most graphic and dramatic warnings to practice restraint in the use of our tongues can be found in the letter of St. James. His remarks are quite lengthy, but are well worth quoting in their entirety. After noting that we put bits in the mouths of horses to make them obey us, and use a very small rudder to guide a ship, James says that "the tongue is something like that. It is a small member yet it makes great pretensions.

"See how tiny the spark is that sets a huge forest ablaze! The tongue is such a flame. It exists among our members as a whole universe of malice. The tongue defiles the entire body. Its flames encircle our course from birth, and its fire is kindled by hell. Every form of life, four-footed or winged, crawling or swimming, can be tamed, and has been tamed, by mankind; the tongue no man can tame. It is a restless evil, full of deadly poison. We use it to say,

'Praised be the Lord and Father'; then we use it to curse men, though they are made in the likeness of God. Blessing and curse come out of the same mouth.

"This ought not to be, my brothers! Does a spring gush forth fresh water and foul from the same outlet? A fig tree, brothers, cannot produce olives, or a grapevine figs; no more can a brackish source yield fresh water" (James 3:1-12).

Lying

There is a story about a dignified preacher who was walking down the street when he noticed a group of boys crowded around a small dog. When he asked them what they were doing, the youngsters replied: "Telling lies. Whoever tells the biggest lie gets the puppy."

"That's shocking!" the preacher exclaimed. "Why when I was your age I never thought of telling a lie."

"You win," the boys shouted in unison. "The dog's yours."

Perhaps lying is not as common as the story might indicate, but of all the violations of the commandment that forbids us to bear false witness against our neighbor, telling lies is the most obvious fault. **A lie is a harmful untruth (by word or deed) told to one who has the right to the truth.** A lie may be harmful either to another individual or to society at large. The direct harm may not be easily perceived, but every lie in some measure breaks down the mutual trust between persons and harms the good order of society. Imagine a relationship between individuals, or between groups or governments, where you could never be sure that the other party was telling the truth. How difficult life would be if we could never trust or believe what someone was telling us.

The underlying presumption here is that in almost all circumstances a person has a right to the truth. When parents ask a teenager where he or she spent the previous evening, they have a right to a truthful answer, even if it's going to get the teenager in trouble. When a lawyer asks a witness in a courtroom whether the defendant committed a particular crime, a truthful answer is required if justice is to be achieved.

But there are rare occasions when a person may conceal the truth for a higher good or for the greater right of another or of society. For instance, a doctor who is asked by a nosy relative about a person's illness is not obliged to give a truthful reply because the relative has no right to that information. Or a government official who is asked by a reporter about a military operation may withhold the truth until after the operation has been successfully completed so as not to jeopardize the lives of the participants.

Lies are usually divided into three types: helpful lies, jocose lies, and harmful lies. The first type (also known as a "white lie," although no lie is blameless) is intended to help oneself or someone else to get out of a difficult situation or to avoid embarrassment. Thus, a friend asks how you like her new dress. You really think that it looks terrible on her, but you don't want to hurt her feelings, so you say that it looks great. This kind of lie is sinful, but it is only slightly sinful since it does not cause serious harm to another.

The second type, a jocose lie, is told merely for amusement. Thus, you tell your friends that you caught a huge fish on your fishing trip, or that you hit a home run to win the game, or that you made the dean's list in college. All of these things are untrue, and your friends may even suspect that they are untrue, but they are told in a spirit of exaggeration and are not intended to hurt anyone. Therefore, they are only venial sins.

The third type, the harmful lie, is aimed at hurting someone or damaging their reputation and can be a mortal sin if the harm caused is great enough. Examples of a harmful lie would be perjury (telling a lie under oath) and calumny (inventing lies to ruin the reputation of another person). Because lying is an abuse of the power of speech and a violation of the eighth commandment, all lies must be avoided, but especially harmful lies since "lying lips are an abomination to the Lord" (Proverbs 12:22). We should follow the advice of St. Paul: "See to it, then, that you put an end to lying; let everyone speak the truth to his neighbor, for we are members of one another" (Ephesians 4:25).

One of the most odious labels a person can be branded with is to be called a liar. No matter what a person's faults may be, no one likes to hear that word applied to him or her. For a liar is rejecting Christ, who is the truth, and imitating the devil, who is the father of lies. "The reason I was born, the reason why I came into the world," Jesus told Pontius Pilate, "is to testify to the truth. Anyone committed to the truth hears my voice" (John 18:37). The devil, on the other hand, who lied to our first parents at the dawn of the human race, "has never based himself on truth; the truth is not in him," said Jesus. "Lying speech is his native tongue; he is a liar and the father of lies" (John 8:44).

While we are never supposed to lie, there are times when it is necessary to conceal the truth for a good reason, such as to protect a secret or to avoid revealing information that would hurt someone's name (mentioning that a neighbor now leading a good life had once spent time in jail). This can be done by the use of a mental restriction or a mental reservation. **A mental restriction is a statement that can be understood in a true sense, but probably will be understood by the hearer in another sense.** For instance, if an annoying salesman calls the office and asks for Mr. Brown, and Mr. Brown is there but has told you that he does not want to talk to that particular salesman, you could say that "Mr. Brown is not available." This is a legitimate mental restriction because people commonly understand that phrase to mean that Mr. Brown is not available to talk to that person.

Another example might be a nurse who was asked how a sick patient was doing. "Oh, he's doing much better," the nurse might say, meaning that the patient had received the Anointing of the Sick and was doing much better spiritually even though his physical condition was still serious. And there is a story told about a time that St. Athanasius was being pursued in a boat by his enemies. When he told the pilot of his boat to turn around and face his enemies, the skipper of the enemy boat shouted, "Have you seen Athanasius?" The pilot of the saint's boat replied, "Just a short time ago he passed this very spot, going up river." The statement was true, but was understood by the enemy in a different sense.

Obviously, mental reservations must be used prudently and only for a very good reason lest they create an atmosphere of mistrust and uncertainty where people are not sure what to believe.

Calumny

Calumny is the injuring of another's good name by lying about him or her. It is a sin against truth because a lie is told. It is a sin against charity because it is a flagrant violation of Christ's fundamental command to love our neighbor. It is a sin against religion, which cannot thrive in an atmosphere of lying and slander. And it is a sin against justice because it harms a person's good name and reputation.

As we saw in connection with the seventh and tenth commandments, a violation of justice requires restitution. When we steal money from someone, we must not only confess the sin, we must also give back the money. So, too, when we rob someone of their good name, we have an obligation to restore it (a task that is nearly impossible in most cases). Which is why we ought to heed the admonition that many of us first heard when we were children: If you can't say something good about somebody, don't say anything.

Before you speak badly of another person, think of the old story about the woman who told a priest that she was guilty of slandering an acquaintance. The priest told her to take a pillow, cut it open, and let the feathers blow wherever they might; then the next day to go out and gather up every feather. "But that would be impossible," the woman said. "Exactly," the priest replied. "It is impossible to repair the harm done by your words." Nevertheless, we still have the obligation to make every effort to repair the damage we have done.

Christ himself knew what it was like to be the object of calumnious statements by his enemies. He who spent his time doing good even for those whom he knew did not appreciate his efforts, who went about healing the sick and bringing sinners back to repentance, was sometimes the target of slanderers. Recall the time that he attended a banquet in Matthew's house with tax collectors and those whom the scribes and Pharisees considered the dregs of Palestinian society. All his good deeds were forgotten as the hypocritical Pharisees derided our Lord for "eating with tax collectors and those who disregard the law." Overhearing their remark, Jesus said, "People who are in good health do not need a doctor; sick people do .... I have come to call, not the self-righteous, but sinners" (Matthew 9:10-13).

No wonder that Christ and the Bible are so emphatic in condemning those who slander others. "Like a club, or a sword, or a sharp arrow is the man who bears false witness against his neighbor" (Proverbs 25:18). And the Bible is just as emphatic about those who listen to calumny as those who spread it: "Never repeat gossip, and you will not be reviled. Tell nothing to a friend or foe; if you have a fault, reveal it not, for he who hears it will hold it against you, and in time become your enemy. Let anything you hear die within you; be assured it will not make you burst. When a fool hears something, he is in labor, like a woman giving birth to a child. Like an arrow lodged in a man's thigh is gossip in the breast of a fool" (Sirach 19:6-11).

If Christ's spirit of love of neighbor is at the basis of our words and actions, then sins of calumny and slander will have no part in our life. The tongue can be a source of drawing souls to Christ, or of pushing souls (including our own) away from Christ. So we must avoid not only calumny and slander, but any kind of mockery and ridicule that we may say is aimed at "getting a laugh," but that more often than not is motivated by pride or envy.

Detraction

One day a group of men visited Abraham Lincoln at the White House and gave him a written statement containing accusations about one of Lincoln's old and faithful friends. The President read the paper and then, looking at the group, asked: "You have given me this paper, so may I do with it as I please?"

"Certainly, Mr. President," was the reply. Lincoln turned to the fireplace behind him, threw the paper into the flames, faced the men, and said, "Good day, gentlemen."

Abraham Lincoln, who was the target of many lies and smears, knew only too well what it was like to have his character maligned. So he was very sensitive to attempts to ruin the good name of another person. He was opposed not only to calumny and slander, but also to detraction. **The sin of detraction involves making known the hidden faults of another when there is no good reason to do so.** It means telling the truth about someone, but a truth that it is not necessary to make public without a very strong reason. For example, if you see your neighbor coming home drunk late at night, there is no good reason for you to make that fact known to others the next day. Nor is there any reason for you to reveal that a public official now in good standing in the community once committed a crime.

One's reputation or good name is one of the most precious earthly possessions we can have. It is far more valuable than wealth. The loss of a spotless reputation by persons with great riches and an abundance of worldly goods has led some almost to despair because when a good name is lost, no amount of money can get it back. Shakespeare put it well when he wrote in *Othello*: "Who steals my purse steals trash; 'tis something, nothing;/'Twas mine, 'tis his, and has been slave to thousands;/But he that filches from me my good name,/Robs me of that which not enriches him/And makes me poor indeed."

The seriousness of the sin of detraction depends on the degree of harm done to another's reputation and, as in the case of calumny, there is an obligation to repair the damage caused. Because detraction involves the truth, one cannot say that the statement was mistaken, as in the case of calumny. One can, however, try to make up for the sin by stressing the good points of the person injured. If the detraction took place in the media, one must use the same forum to undo it. If the injury to another's reputation was made in a group of people, the detractor must make sure that all those who heard the statement and perhaps passed it along to others also spread the reparation, too. The obligation to repair the damage would cease if there was reason to believe that enough time had gone by so that people had forgotten about the matter, or if it might do more harm than good to bring it up again.

Rash Judgment

It was during his famous Sermon on the Mount that Jesus spelled out for all ages and for all people his condemnation of rash judgment, hypocrisy, and deceit. "If you want to avoid judgment, stop passing judgment," Christ told his audience. "Your verdict on others will be the verdict passed on you. The measure with which you measure will be used to measure you. Why look at the speck in your brother's eye when you miss the plank in your own? How can you say to your brother, 'Let me take that speck out of your eye,' while all the time the plank remains in your own? You hypocrite! Remove the plank from your own eye first; then you will see clearly to take the speck from your brother's eye" (Matthew 7:1-5).

Rash judgment is the willingness to believe, without sufficient evidence, that a person is guilty of some evil. We might also call it "jumping to conclusions" or "judging a book by its cover." An example would be the person who saw a neighbor go out at odd hours of the night and suspected that the neighbor was involved in some kind of illegal or immoral activity, when in fact the neighbor was attending Nocturnal Adoration services and praying to Jesus in the Blessed Sacrament at a church in the next town. Our Lord himself was rashly judged when he associated with people perceived to be great sinners. What those doing the judging did not know was that former sinners like Mary Magdalene and Zaccheus had reformed their lives due to the influence of Christ.

That is why Jesus is so emphatic in warning us not to judge others. We see only the outward appearances, while God sees the inner person. Of course, we must always exercise caution, especially with those who have been known to commit evil actions in the past. We are not expected to be gullible; otherwise we might suffer some harm to ourselves or to our loved ones. But in exercising caution, we must not attempt to pass judgment on the state of a person's conscience. That is for God to determine.

It is also important to remember that not judging others means not judging their motives, or not trying to guess at the reasons for their actions. It does not mean that we cannot call a crime a crime, or a sin a sin. If someone steals your car, there is nothing wrong with calling the guilty party a thief. If a physician makes a living killing unborn babies, there is nothing wrong with calling him an abortionist. We are simply stating a fact in both instances and are not attempting to judge the motivations of the individuals performing the actions. We may condemn the sin, but we must not condemn the sinner. We are called to hate the sin but to love the sinner, which means that we must pray for the sinner that he or she will repent of their evil lifestyle and turn back to God.

In rash judging, we often judge others by our own standards. Our leaning toward a particular sin is liable to mislead us into thinking that other people have the same leaning. Bad people quickly suspect evil of others because they are so caught up in evil themselves. That is why thieves often argue among themselves, why two-timing spouses often accuse the other party of being unfaithful, why the person who cheats the most in examinations is the first one to attribute another's high marks to cheating. Just as molten lead takes the form of the mold into which it is poured, so our judgment of what we see and hear often takes shape from our own feelings. A corrupted mind takes an evil view of things, whereas a good person puts the best interpretation on everything.

St. Anselm said that he would much rather be wrong by thinking good of a bad man, than by thinking evil of a good man. Even when an action is without doubt an evil one, the man or woman filled with the charity of Christ does not judge the person, but leaves that judgment to God. Our words and actions will never be Christ-like until we first train our minds to think good thoughts about our brothers and sisters in Jesus Christ.

Secrets and Promises

A follower of Christ ought to be trustworthy in all dealings with others, and this includes being faithful to our word by keeping secrets and holding to promises. There are three kinds of secrets: natural, promised, and official or professional. **A natural secret is one which by its very nature ought to be kept from others.** If I learn some hidden fault about my neighbor (he watches pornographic movies), I have an obligation to keep that information to myself and not spread it around the neighborhood.

A promised secret is one that must be kept because the person promised to do after he became aware of the secret. Suppose I find out from an organization that they are going to give a friend of mine a prestigious award, but it's a surprise. I promise that I will not reveal that secret to my friend, and I am bound by that promise.

An official or professional secret is one which comes within the scope of a person's job or profession. Thus, public officials, doctors, lawyers, priests, etc., are to keep secret any information they receive in confidence from their superiors, patients, clients, or penitents. The "seal of the confessional" is particularly comforting to Catholics because it means that a priest can never, under any circumstances, reveal what he has heard while extending God's forgiveness in the sacrament of Reconciliation.

Because we have as much right to our secrets as we do to our property and to our good name, it is a sin to make another's secrets known against his or her will. The sin may be either mortal or venial depending on the harm that is caused by revealing a particular secret. Revealing the hidden faults of a neighbor could be a venial sin if it only caused the neighbor embarrassment, or it could be a mortal sin if it cost the neighbor his job and his means of supporting his family.

Ordinarily the revelation of a promised secret would be a slight sin, while the breaking of an official secret would normally be a serious sin. It would be a mortal sin, for example, for a government official to make defense secrets known to the enemy since this would jeopardize the lives and possibly the freedom of his fellow citizens. It would also be a serious sin for a public official to let it be known that a certain parcel of land was going to become very valuable, thus allowing a friend to use this advance knowledge to make a lot of money.

The only times that an official secret could be made known – with the exception of a confessional secret, which can never be revealed – would be if the matter had already become public in another way, if the person with the secret gave permission to make it known, or if the good of society or of an individual required it. The good to be accomplished must outweigh the evil of giving away the secret. If you learned that a candidate for public office was a tool of organized crime, you would not be wrong to make the information public. Or if a doctor discovered that a young man scheduled to be married had a sexually transmitted disease, he would be obligated to tell the fiancee if the man was not willing to do so.

Not only do we have a serious duty to keep a secret, but it would also be wrong to attempt to discover someone's secrets, say, by eavesdropping on their telephone conversations or by reading their mail. But there are exceptions here as well. It is not wrong for the police to seek judicial approval to wiretap the phones of criminals in order to obtain evidence of criminal activity since the public good is at stake. Nor would it be wrong for parents to read the mail of their children if they had strong reason to believe that doing so might keep the children from serious harm. In general, however, we must respect the right of others to have secrets.

A Saint's Reminder

St. Gertrude reminds us that "the tongue is privileged above the other members of the body, as on it reposes the Sacred Body and Precious Blood of our Lord." These words ought to inspire us to redouble our efforts to avoid the common sins resulting from the misuse of our marvelous faculty of speech.

There is something intriguing about listening to our voice on tape. We have trouble believing that it is our voice, for one thing. It is also interesting to hear the voice of someone who is no longer alive, perhaps even a departed grandparent or parent. But suppose that all our conversations in the past had been recorded on tape and were played back to us. Would there be any lies, calumnies, detractions, rash judgments, and other sins of the tongue to cause us shame and embarrassment? Probably more than we would care to acknowledge. Yet we should not forget that every word that falls from our lips is recorded in the eternal memory of God, and he has promised to hold us accountable for all of these unguarded words (Matthew 12:36-37).

So let us make a conscious effort every day to eliminate these faults of speech and to use our tongue to glorify, praise, and thank God for the many blessings given to us, and to demonstrate love and concern for our friends and neighbors, and even for our enemies.

Chapter 11

The Church and You

The Roman Pontiff and the bishops, as authentic teachers, preach to the People of God the faith which is to be believed and applied in moral life. It is also incumbent on them to pronounce on moral questions that fall within the natural law and reason. – *Catechism of the Catholic Church*, n. 2050

When a teenager from the Midwest was told that his younger brother, age six, needed a blood transfusion immediately, he volunteered to give a pint of his own blood. After the donation had been completed, the little boy was told what his older brother had done for him. "Mom, will he die now – like Jesus?" the youngster asked his mother. Of course, his mother explained that a person can donate blood to help someone else without doing any harm to himself.

The same principle holds true with reference to the mutual spiritual assistance that exists among the members of the Catholic Church, which is sometimes called the Mystical Body of Christ. If one member is failing spiritually, another may come forward and help restore him or her to spiritual health. Unfortunately, there are members of the Church who are spiritually sick, anemic, or dying; they need the help of more healthy members. Fortunately, spiritual blood transfusions are available for those who need them and, like a physical transfusion, they do not drain us, but rather make us stronger as we give to others.

There is an old saying that the good or evil done to others is good or evil done to Christ. The saying comes from the story of St. Paul's conversion from a fierce persecutor of the Church to one of its greatest apostles. You will recall that Paul, who was known as

Saul in those days, was on his way to Damascus, "breathing murderous threats against the Lord's disciples," when a flash of light from the sky knocked him to the ground. He heard a voice saying, "Saul, Saul, why do you persecute me?" When Saul asked who was speaking, the voice said: "I am Jesus, the one you are persecuting" (Acts 9:1-5). It was not Christ whom Saul was persecuting, but his followers – and yet those words rang in Saul's ears: "Why do you persecute me?"

After Paul became a disciple of Jesus, the Apostles gave him further evidence that the good or evil done to others is good or evil done to Christ when they told him what the Lord had said about the last judgment. At that final judgment of the whole world, Jesus will call all the just and say to them: "Come, you have my Father's blessing! Inherit the kingdom prepared for you from the creation of the world. For I was hungry and you gave me food, I was thirsty and you gave me drink. I was a stranger and you welcomed me, naked and you clothed me. I was ill and you comforted me, in prison and you came to visit me."

When the just ask when they did all of these things, Jesus will reply: "I assure you, as often as you did it for one of my least brothers, you did it for me" (Matthew 25:34-40). Christ also made clear that failure to do these things will bring eternal punishment, saying: "I assure you, as long as you neglected to do it to one of these least ones, you neglected to do it to me" (Matthew 25:45).

The Mystical Body of Christ

The bond among all Christians in the Mystical Body of Christ is the same as the bond that exists among members of the human body, as St. Paul made clear in his First Letter to the Corinthians (12:12-31). Christ is the head of the body, and we are the members. If a member of the human body is cut off from the head, it is useless. But if it remains in contact with the head, it will work for its own good and the good of all the other members. So, too, if a Catholic, a member of Christ's Mystical Body, remains in contact with Christ the head, he or she will benefit themselves and others.

If the eye sees a rock sailing through the air toward the chest, the eye does not say, "That is not going to hit me, I'll let my chest worry about that." Rather, the eye does everything possible to prevent injury to the chest, for both are parts of one and the same body. This means that we cannot be indifferent to the fate and well-being of other members of the Mystical Body, for when the

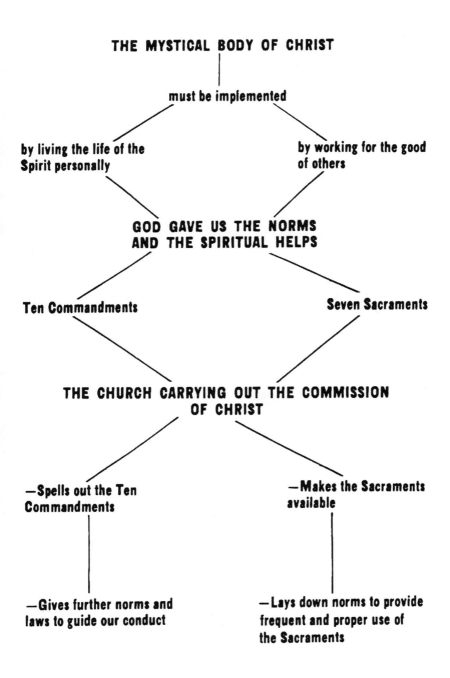

THE MYSTICAL BODY OF CHRIST

must be implemented

by living the life of the
Spirit personally

by working for the good
of others

GOD GAVE US THE NORMS
AND THE SPIRITUAL HELPS

Ten Commandments

Seven Sacraments

THE CHURCH CARRYING OUT THE COMMISSION
OF CHRIST

—Spells out the Ten
Commandments

—Makes the Sacraments
available

—Gives further norms and
laws to guide our conduct

—Lays down norms to provide
frequent and proper use of
the Sacraments

Church in any part of the world suffers, we suffer since we are all members of the body headed by Christ. And by the same token when any member of the body rejoices, we also share in their joy for we are all linked together.

This bond was emphasized by the Second Vatican Council: "As all the members of the human body, though they are many, form one body, so also are the faithful in Christ. Also, in the building up of Christ's body there is a flourishing variety of members and functions. There is only one Spirit who, according to his own richness and the needs of the ministries, distributes his different gifts for the welfare of the Church. Among these gifts stands out the grace given to the Apostles. To their authority, the Spirit himself subjected even those who were endowed with charisms. Giving the body unity through himself and through his power and through the internal cohesion of its members, this same Spirit produces and urges love among the believers. Consequently, if one member suffers anything, all the members suffer it too, and if one member is honored, all the members rejoice together" (*Dogmatic Constitution on the Church*, n. 7).

In another of its sixteen documents, the Council said that "God, who has fatherly concern for everyone, has willed that all men should constitute one family and treat one another in a spirit of brotherhood. For having been created in the image of God, who 'from one man has created the whole human race and made them live all over the face of the earth,' all men are called to one and the same goal, namely, God himself" (*Pastoral Constitution on the Church in the Modern World*, n. 24).

This means that "a special obligation binds us to make ourselves the neighbor of absolutely every person, and of actively helping him when he comes across our path, whether he be an old person abandoned by all, a foreign laborer unjustly looked down upon, a refugee, a child born of an unlawful union and wrongly suffering for a sin he did not commit, or a hungry person who disturbs our conscience by recalling the voice of the Lord: 'As long as you did it for one of these, the least of my brethren, you did it for me'" (*Pastoral Constitution on the Church in the Modern World*, n. 27).

The Church can be compared to a baseball team. If one player strikes out, it not only pulls down his average, but it hinders the team as well. If a member hits a home run, it boosts his average and helps the whole team. Thus, we are all joined together on the team that is headed by Christ, and there should be no such thing as an isolated Christian. Wherever a Christian is anywhere in the world, he or she is not alone, but is linked to millions of other Christians. Just as the whole team benefits by the home run of one player, so all Christians share in the spiritual riches of the Church (cf. *Catechism of the Catholic Church*, n. 953),

Every Catholic shares in the fruits of the Mass, wherever it may be said. Through our own prayers and sacrifices, we not only help ourselves, but also give a spiritual blood transfusion to other members of the Church throughout the world. The faithful on earth can as members of the Mystical Body of Christ help one another by practicing supernatural charity, by prayers, and by performing the corporal and spiritual works of mercy. The Catholic doctrine of the Mystical Body is not a static thing, but implies action:

"For this the Church was founded: that by spreading the kingdom of Christ everywhere for the glory of God the Father, she might bring all men to share in Christ's saving redemption; and that through them the whole world might in actual fact be brought into relationship with him. All activity of the Mystical Body directed to the attainment of this goal is called the apostolate, and the Church carries it on in various ways through all her members. For by its very nature the Christian vocation is also a vocation to the apostolate.

"No part of the structure of a living body is merely passive but each has a share in the functions as well as in the life of the body. So, too, in the Body of Christ, which is the Church, the whole body, 'according to the functioning in due measure of each single part, derives its increase.' Indeed, so intimately are the parts linked and interrelated in this body that the member who fails to make his proper contribution to the development of the Church must be said to be useful neither to the Church nor to himself" (*Decree on the Apostolate of the Laity*, n. 2).

Read that last sentence again. It says that our bond with our brothers and sisters in the Body of Christ is so intimate that if we fail to help them, and fail to build up the Church, we are useful neither to the Church nor to ourselves. That indicates what a solemn and important responsibility we have to be active members of the Mystical Body of Christ.

The Communion of Saints

But there is still another bond of unity that affects us. This is the bond that exists between the saints in heaven, the souls in purgatory, and all of us on earth. Known as the Communion of Saints, the three groups have been described as the Church Triumphant, those who led lives of holiness on earth and are now receiving their reward in heaven; the Church Suffering, those who are making up for their sins in purgatory, being purified for heaven; and the Church Militant, those on earth who are fighting against the world, the flesh, and the devil to attain heaven (cf. *Catechism of the Catholic Church*, nn. 954-959).

All members of this community can share in the spiritual treasury of the Church and can aid one another by prayers and good works. Those already in heaven, of course, have no need of our prayers, but we can honor and imitate them, and they can intercede with God for us and for the souls in purgatory. Those in purgatory cannot pray for themselves, but they can pray for us. And we can pray for each other and for the souls in purgatory. Just as one person can take care of the monetary debts of another person, so by our prayers and good works can we help those who have accumulated spiritual debts. "Pray for one another," St. James tells us, "so that you may find healing" (James 5:16).

Monica became a saint because of her prayers for her wayward son, the future St. Augustine. And Scripture tells us that prayers for the dead are a "holy and pious thought" (2 Maccabees 12:45). What a wonderful privilege and consolation it is to be able to pray for our departed loved ones knowing that by our prayers we may shorten the time of their purification and speed up their entry into heavenly bliss! And can we doubt that when those we helped out of purgatory reach heaven, they will intercede for us?

St. Paul asked his converts and the faithful of the early Church to "pray for us" (1 Thessalonians 5:25). We often ask friends to pray for us, so why not ask friends who have left this world and are now in heaven to pray for us, too? There are those who scoff at such an idea, but isn't it reasonable to think that those who were close to us in this life would still be interested in us in heaven and would be aware of our needs? It was Christ himself who assured us: "I tell you, there will likewise be more joy in heaven over one repentant sinner than over ninety-nine righteous people who have no need to repent" (Luke 15:7).

How can this be true if those in heaven have no knowledge of or interest in us? When one reaches heaven and sees more clearly the needs of those on earth, he or she will as a saint use his or her powers of intercession with God all the more. St. Jerome saw this very clearly in the fourth century, and his words reflect the belief of the Catholic Church in our own century: "If apostles and martyrs while still in the flesh and still needing to care for themselves, can pray for others, how much more will they pray for others after they have won their crowns, their victories."

The Church's Right to Make Laws

By living as an active member of the Mystical Body and the Communion of Saints, the individual Catholic works toward his or her own individual salvation and tries to help others achieve that same lofty goal. As we have already seen, the ten Commandments were given to us by God to serve as guidelines for Christian living. The Church is not only the guardian and teacher of the ten Commandments, but she also carries on the work of Christ by making additional rules and precepts to help her members live this present life in a way that will best prepare them for the life to come. Where does the Church get the authority to do such a thing? From Christ, of course.

One day when Jesus and the Apostles were in northern Palestine, near the city of Caesarea Philippi and within sight of the magnificent temple of Augustus, which sat high on a majestic rock that towered over the city, our Lord conducted the first public opinion poll by asking the Apostles: "'Who do people say that the Son of Man is?' They replied, 'Some say John the Baptizer, others Elijah, still others Jeremiah or one of the prophets.' 'And you,' he said to them, 'who do you say that I am?'

"'You are the Messiah,' Simon Peter answered, 'the Son of the living God!' Jesus replied, 'Blest are you, Simon, son of Jonah! No mere man has revealed this to you, but my heavenly Father. I for my part declare to you, you are "Rock," and on this rock I will build my Church, and the jaws of death shall not prevail against it. I will entrust to you the keys of the kingdom of heaven. Whatever you declare bound on earth shall be bound in heaven; whatever you declare loosed on earth shall be loosed in heaven" (Matthew 16:13-19).

This is where the Church founded by Christ receives its mandate to make the laws and precepts for us to follow if we wish to get to heaven. The incident shows our Lord acting out part of his triple function on earth as teacher, priest, and shepherd. Christ was a teacher who spent much of his time during the three years of his public life teaching individuals and groups of people to follow him as the way, the truth, and the life. He also exercised the function of priest by forgiving sins and offering the greatest sacrifice of all – his own life – for our sanctification. And Christ was a spiritual shepherd, guiding and feeding his sheep with the solid food of truth, reproving and correcting them when they strayed from the right path.

Before leaving the earth, Jesus passed along this triple function of teacher, priest, and shepherd to the Church that carrries on his mission in the world. The Catholic Church teaches the doctrine of Christ (Pope John XXIII began his famous encyclical letter *Mater et Magistra* by saying that "the Catholic Church has been established by Jesus Christ as MOTHER AND TEACHER of nations"). The Catholic Church ministers to the spiritual needs of Christ's flock through the Sacraments, and the Church acts as a shepherd, laying down necessary laws and precepts, reproving and correcting when necessary.

That Jesus Christ established a Church to continue his work on earth is clear. It is equally clear, although it is disputed by people who call themselves followers of Christ, that Jesus gave the leaders of his Church the power to make laws related to the spiritual welfare of the members of that Church. When our Lord told Peter, "Whatever you declare bound on earth shall be bound in heaven," he was saying that whatever laws Peter and his successors made, he would ratify them in heaven.

"Refer It to the Church"

To make his intentions absolutely clear, our Lord, after appointing a group of seventy-two men to aid the Apostles in their work, and before sending them on their first missionary journey, assured them of their spiritual power when acting in his name and said: "He who hears you, hears me. He who rejects you, rejects me. And he who rejects me, rejects him who sent me" (Luke 10:16).

On another occasion, Christ told the Apostles that if a member of the Church "should commit some wrong against you, go and point out his fault, but keep it between the two of you. If he listens to you, you have won your brother over. If he does not listen, summon another, so that every case may stand on the word of two or three witnesses. If he ignores them, refer it to the church. If he ignores even the Church, then treat him as you would a Gentile or a tax collector. I assure you, whatever you declare bound on earth shall be held bound in heaven, and whatever you declare loosed on earth shall be held loosed in heaven" (Matthew 18:15-18).

Any large society needs laws if it is to function smoothly and in accordance with the plan of its founder. The same is true of the worldwide society of Jesus Christ, the Catholic Church. The task of getting to heaven is not an easy one; it requires effort and discipline. And since human nature is weakened by original sin, we need all the guidance we can get to do good and avoid evil. This additional guidance is available to us through the Church of Jesus and the laws and precepts it has adopted over the centuries. And remember that these laws were made under the guidance of the Holy Spirit, "the Spirit of truth," whom Christ promised would be with his Church always (John 14:16-17).

The Precepts of the Church

In addition to the ten Commandments, the Church has from time to time spelled out certain specific duties of Catholics. The basic list of six precepts (cf. *Catechism of the Catholic Church*, nn. 2041-2043) was expanded to seven and fleshed out with more detail in the *Basic Teachings for Catholic Religious Education* that was issued by the Catholic Bishops of the United States. The precepts listed there are as follows:

1. To keep holy the day of the Lord's Resurrection: to worship God by participating in Mass every Sunday and Holy Day of Obligation: to avoid those activities that would hinder renewal of soul and body, e.g., needless work and business activities, unnecessary shopping, etc.

2. To lead a sacramental life: to receive Holy Communion frequently and the Sacrament of Penance regularly — minimally, to receive the Sacrament of Penance at least once a year (annual confession is obligatory only if serious sin is involved) — minimally, to receive Holy Communion at least once a year, between the First Sunday of Lent and Trinity Sunday.

3. To study Catholic teaching in preparation for the Sacrament of Confirmation, to be confirmed, and then to continue to study and advance the cause of Christ.

4. To observe the marriage laws of the Church: to give religious training (by example and word) to one's children; to use parish schools and religious education programs.

5. To strengthen and support the Church: one's own parish community and parish priests; the worldwide Church and the Holy Father.

Chapter 12

Our Share in God's Life

"The purpose of the sacraments is to sanctify men, to build up the Body of Christ, and, finally, to give worship to God. Because they are signs they also instruct. They not only presuppose faith, but by words and objects they also nourish, strengthen, and express it. That is why they are called 'sacraments *of faith.*'" – *Catechism of the Catholic Church*, n. 1123

There is an old story about a man who was walking through the fields of northern Italy just before the turn of this century. As he stopped to meditate at the Oropa Shrine, an exciting and wonderful thought came to him. He descended the hillside from the shrine to the city early in the evening and met a friend, a poet and journalist named Abate. "Giuseppe," the man said to his friend, "up there at the chapel a sudden, wonderful idea struck me." That wonderful idea is described today on a tablet on the golden door of the shrine. The tablet bears this inscription:

"From the cloisters of the mountains of Oropa, Guglielmo Marconi drew inspiration for his great discovery. May wireless telegraphy, under the auspices of Mary, bring the peace of Christ to mankind."

It was while communicating with his God that the famous electrical engineer and inventor got his inspiration for a better way of communicating with his fellow human beings.

In this chapter, we begin a study of the seven Sacraments, each of which is a unique communication between God and us. These special encounters between divinity and humanity give us a share, or increase our share, in God's life, which is known as sanctifying grace. And these encounters come at the particular times in our lives when we need them. When we first come into the world stained with original sin and in need of cleansing in order to join the family of Christ ("No one can enter into God's kingdom without being begotten of water and Spirit" – John 3:5), there is the sacrament of Baptism. When we reach the age of reason, usually about seven, and know the difference between right and wrong and can understand the Real Presence of Jesus in Holy Communion and our need for this spiritual nourishment, we receive the sacraments of Penance and the Holy Eucharist for the first time.

For many of us as we reached our teenage years (the age for Confirmation has varied from infancy to the teens), and found that we had more temptations to face and more problems to solve, there was the sacrament of Confirmation to give us the special gifts of the Holy Spirit. Those gifts are wisdom, understanding, counsel, fortitude (or courage), knowledge, piety, and fear of the Lord (or wonder and awe at the power of God). When the time comes for us to choose a vocation in life, there are the sacraments of Holy Orders (for men entering the priesthood) and Matrimony (for couples desiring to spend the rest of their lives together in marriage). And when we reach old age, or when we are seriously ill at any age, there is the sacrament of the Anointing of the Sick to help us to deal with pain and suffering and to prepare us to meet God if the illness should lead to death.

Signs and Symbols

Every day we find ourselves regulating our actions – doing this and avoiding that, or acting in one way rather than another – according to the many signs and symbols that we see. When we see a red traffic light, for instance, we know that it means we should stop the car. When we see an umpire in a baseball game raise his right hand to the sky, it usually means that a player is out. When we enter the supermarket, we follow the signs to find the aisle that has the particular food we want to buy. The motion of our hand one way or the other can mean "Come here" or "Go away." Signs and symbols that represent a thought or a command or an invitation play an important part in our daily life.

It is therefore the most logical thing in the world that signs should also play a part in the religious sphere of our life too, that there should be symbols that express something about our relationship with God, or about his relationship with us. In Japan, there is a custom whereby a pagan boy or girl will sometimes write out petitions and prayers on a slip of paper and tie it to the leg of their stone fox-god. It is an expression – a sign – of belief and confidence in that god. That same symbolic expression of reliance on the true God is also demonstrated by Christians who write out petitions and prayers to Jesus, to his mother Mary, and to the saints. The use of signs and symbols is very much a part of our secular and religious lives.

And yet there are some people who claim that the Catholic Church has too many ceremonies, too many liturgical gestures and vestments and vessels. They say that "we just want to pray to God without external religious signs and ceremonies." That is very similar to saying that "we just want health and strength – let's do away with all the medical procedures and machines and instruments, all those external trappings."

No, we cannot do away with all those things and still have good health. Neither can we do away with all the external rites and accouterments of religion without diminishing the honor and reverence that is due to God, and without denying ourselves the beauty and significance of those ceremonies and sacred objects.

Christ himself gave many indications of how important religious signs and symbols are to our spiritual life. His many miracles – changing water into wine, curing a blind man with mud, feeding more than 5,000 with five loaves of bread and two fish, etc. – had great sign value to those who witnessed them. "These very works which I perform," Jesus said, "testify on my behalf that the Father has sent me" (John 5:36). His wondrous deeds were seen by hundreds and even thousands of people, and what they saw changed many of their lives forever.

We are composed of body as well as soul, not completely spiritual as angels are but with a material part of our existence that conceals the spiritual dimension. This is an example of God using something material that we can see to express or bring about spiritual realities that we cannot see. As St. John Chrysostom said many years ago, "If you were without a body, God would have given you invisible gifts, but since your soul is united to a body he gives you spiritual things within visible things."

God has done just that in giving us the seven Sacraments. He has taken ordinary elements of life – bread, water, and oil, for example – and commanded that they be used to express and accomplish extraordinary spiritual results. Yes, there are many external ceremonies in the Church, but there are seven rituals that stand in a class by themselves. They are the seven Sacraments.

To convey an idea to other people, we make use of signs. Some of these signs are natural – tears indicate that a person is sad, laughter indicates happiness. But most signs do not spring from natural reactions, they are artificial. They take on a meaning through mutual agreement and understanding. One example is language, by which a group of people agree that certain sounds will have a certain meaning. And once all members of the group come to know the meaning of the various sounds, they will be able to communicate effectively with each other.

God likewise makes use of signs to reveal and indeed to make operative his plan of salvation. But because he is infinite, no sign can completely express his meaning; and because we are finite, we cannot completely grasp the meaning of God. So we are confronted with what the Church calls a "mystery," that is, a divinely revealed truth that is beyond our comprehension but that we accept as true on the word of God, who is all Truth and who would never deceive us.

St. Paul has described well the infinite nature of the Almighty: "How deep are the riches and the wisdom and the knowledge of God! How inscrutable his judgments, how unsearchable his ways!" (Romans 11:33).

In the Eastern churches, the seven Sacraments are most often referred to as Mysteries. They are seven vital channels through which Christ in a mysterious way brings salvation to us. They are also signs which not only convey a meaning but also accomplish in us what they signify. Water, for instance, is recognized as a cleansing agent, and so in the sacrament of Baptism it not only conveys this meaning, but it also achieves the cleansing of our soul from original sin and any personal sin.

Why the Sacraments?

By his life, death, and resurrection, Christ gained for us the title to heaven. He filled to overflowing a reservoir of grace, providing all the assistance that we would ever need to get to heaven. But how were the fruits of Christ's life to reach the countless generations that would come after him? How was this reserve supply of grace to become a personal living reality in our own lives? How was this vast ocean of graces and blessings won by our Lord to be applied to our individual souls? Of what value would it be to us if we could never tap into it?

If you have ever traveled through large areas of farmland, perhaps you have noticed the presence of irrigation systems, a complex web of pipes and canals to bring water to each tree or plant. It is not only necessary to have a huge supply of water, but there must be some means to bring this life-giving liquid to the crops. No matter how much water is contained in a lake or reservoir, if there are no pipes or canals to carry it to each tree or plant, there will be no crop at harvest time.

By his life and death, Jesus filled the reservoir of grace to overflowing, but it is still necessary for each person to be able to draw from that reservoir. The Sacraments are the means provided for us by God – they are the channels of divine grace to our souls.

The enemies of Christ and his Church have always recognized the power of the Sacraments, and have tried to cut people off from them. This was particularly true when Marxism-Leninism ruled many countries of the world. In Romania, for instance, the Communist authorities put a heavy tax on the reception of the Sacraments. The Minister of Religion announced that for Baptism a tax amounting to three times the monthly income of an average worker would be imposed. Those wishing to receive the sacrament of Matrimony were told to come up with seven times an average worker's monthly income. In this way the atheistic regime was able to neutralize the potent influence of the Catholic sacramental system.

How ironic that many Catholics who live in freedom today, and who could receive the Sacraments easily and frequently, choose not to do so for one reason or another. They know that failure to tap into the city or regional water supply would soon cause their physical death, but they seem blithely unconcerned about the possibility of spiritual death if they do not take advantage of the life-giving graces available to us through the Sacraments.

What Is a Sacrament?

According to the *Catechism of the Catholic Church*: **"Sacraments are efficacious signs of grace, instituted by Christ and entrusted to the Church, by which divine life is dispensed to us"** (n. 1131). They are also visible signs of an invisible reality – namely, God's love. They are actions through which Christ gives his Spirit to us and makes us a holy people. They are encounters in which we meet God and God meets us.

But whatever definition we use, it is important to understand that the Sacraments, in the words of the *Basic Teachings for Catholic Religious Education*, "are always to be thought of as actions of Christ himself, from whom they get their power. Thus, it is Christ who baptizes, Christ who offers himself in the Sacrifice of the Mass through the ministry of the priests, and Christ who forgives sins in the sacrament of Penance" (n. 10). But let us for the sake of clarity use the *Catechism* definition and break it down into its parts.

First of all, a sacrament is an **efficacious sign**, one that brings about a desired result. For instance, in Baptism the outward sign is the pouring of water and the saying of the words, "I baptize you in the name of the Father, and of the Son, and of the Holy Spirit." In the Anointing of the Sick, it is the anointing with oil and the words of the priest. These external signs or ceremonies were established by Christ in order that the invisible grace given might be represented to us and made apparent to us in a visible way. Oil has been used for centuries by athletes to give strength to their bodies, so oil is a fitting symbol for Confirmation to represent the spiritual strength we get from the Holy Spirit.

Our Lord could have given us grace and spiritual benefits through a mere thought or word on his part, but he chose to make use of some external sign. When Jesus was on earth, he could have healed people with a word, but he chose instead to use mud to heal a blind man, saliva to restore hearing to a deaf man, and the touch of his hand to cure a leper. So in the Sacraments Christ makes use of external gestures and elements too. The seven Sacraments are like a mirror in which we can see the reflection of what goes on in the soul.

The Sacraments were **instituted by Christ**, and there are only seven of them given that official designation (cf. *Catechism of the Catholic Church*, n. 1117). There are other things that could come under the definition quoted above, such as the Church itself, which is certainly an efficacious sign instituted by Christ to give us grace or divine life. There are also other ceremonies and prayers and objects in the Church's life that are known as sacramentals, such as crucifixes, holy water, religious medals and scapulars, rosaries, and blessings, but when we talk in this book about a sacrament, we are referring only to the seven formal rituals of Baptism, Confirmation, Holy Eucharist, Penance/Reconciliation, Anointing of the Sick, Holy Orders, and Matrimony. That all of these were given to us by Christ will be demonstrated as we go along.

The purpose of the Sacraments is to **give us grace** or a share in the divine life of God. As we have already seen, grace is spiritual health and may be compared to bodily health. One person may have good health and another may not because of some disease. Of those who are healthy, some may be healthier or stronger than others because of heredity, diet, exercise, or some other reason. So too, one person may have good spiritual health, an abundance of sanctifying grace, while another may be deprived of this because of the disease of sin. And just as one person may be physically healthier than another, so one person may have more or less sanctifying grace than another, depending on the holiness of their lives, or even no sanctifying grace at all if one is in mortal sin.

Categories of Sacraments

The seven Sacraments can be divided into different categories. They can be separated into the Sacraments of the Living (Confirmation, Holy Eucharist, Anointing of the Sick, Holy Orders, and Matrimony) because one must be spiritually alive, already in the state of grace and free from mortal sin, in order to receive them worthily, and the Sacraments of the Dead (Baptism and Penance) because the soul is spiritually dead when we receive them. Or the seven can be divided into the Sacraments of Initiation (Baptism, Confirmation, and Holy Eucharist) because they bring us into the Church, strengthen us, and feed us the Body of Christ to unite us ever more closely with Jesus; the Sacraments of Healing (Penance/Reconciliation and Anointing of the Sick) because they restore our soul to spiritual health; and the Sacraments of Vocation or Service (Holy Orders and Matrimony) because they give us the divine assistance we need to live our vocation to the fullest and to serve others.

Three Sacraments may be received only once in a lifetime (Baptism, Confirmation, and Holy Orders), and they imprint on the soul a spiritual character that lasts forever. St. Thomas Aquinas called this character a "spiritual power" which enables the baptized to participate in the Church's worship, especially in the Eucharistic Sacrifice. It is not a visible sign, said Pope John Paul II, "although in many baptized persons certain of its effects are visible, such as the sense of belonging to Christ and the Church, which is shown in the words and deeds of truly faithful Christians, both priests and laity" (General Audience, March 25, 1992).

In that same talk, the Holy Father stressed that "the capacity involved in the character entails a mission and, thus, a responsibility: Whoever has received the holiness of Christ must show it to the world 'in every aspect of his conduct' (1 Peter 1:15) and, therefore, he must nourish it with the sacramental life, more particularly through participation in the Eucharistic Banquet."

In our day, every opportunity is given for frequent reception of those Sacraments we can receive more than once, especially the Holy Eucharist and Penance. But with that opportunity also comes a difficulty, for we sometimes do not appreciate those things that are most valuable to us. We sometimes neglect those things that come easiest to us. Who would deny that there is a lack of interest in the Sacraments among too many Catholics today? This is quite a different situation from that which existed in the early days of Christianity, when there was great reverence and respect for these gifts from God. For instance, before an adult was admitted to Baptism back then, he or she had to go through two years of probation.

People today will go to amazing lengths, and put themselves through agonizing regimens, to regain or preserve their physical health. But how many of these same people will not take even routine and ordinary steps to regain or preserve their spiritual health? The Sacraments were given to us by Christ to help us spiritually all through life. As there are ports or harbors where ships may take on supplies and fuel, so the Sacraments provide special opportunities for us to stock up on spiritual supplies and to refuel our weary souls for the journey toward heaven.

But all too often, Catholics do not take full advantage of the Sacraments. They put off Baptism and Confirmation for their children, or they receive the sacraments of Reconciliation and the Holy Eucharist rarely, if at all. What a shame to miss out on this great source of spiritual restoration! What a shame to disregard the consoling words of our Lord: "Come to me, all you who are weary and find life burdensome, and I will refresh you" (Matthew 11:28).

Sacramental Grace

As we have already noted, sanctifying grace is either given or increased every time we receive a sacrament worthily. But beyond this there is a particular bonus attached to each sacrament that we call sacramental grace. The sacrament of Matrimony, for example, gives a couple special helps to carry out the duties and to make the sacrifices of married life. Confirmation gives the recipient the strength necessary to practice one's faith in a world that is largely hostile to religious beliefs and practices. Holy Orders conveys to a man not only the powers of the priesthood, but also all the spiritual assistance necessary to act in the person of Christ.

There is both a personal and a social dimension to the Sacraments. Each one gives or increases sanctifying grace for individuals, and also confers a specific grace geared to fulfilling the purposes of the particular sacrament. But in addition, the graces that flow over us also flow over others since we are all members of the Mystical Body of Christ and share in each other's joys. In other words, the Sacraments are not strictly personal. What happens to us affects others.

When a person is confirmed, something good happens to him or her, but the benefits do not stop there. Like the ripples from a stone tossed into a pond that spread to the farthest shore, so there are spiritual ripples that extend far beyond the individual who received the sacrament. In the words of Vatican II: "For their part, the Sacraments, especially the Most Holy Eucharist, communicate and nourish that charity which is the soul of the entire apostolate" (*Decree on the Apostolate of the Laity*, n. 3).

The Sacraments do not work on us like magic. We must cooperate with God in receiving them willingly and worthily. We can prevent them from having a good effect on us by bad will on our part. So if a person were to receive Holy Communion, Confirmation, or Matrimony while knowingly in the state of serious sin, not only would the spiritual effects of the sacrament be cut off, but there would be an additional sin of sacrilege, the misuse of something that is sacred and holy.

The sun cannot enter a room with the blinds drawn. When the blinds are opened, the sun will light up and warm the room. If the blinds are only partially opened, some sunlight and warmth will enter the room. In the same way, the effects of the Sacraments depend on our dispositions. We can open ourselves up to them wholeheartedly, we can receive them in a lukewarm manner, or we can approach them while still enveloped by the darkness of sin. God presents these wonderful channels of grace to us, but it is our responsibility to make sure that we receive them joyfully and honorably.

We know from history that some ancient civilizations depended for their very existence upon aqueducts, conduits that brought water from distant places. A civilization that depends on aqueducts is in constant peril because of the possibility that an enemy or some natural disaster could destroy the life-giving waterways. This indeed happened to some ancient cities which fell into ruin once their aqueducts no longer brought water to them. The Sacraments are aqueducts of grace. But they too can be broken, either by our enemy Satan or by a failure on our part to keep these channels open and well-maintained. We must do all in our part to prevent this from happening.

The Power of the Sacraments

In addition to being signs and symbols expressing what takes place spiritually, the Sacraments go a step further; they actually accomplish what they signify. Of course, the external rites and the material used – water, oil, bread – have no power of themselves. But God works his power through these substances so that they can bring about a spiritual result, and God remains the principal cause of what happens. When a saw used by a carpenter cuts through a board, it is really the saw that does the cutting, but only because it is an instrument in the hand of the carpenter. Water has no power to take away original sin, nor could any human being give it that power. But when God determines that such a result should come about from the pouring of water and the recitation of a few words, then the power of God will see that such a result does come about.

Our struggle to get to heaven is not an easy one. We must do battle daily with the forces of evil who seek to send us down the road to hell. One could put the struggle in military terms by saying that Baptism makes us a citizen in the kingdom of Christ that has begun here on earth; that Confirmation prepares us to be a soldier in the army of Christ by more fully equipping us to deal with the attacks of Satan; that the Eucharist nourishes and strengthens us for the long struggle; that Penance helps to bind up and heal spiritual wounds; and that the Anointing of the Sick gets us ready for the final victory.

It is in these Sacraments "which flow forth from the pierced side of the Redeemer," as Pope John Paul said, "that believers find the grace and the strength always to keep God's holy law, even amid the gravest of hardships" (*Veritatis Splendor*, n. 103).

Who would have suspected that the all-powerful and infinite God could give us his help in such ordinary ways and through such commonplace substances? Actually, we should not be any more surprised at this than at God's choice of ordinary and unspectacular fishermen to head his Church and to bring his love and mercy and justice to a world desperately in need of all three. Whatever physical qualities or strength or resources an individual or a nation might possess, it all counts for little without a spiritual dimension. Anyone who is lacking the Sacraments has a huge, unbridged gap between him or her and God. The Sacraments are reservoirs that must be tapped if their spiritual energy is to do us any good in this life or in the next. We must use them well and often if we expect to share all eternity with the God who made our salvation possible by dying on the cross and leaving us this wonderful spiritual treasure.

Christ came not merely to teach us how to attain heaven, but to help us get there. The Sacraments are seven steps toward heaven.

THE SACRAMENT OF BAPTISM: In his final appearance to the Apostles, Jesus told them: "Go, therefore, and make disciples of all the nations. Baptize them in the name of the Father, and of the Son, and of the Holy Spirit" (Matthew 28:19).

THE SACRAMENT OF CONFIRMATION: Peter and John, while visiting the Christian community in Samaria, found that the people there "had only been baptized in the name of the Lord Jesus" and had not received Confirmation. So Peter and John "imposed hands on them and they received the Holy Spirit" (Acts 8:16-17).

THE SACRAMENT OF THE HOLY EUCHARIST: After taking bread and wine in his hands at the Last Supper, Jesus said, "This is my body .... This is my blood .... Do this as a remembrance of me" (Matthew 26:28, Luke 22:19, 1 Corinthians 11:23-25).

THE SACRAMENT OF PENANCE: In his appearance to the Apostles on the first Easter Sunday night, Jesus "breathed on them and said: 'Receive the Holy Spirit. If you forgive men's sins, they are forgiven them; if you hold them bound, they are held bound' " (John 20:22-23).

THE SACRAMENT OF THE ANOINTING OF THE SICK: "Is there anyone sick among you? He should ask for the presbyters of the Church. They in turn are to pray over him, anointing him with oil in the Name of the Lord. This prayer

uttered in faith will reclaim the one who is ill, and the Lord will restore him to health. If he has committed any sins, forgiveness will be his" (James 5:14-15).

THE SACRAMENT OF HOLY ORDERS: At the Last Supper, Jesus told the Apostles, his first priests, to offer up bread and wine "as a remembrance of me" (Luke 22:19). In each church to which they traveled, Paul and Barnabas "installed presbyters and, with prayer and fasting, commended them to the Lord in whom they had put their faith" (Acts 14:23).

THE SACRAMENT OF MATRIMONY: "Husbands, love your wives as Christ loved the church .... For this reason a man shall leave his father and mother, and shall cling to his wife, and the two shall be made into one" (Ephesians 5:25, 31).

The teaching of the Catholic Church on the Sacraments is tersely summed up in the Second Vatican Council's *Dogmatic Constitution on the Church*, n. 11):

BAPTISM: "Incorporated into the Church through Baptism, the faithful are consecrated by the baptismal character to the exercise of the cult of the Christian religion. Reborn as sons of God, they must confess before men the faith which they have received from God through the Church."

CONFIRMATION: "Bound more intimately to the Church by the sacrament of Confirmation, they are endowed by the Holy Spirit with special strength. Hence they are more strictly obliged to spread and defend the faith both by word and by deed as true witnesses of Christ."

HOLY EUCHARIST: "Taking part in the Eucharistic Sacrifice, which is the fount and apex of the whole Christian life, they offer the divine Victim to God, and offer themselves along with it .... Strengthened anew at the holy table by the Body of Christ, they manifest in a practical way that unity of God's People which is suitably signified and wondrously brought about by this most awesome sacrament."

PENANCE: "Those who approach the sacrament of Penance obtain pardon from the mercy of God for offenses committed against him. They are at the same time reconciled with the Church, which they have wounded by their sins, and which by charity, example, and prayer seeks their conversion."

ANOINTING OF THE SICK: "By the sacred Anointing of the Sick and the prayer of her priests, the whole Church commends those who are ill to the suffering and glorified Lord, asking that he may lighten their suffering and save them."

HOLY ORDERS: "Those of the faithful who are consecrated by Holy Orders are appointed to feed the Church in Christ's name with the Word and the grace of God."

MATRIMONY: "Christian spouses, in virtue of the sacrament of Matrimony, signify and partake of the mystery of that unity and fruitful love which exists between Christ and his Church. The spouses thereby help each other to attain to holiness in their married life and by the rearing and education of their children."

Chapter 13

Gifts from God's Church

"Holy Mother Church has, moreover, instituted sacramentals. These are sacred signs which bear a resemblance to the sacraments. They signify effects, particularly of a spiritual nature, which are obtained through the intercession of the Church." – *Catechism of the Catholic Church*, n. 1667

Sacramentals are certain rites or objects, such as blessings or medals, which are used to win God's help by reason of our own devotion plus the prayers of the Church on our behalf. As the *Catechism* pointed out, sacramentals have some outward resemblance to the Sacraments – both are external, visible, spiritual ceremonies. But the Sacraments were instituted by Christ, while the sacramentals were instituted by the Church. The Church can change or add to the sacramentals; the Church cannot change the Sacraments.

While the Sacraments confer grace directly, the sacramentals give grace by virtue of the devotion of the person using them, and also by virtue of the official prayers and intercession of the Church. Our Lord gave the Apostles certain power to banish Satan and to cure diseases at times. The Church carries on with that power, blessing objects, praying that those who use them might be shielded against the attacks of the devil, and praying for the cure of illnesses.

In the use of the sacramentals, prayers are said in the name of the Church for certain spiritual or temporal blessings, and some visible sign is employed, such as holy water or a crucifix. The sacramentals are not necessary for salvation, but they can help us get to heaven.

Far from being deemphasized in recent years, the sacramentals were given renewed emphasis by Vatican II (and in the *Catechism of the Catholic Church*), which urged that they be administered by lay people in order that they might be more readily available to the faithful:

"Thus, for well-disposed members of the faithful, the liturgy of the sacraments and sacramentals sanctifies almost every event in their lives; they are given access to the stream of divine grace which flows from the paschal mystery of the passion, death, and resurrection of Christ, the fountain from which all sacraments and sacramentals draw their power. There is hardly any proper use of material things which cannot thus be directed toward the sanctification of men and the praise of God" (*Constitution on the Sacred Liturgy*, n. 61).

The Council also called for a revision of the sacramentals that would enable the faithful to participate in them "intelligently, actively, and easily," and said that "in special circumstances and at the discretion of the Ordinary," the sacramentals "may be administered by qualified lay persons" (*Constitution on the Sacred Liturgy*, n. 79). These revisions have taken place since the Council, and qualified lay persons are now permitted to do a number of things once reserved to a priest or deacon, including the blessing of throats and the placing of ashes on the foreheads of the faithful on Ash Wednesday.

Kinds of Sacramentals

There are three primary categories of sacramentals: blessings, objects of devotions, and exorcisms. A blessing is the invocation of God's favor on people (mothers, children, the sick) and on objects (schools, homes, cars). Objects of devotion are various items used for pious purposes, such as holy water, crucifixes, candles, rosaries, scapulars, medals, palms (on Palm Sunday), ashes, and pictures or statues. Exorcisms are prayers said in the name of the Church to banish evil spirits from persons or buildings. Exorcisms are not frequent occurrences, but they are important from time to time to deal with diabolical possession or obsession.

The sacramentals can benefit us in a variety of spiritual and temporal ways. They are channels of grace through which we can **obtain actual graces,** which are passing helps provided by God for our mind or will; they can bring us back to the practice of our faith or give us an extra "push" toward heaven. The graces which a sacramental gives might help us to perform better the duties of our particular state in life, say, for instance, the religious life or the married life, or they might assist us in obtaining some favor or special need.

Sacramentals have the power to **obtain pardon for venial sin**. Thus, reciting the rosary, saying a prayer of sorrow, using blessed ashes, or saying the Stations of the Cross can have a powerful effect in taking away venial sin. The sacramentals can also remit temporal punishment due to sin, that is, the punishment for forgiven sin that must be taken care of either in this life or in purgatory. So frequent use of sacramentals can reduce our period of purification before reaching heaven.

Sacramentals have the power to **obtain health of body and material blessings**, provided that they would be for the good of our soul. There are, for example, blessings for the sick, blessings of homes to protect the inhabitants, and blessings of automobiles and other vehicles to keep drivers and passengers from harm. As for obtaining material things, sacramentals will not infallibly produce these effects, especially if they would not be in our best interests, but they may bring them about if God sees that they will be for our good.

Sacramentals give **special protection against the powers of the devil**. By obtaining extra spiritual strength, by securing the help of the good angels, by weakening the sway of Satan and his minions, the sacramentals can be a means of resisting evil. They can help in times of serious temptation. Some of the saints have emphasized the tremendous power of holy water to drive away the devil. Holy water and crucifixes are an essential part of the rite of exorcism.

While sacramentals employed by the Catholic Church are usually meant primarily for Catholics in good standing, others can benefit from them also. Those who are not yet baptized Catholics, but who are preparing for Baptism, as well as those who are not of the Catholic Faith, can receive spiritual and temporal benefits from them. For instance, a non-Catholic who receives the blessing of a priest, or makes use of religious medals or the rosary or holy water, can obtain the good effects of these sacramentals. But a Catholic who has been excommunicated from the Church loses much of the spiritual help that the sacramentals would ordinarily provide.

Sacramentals vs. Superstition

Persons not familiar with the theology of sacramentals, including some Catholics, have been known to accuse those who use them of superstition, of giving to some object or gesture powers that it does not possess. So is it superstitious to put a medal or rosary in one's car? Or to wear a scapular around one's neck? Or to keep a small holy water font near the door of one's home or apartment? Certainly not! There is a world of difference between the person who carries a rabbit's foot and the one who wears a medal or scapular. The rabbit's foot has no power to bring a person good luck, but the religious objects can produce that effect through the power of Christ by virtue of the official prayer of the Church and the devotion of the person involved. Obviously, the mere presence of a sacramental will not obtain spiritual benefits if the person employing one is indifferent or even hostile to its religious significance. We must will the good effect if we hope to receive it.

During his time on earth, Jesus blessed the loaves and the fishes (Matthew 14:19). He blessed the little children who were brought to him (Mark 10:16). He blessed the bread and wine before transforming them into his Body and Blood at the Last Supper (Mark 14:22, Luke 22:17). He blessed the Apostles before ascending into heaven (Luke 24:50). Christ also healed the sick and cast out devils, and the Church which he founded carries on those functions in the modern world through the sacramentals. Let us look a little more closely at some of the more familiar sacramentals of the Catholic Church.

Blessings

A blessing is the placing of a person or a thing under the care of God. In *The Roman Ritual*, which was revised by decree of the Second Vatican Council, there are more than 200 blessings, some of which can only be administered by those with special faculties, such as certain priests and bishops. The various kinds of blessings, and the words and ceremonies to be used, can be found in the *Book of Blessings*. The simplest kind of blessing involves making the Sign of the Cross, and it is sometimes accompanied by the sprinkling of holy water, as when the celebrant at Mass blesses the congregation, or when the priest blesses or consecrates such sacred objects as the chalice and other vessels, vestments, and candles used for religious ceremonies either in church or elsewhere. Palms are blessed for Palm Sunday and then, nearly a year later, the old dried-out palms are burned and the ashes from them are used on Ash Wednesday.

A natural element for cleansing, water has always been symbolic of interior cleansing and purity. Holy water has been used in the Catholic Church since its earliest days. It gains its spiritual value through the devotion of the person using it and the prayer of the Church. It is used at special liturgical celebrations, such as the Mass or the sacrament of Baptism, as well as to bless persons, places, and objects. When one moves into a new house or apartment, it is a good idea to have the residence blessed so that those living there will be protected from harm and may receive both spiritual and temporal blessings.

Objects of Devotion

The most commonly used sacramentals are crucifixes, medals, scapulars, and rosary beads. Since Catholics are saved by the power of the cross, what better reminder to us of our debt of gratitude to Jesus, and of the probability that we will have our own crosses to carry in this life if we are to be true followers of Christ, than to put crucifixes on the walls of our homes or to wear one on our person? There are many religious medals that we can wear to honor the Blessed Mother and many of the saints. We do not attribute power to these objects, nor do we worship them. Just as we carry pictures of loved family members, whether living or deceased, to remind us of them, so too we wear medals to remind us of our favorite saint and to invoke that saint's help in our daily lives.

A scapular is two small pieces of cloth joined by strings and worn around the neck and under the clothes. It originated with certain religious orders and was meant to symbolize the yoke of Christ. The Church has approved nearly twenty different scapulars, many of them of different colors, with the most widely used being those of Our Lady of Mount Carmel (brown), the Passion of our Lord (red), the Seven Dolors (black), the Immaculate Conception (blue), and the Holy Trinity (white). There is also a scapular medal that was approved by Pope St. Pius X as a substitute for the cloth ones. Those who wear the scapular share in the merits and good works of the particular group which originated it.

The rosary has long been one of the most powerful prayers at the disposal of a Catholic, and the Blessed Virgin Mary has on many occasions promised great spiritual and temporal rewards, including peace in the world, to those who pray this devotion faithfully. Popes in this century have written encyclicals praising and encouraging recitation of the rosary, rosary crusades have led to major victories for Christian civilization, and many family crises have been avoided or solved by devoutly adhering to this practice of meditating on the events in the lives of Jesus and his Blessed Mother while reciting prayers to them.

The fourteen Stations of the Cross are a wonderful way to accompany our Lord spiritually on his sorrowful journey during those long and painful hours on that first Good Friday. It is not only a beautiful and consoling devotion, but it is also a great sacramental. Many of us will never have the opportunity to visit the Holy Land and to reverence the places where Jesus lived and taught and died. But the Way of the Cross affords us the chance to pause at each of the fourteen places along the road from Pontius Pilate's fortress to the hill of Calvary. This devotion began when the Turks captured the Holy Land, and Christians were no longer able to make pilgrimages there. So the Church decided to do the next best thing – to use paintings and sculptures to mark out along the walls of our local churches the fourteen events that lead us through the passion and death of Christ.

Exorcisms

Though the Church's ritual for expelling evil spirits from persons or places is not often used, it remains an important function of the Church and can be carried out only with the permission of the bishop and by persons, usually priests, who are "endowed with piety, knowledge, prudence, and integrity of life" (*Code of Canon Law*, n. 1172).

Great care must be taken to make sure that there is diabolical possession, and that the person is not merely suffering from some emotional disorder. Once the determination of possession by evil spirits has been established, the rite of exorcism includes many sacramentals, including signs of the cross and the use of holy water. There are also special prayers to St. Michael the Archangel, recitation of the Psalms and the Athanasian Creed, use of the crucifix, invocation of the name of Jesus, and periodic commands demanding that the devil come out of the person possessed.

Those Wonderful Sacramentals

All the Sacraments are so great that they are truly incomparable – they cannot be compared to anything on earth. They are the channels by which the graces won by the passion and death of Christ two thousand years ago are brought into our souls today. But how fortunate we are that in addition to these unique Sacraments, the Church has also made available to us so many wonderful sacramentals. One writer has said that "the sacramentals are extensions and radiations of the Sacraments and have the same cause – the passion, death, and resurrection of Christ. They continue the work of the Sacraments or prepare for their reception."

He explained further:

"Thus, Baptism can be followed by the sacramentals of holy water, the sprinkling of water at the beginning of the Sunday Eucharist, and the blessing of infants and children. Confirmation is extended by the blessings of a school, library, archive, or typewriter. The Eucharist may be prolonged by Benediction of the Blessed Sacrament. Holy Orders is followed by the consecration or blessing of virgins. Marriage is prolonged by the blessings of a bridal chamber, an expectant mother, and a house and the various blessings of material things used in a home. Penance is extended in the Sacrament of the Confiteor, absolutions, the Papal Blessing at the hour of death, and exorcisms. The Anointing of the Sick flows into blessing of the sick, the blessing of oil, medicine, and linens, and the blessing of a deceased at the grave" (Rev. Jovian P. Lang, O.F.M., *Dictionary of the Liturgy*, pp. 560-561).

Chapter 14

No Longer Strangers

Holy Baptism is the basis of the whole Christian life, the gateway to life in the Spirit (*vitae spiritualis ianua*), and the door which gives access to the other sacraments. Through Baptism we are freed from sin and reborn as sons of God; we become members of Christ, are incorporated into the Church and made sharers in her mission. – *Catechism of the Catholic Church*, n. 1213

It was during wartime that an Air Force chaplain baptized a fighter pilot. A few hours later, the new convert flew on a dangerous mission but managed to return safely to the carrier that night. When the chaplain asked the pilot how he could fly into danger with no apparent sign of fear, the pilot replied: "Well, I was a little bit afraid, but then I thought there is no reason to worry since I was just baptized this morning. If anything happened to me, I would go right to heaven."

The young convert to Catholicism showed a simple but deep appreciation of the effects of Baptism; he knew that he was completely prepared for heaven. He had learned from his religious instructions what every Catholic should know: that Baptism is the sacrament which gives our souls the new life of sanctifying grace and makes us children of the Father, brothers and sisters of Jesus, members of the family of God that we call the Church, and heirs to heaven.

A New Birth

One night early in his public life, a Pharisee named Nicodemus came to see Christ to inquire about the teachings of our Lord. In the course of their conversation, Jesus told Nicodemus about the necessity of Baptism if one is to get to heaven: "I solemnly assure you, no one can enter God's kingdom without being begotten of water and Spirit" (John 3:5). That is why the Catholic Church requires the sacrament of Baptism for all its members, including infants, since it was the custom in the early Church to baptize entire households and families, which presumably meant children too (cf. Acts 16:15 and 16:33, and 1 Corinthians 1:16). Parents who neglect to have their children baptized within the first few weeks after they are born will have to give an account of their neglect.

All of us are born in the state of original sin. It is not a personal sin of ours, but something that we inherit from our first parents, Adam and Eve. They were created in a state of sanctifying grace, giving them a right to heaven, but they disobeyed God and lost their share in God's life and their right to heaven. The Second Vatican Council described their fall in these words: "Although he was made by God in a state of holiness, from the very dawn of history man abused his liberty, at the urging of personified Evil. Man set himself against God and sought to find fulfillment apart from God. Although he knew God, he did not glorify him as God, but his senseless mind was darkened and he served the creature rather than the Creator" (*Pastoral Constitution on the Church in the Modern World*, n. 13).

Fortunately, God did not abandon us, but sent his only Son to die for our sins and to give us the sacrament of Baptism that would return us to the state of holiness that Adam and Eve were in before they sinned. That is why Baptism is necessary for everyone if they want to get to heaven. In fact, Baptism is so important that it is the only sacrament that can be administered by a person who is not even a Catholic, or even a believer in God. All that is required is that the person performing the Baptism, perhaps even a Hindu nurse in a hospital, pour water over the baby's head while saying, "I baptize you in the name of the Father, and of the Son, and of the Holy Spirit." If the person pouring the water intends to do what the Church intends, and uses the trinitarian formula, then the Baptism is valid.

At the moment of Christ's baptism by John in the Jordan River (Matthew 3:13-17), a baptism that Jesus did not need but to which he submitted to show the credibility of John the Baptist and the importance of baptism, plain natural water took on a new significance through contact with God. Christ could have given his grace to us without the aid of material elements, but he chose water to be the instrument by which our souls would be cleansed of original sin and made ready for the indwelling of the Spirit.

God always chooses the simple things of the world to manifest sublime spiritual truths. Just as he chose to manifest his birth on earth by a star, so he has made the common element of water the key to our supernatural birth. It is a substance that is within reach of everyone, and any person, as we have mentioned, may baptize in case of necessity.

The sacrament of Baptism is the ordinary means of entrance into heaven, but for those who through no fault of their own have not received baptism of water, there are two emergency exits from the death of sin to the life of grace. One is baptism of blood or martyrdom, whereby a person lays down his or her life for Christ, say, by refusing to reject belief in Jesus when threatened with death. The other is baptism of desire, whereby a person has a strong desire to belong to the Church of Christ and to do all that is necessary for salvation even though he or she may not know which Church is the one established by Christ as the surest route to heaven.

"The divine design of salvation embraces all men," said Pope Paul VI in his *Credo of the People of God*, "and those who without fault on their part do not know the Gospel of Christ and his Church, but seek God sincerely, and under the influence of grace endeavor to do his will as recognized through the promptings of their conscience, they, in a number known only to God can obtain salvation" (cf. *Catechism of the Catholic Church*, n. 1260).

Baptism not only completely washes away original sin, but for those past the age of reason also any personal sins. Something of what happens on the day of baptism is expressed in the inspired words of Scripture: "Though your sins be like scarlet, they may become white as snow; though they are crimson red, they may become white as wool" (Isaiah 1:18).

That is why King Louis of France used to observe each year the anniversary of his baptism, counting that day of greater importance than the day on which he was crowned King of France. "I think more of the chapel where I was baptized," he once said, "than the cathedral ... where I was crowned." He explained that through baptism he was given the dignity of a child of God, which is greater than being the ruler of a country. The latter will be lost at death, while the former will remain as a passport to everlasting glory.

The Origins of Baptism

During the three years of his public life, Jesus spent day after day teaching the Apostles and the crowds that followed him. Whether at prayer services in synagogues, before the sophisticated people of Jerusalem, or to the simple folk in small villages of Galilee, Christ told those who would listen how they should live and what they must do to get to heaven. But after all that, these were his final words to his Apostles: "Go, therefore, and make disciples of all the nations. Baptize them in the name of the Father, and of the Son, and of the Holy Spirit" (Matthew 28:19).

Baptism was considered of prime importance by Jesus. Lest there be any doubt about its necessity for salvation, our Lord told Nicodemus that "no one can enter into God's kingdom" without baptism (John 3:5). St. Paul talked about the necessity of putting aside the sinful life and taking on the new life of grace: "Are you not aware that we who are baptized into Christ Jesus were baptized into his death? Through baptism into his death we were buried with him, so that, just as Christ was raised from the dead by the glory of the Father, we too might live a new life" (Romans 6:3-4).

In the Old Testament, there were foreshadowings of baptism in the Great Flood that washed away all but eight members of a sinful humanity (Genesis 6-9), and in the crossing of the Red Sea that took the people of Israel from slavery in Egypt to the Promised Land (Exodus 14). St. Paul, in the New Testament, saw the connection between the crossing and baptism: "Our fathers were all under the cloud and all passed through the sea; by the cloud and the sea all of them were baptized into Moses" (1 Corinthians 10:1-2). So the power of water to wash away sin has a long history that gives it considerable significance as the outward sign of baptism.

To the eyes of a world dulled by constant daily contact with the merely physical there is little appreciation of the spiritual. Perhaps that is why Christ, in instituting the Sacraments as channels through which the spiritual graces and blessings of his redemption are applied to our souls, linked them to external signs that would be easily recognized and understood. Thus, a person who witnesses the simple act of pouring water over the forehead of an infant or an adult, and hears the recitation of the formula of baptism, should have no difficulty grasping what is taking place.

Sherlock Holmes, the great fictional detective, once said: "It has long been an axiom of mine that the little things are infinitely the most important." This might well be applied to the simple act of baptism, which is one of the most important things in our life.

If we had to rely on our own human efforts, there is no way that we could reach the divine life. The abyss that exists between God and us when we are born can be bridged by the action of God alone. Though we were cut off from God by the chasm of original sin, he spanned this chasm with the sacrament of Baptism. Which is why Baptism has been termed the "gateway to faith," for in passing through this gateway we become a child of God and a member of Christ's Church with the right to receive all of the other Sacraments. As Pope John Paul has pointed out: "The recently published *Catechism of the Catholic Church* devotes seventy-one paragraphs (nn. 1213-1284) with eighty-five explanatory notes to Baptism, and emphasizes that it 'is the foundation of all Christian life, the vestibule for entrance into life in the Spirit, and the door which gives access to all the other Sacraments' " (General Audience, January 2, 1993).

The Holy Father went on to say that "the teaching about Baptism, which the *Catechism* explains so simply and clearly, yet solemnly and persuasively, must be a topic of stimulating meditation for each person in order to understand fully the transcendent reality of this sacrament and to live it with conviction and consistency. 'Baptism,' we read, 'is the most beautiful and magnificent of God's gifts .... We call it a gift, grace, anointing, enlightenment, garment of immortality, waters of rebirth, and the seal of all that is most precious.' Referring to the words of St. Peter, it adds: 'The baptized have become living stones for building a spiritual house, for a holy priesthood' (cf. 1 Peter 2:5)."

The Results of Baptism

By baptism a person becomes a member of the Church, a member of Christ's Mystical Body of believers on earth. We sometimes hear the term "identity crisis" today, meaning that one is not sure of one's place in life. But if you are baptized and have come to the realization of what that means, then at least one aspect of your identity crisis has been solved. You are a member of the community of the Church whose members have a definite identity as children of God and brothers and sisters of Jesus. You belong to Christ.

Listen to how St. Paul expressed this truth: "All of you who have been baptized into Christ have clothed yourselves with him. There does not exist among you Jew or Greek, slave or freeman, male or female. All are one in Christ Jesus" (Galatians 3:27-28).

Baptism confers sanctifying grace. Original sin is taken away and we share in the death and resurrection of Christ and in his victory over the forces of evil. "This is the meaning of the baptismal rite," said Pope John Paul II, "in which the candidate is asked: 'Do you reject Satan?' He is asked to make a personal commitment to total freedom from sin and, thus, from the power of Satan – the commitment to fight, throughout his earthly life, against the seductions of Satan. It will be a 'good fight,' which will make the individual more worthy of his heavenly calling, but also more perfect as a human person" (General Audience, March 25, 1992).

Baptism marks the soul as Christian. The "mark" or "character" of Baptism lasts forever and cannot be repeated. It is a sign of belonging whereby the baptized person becomes the property of Christ, the property of God. One who is baptized is forever different from one who is not baptized. The very early Christian writers and Fathers of the Church compared the character conferred on the soul by Baptism, Confirmation, and Holy Orders to a badge of military service, or to a brand that an owner puts on his livestock. Grace may be lost, but the character of these three sacraments remains forever. And this character, which St. Thomas Aquinas called a "spiritual power," though not a visible sign, should be visible to others in the way that we live "as children of light" (Ephesians 5:8), in the way that we worship at Mass, and in the way that we publicly profess our faith in Jesus Christ (cf. *Catechism of the Catholic Church*, nn. 1272-1274).

Baptism confers the priesthood of the laity. The newly baptized is anointed with oil during the ceremony. This means, according to St. Ambrose, that "you have been anointed as an athlete of Christ, as if you were about to engage in a contest. You have professed your willingness to undertake a contest." The anointing with the "chrism of salvation" gives the baptized person a share in the priesthood of Christ, who was also anointed Priest, Prophet, and King. The baptized is also clothed with a white garment, indicating that "you have become a new creation, and have clothed yourself in Christ," and is given a lighted candle that symbolizes the "light of Christ." The parents and godparents of the new Christian are instructed to keep that light of Christ always "burning brightly."

Speaking of godparents or sponsors, at least one is required for the person being baptized, and the one chosen by the parents must be a practicing Catholic who has received the sacraments of Baptism, Confirmation, and the Holy Eucharist. The sponsor's role is to assist the baptized person, by word and example, to lead a good Christian life. While it is not required that those to be baptized choose the name of a saint, it is certainly a good idea since it would give them a patron in heaven whom they can imitate in their own lives and who can intercede for them.

The Glory of Baptism

As noted earlier, Jesus had no need of baptism, yet he submitted to baptism by John:

"Later Jesus, coming from Galilee, appeared before John at the Jordan to be baptized by him. John tried to refuse him with the protest, 'I should be baptized by you, yet you come to me.' Jesus answered: 'Give in for now. We must do this if we would fulfill all of God's demands.' So John gave in. After Jesus was baptized, he came directly out of the water. Suddenly the sky opened and he saw the Spirit of God descend like a dove and hover over him. With that, a voice from the heavens said, 'This is my beloved Son. My favor rests on him' " (Matthew 3:13-17).

The baptism of Jesus was different from other baptisms by John in that there was no acknowledgement of sin on the part of our Lord. And when Jesus emerged from the river, a voice from heaven identified him as God's Son, just as Baptism makes us children of God. Much the same thing happened at our baptism. Like Jesus, we had water poured over us, certain words were spoken, the Holy Spirit descended on us (invisibly), and the Father said to us, "This is my beloved son [or daughter]. My favor rests on him [or her]."

The sacraments of Baptism, Confirmation, and the Holy Eucharist are called the Sacraments of Christian Initiation because they are the channels through which we not only become children of God but come to the fullness of union with him. Through Baptism a person is enabled to offer true and full worship to God and to share in Christ's redemptive work. Through Confirmation a person is given the special strength to witness fully to the Catholic Faith. Through the Holy Eucharist a person is fed with the Bread of Life and given the spiritual nourishment necessary to live up to the commitment made at Baptism and Confirmation. By these three sacraments, we are fully initiated into the life and mission of Christ and prepared to carry out that mission in the world.

In the words of Pope John Paul II, "the lay faithful are sharers in the priestly mission for which Jesus offered himself on the cross and continues to be offered in the celebration of the Eucharist for the glory of God and the salvation of humanity. Incorporated in Jesus Christ, the baptized are united to him and to his sacrifice in the offering they make of themselves and their daily activities (cf. Romans 12:1).

"Speaking of the lay faithful, the Council says: 'For their work, prayers, and apostolic endeavors, their ordinary married and family life, their daily labor, their mental and physical relaxation, if carried out in the Spirit, and even the hardships of life if patiently borne – all of these become spiritual sacrifices acceptable to God through Jesus Christ (cf. 1 Peter 2:5). During the celebration of the Eucharist, these sacrifices are most lovingly offered to the Father along with the Lord's Body. Thus, as worshipers whose every deed is holy, the lay faithful consecrate the world itself to God' " (*Christifidelis Laici*, n. 14).

Far from being considered a burdensome duty as is too often the case today, Baptism, when seen in its true light, is one of the greatest privileges God has given to us. That is undoubtedly why St. Paul enthusiastically exclaimed to those whom he had baptized: "This means that you are strangers and aliens no longer. No, you are fellow citizens of the saints and members of the household of God" (Ephesians 2:19).

Chapter 15

Strength for Service

It must be explained to the faithful that the reception of the sacrament of Confirmation is necessary for the completion of baptismal grace. For "by the sacrament of Confirmation, [the baptized] are more perfectly bound to the Church and are enriched with a special strength of the Holy Spirit. Hence they are, as true witnesses of Christ, more strictly obliged to spread and defend the faith by word and deed." – *Catechism of the Catholic Church*, n. 1285

John Ruskin, the social commentator of the nineteenth century, once made this interesting statement: "The great cry which rises from our manufacturing cities, louder than their furnace blast, is all in very deed for this, that we manufacture there everything but men; we bleach cotton, and strengthen steel, and refine sugar, and shape pottery; but to brighten, strengthen, refine, or to form a single living spirit does not enter into our estimate of advantages."

Yes, in modern times the stress is on scientific and industrial progress. But Christ's emphasis, and the job that he entrusted to his Church, was not to temper steel but to strengthen human beings spiritually; not to refine sugar but to purify and revitalize souls; not to shape pottery but to form men and women for heaven. Christ gave us the means to accomplish that task – the seven Sacraments. And he gave us one special sacrament – Confirmation – to strengthen and revitalize our spiritual lives so that we could bring his love and mercy and justice to modern society.

Confirmation is the sacrament that completes Baptism and through which the Holy Spirit comes to us in a special way to make us strong and perfect Christians and courageous witnesses and apostles of Jesus Christ. A person who receives Confirmation is strengthened, refined, reformed, and bound in a special relationship with the Holy Spirit. Christ has assured us that we receive these helps from the third Person of the Blessed Trinity, particularly through the sacrament of Confirmation. By his life and death, Jesus filled up a reservoir of grace and spiritual strength; the Holy Spirit controls the channels from that reservoir.

A Strong, Driving Wind

Each year the feast of Pentecost reminds us of the sometimes forgotten Person of the Blessed Trinity, the Holy Spirit. But how many Catholics have a real devotion to the Holy Spirit, the "Spirit of truth" that Jesus promised to send to his Church (John 14:17)? How many of us appreciate the great things that he can do for us personally if we only give him the chance? We need to read Pope John Paul II's wonderful letter on the Holy Spirit in the life of the Church and the world and, in the words of the Holy Father, to fix our eyes "on him who is the love of the Father and the Son" and who is also "the Spirit of peace" who "does not cease to be present in our human world, on the horizon of minds and hearts, in order to 'fill the universe' with love and peace" (*Dominum et Vivificantem*, n. 67).

It was the tenth day after the ascension of Jesus into heaven, the fiftieth day after the first Easter Sunday, and the Apostles were gathered together in the city of Jerusalem when "suddenly from up in the sky there came a noise like a strong, driving wind which was heard all through the house where they were seated. Tongues as of fire appeared, which parted and came to rest on each of them. All were filled with the Holy Spirit. They began to express themselves in foreign tongues and make bold proclamations as the Spirit prompted them" (Acts 2:1-4).

The Holy Spirit could have come to the Apostles quietly and invisibly, but the third Person of the Trinity chose to make his presence known and felt on that first Pentecost in a never-to-be-forgotten way. This external miracle was accompanied by a no-less-startling interior marvel. For the Apostles gathered in that room – simple fishermen, unlearned, weak in faith – were immediately transformed into zealous, courageous, and articulate missionaries who not only converted three thousand people that very day but went forth and willingly gave their lives spreading a message that would eventually reach the far corners of the world.

We commemorate this event each spring on the feast of Pentecost, the birthday of the Church, not only by recalling it in song and prayer but also by renewing it in our own lives. We ask the Holy Spirit to exercise as much power over us as he did on the first Pentecost over the Apostles. Is this asking too much, or is it possible that the Holy Spirit can actually live in us today? Can he give us something of what he gave St. Peter two thousand years ago? Or what he gave to those in the early Church?

Recall that Philip, the deacon, not the Apostle, had gotten a great number of converts in Samaria, baptizing them but not confirming them. So Peter and John "went down to these people and prayed that they might receive the Holy Spirit. It had not as yet come down upon any of them since they had only been baptized in the name of the Lord Jesus. The pair upon arriving imposed hands on them and they received the Holy Spirit" (Acts 8:14-17).

The new converts had been received into the Church through Baptism, but something was lacking. The Bible does not use the word "confirmation," but this passage describes the administration of this sacrament only a short time after Christ had promised that "you will receive power when the Holy Spirit comes down on you; then you are to be my witnesses in Jerusalem, throughout Judea and Samaria, yes, even to the ends of the earth" (Acts 1:8).

Light and Strength

On the day of a Catholic's baptism, the priest asks the parents and godparents if they reject Satan and all his works and all his empty promises. Once Satan is banished, the Holy Spirit comes into the soul of the newly baptized person. That presence of the Holy Spirit is renewed and strengthened on Confirmation day. Baptism is the sacrament of spiritual birth; Confirmation is the sacrament of spiritual strength that completes what was begun when we were baptized. The day of our Confirmation is, in a sense, our Pentecost, the day when the Holy Spirit gives us the grace and courage to become missionaries for Christ. St. Thomas Aquinas explained it this way:

"The sacrament of Confirmation is, as it were, the final completion of the sacrament of Baptism, in the sense that by Baptism (according to St. Paul) the Christian is built up into a spiritual dwelling (cf. 1 Corinthians 3:9), and is written like a spiritual letter (cf. 2 Corinthians 3:2-3); whereas by the sacrament of Confirmation, like a house already built, he is consecrated as a temple of the Holy Spirit, and as a letter already written, is signed with the sign of the cross."

Did not St. Paul assure those whom he had baptized and confirmed that they were tabernacles in which God really dwelt until dismissed through sin? "You must know that your body is a temple of the Holy Spirit, who is within – the Spirit you have received from God," said Paul (1 Corinthians 6:19). If the Holy Spirit is really within us, then we ought never do anything or say anything, or even think anything that we would not want God to hear or see.

What happens when the Holy Spirit is allowed to take an active part in our lives? He will *enlighten us*, as he did the Apostles, thus helping us to know the truths of God more clearly. He will *give us supernatural strength*, as he did the Apostles, so that we will carry out the will of God in our daily lives. "In him who is the source of my strength," said St. Paul, "I have strength for everything" (Philippians 4:13). And he will *sanctify us*, as he did the Apostles, so that our holiness will shine like a light in the darkness. This is what the Holy Spirit will do for us in the sacrament of Confirmation if we are open to his grace and assistance.

The Rite of Confirmation

The sacrament of Confirmation is usually administered by a bishop, although in certain circumstances a priest may take the bishop's place in extending his hands over those who are to be confirmed. This is a reminder of the descent of the Holy Spirit on the Apostles on Pentecost. The bishop then anoints the head of each candidate with a holy oil to symbolize the healing and strengthening qualities for which oil has been used for centuries. This holy oil is called chrism. It is made of olive oil and a perfume called balm or balsam and is specially blessed by the bishop each year on Holy Thursday. The bishop makes the Sign of the Cross on the forehead of the candidate, saying, "N., be sealed with the gift of the Holy Spirit," and the candidate responds, "Amen."

Thus, the outward sign of Confirmation is threefold: (1) the imposition of hands; (2) the signing with the cross; and (3) the anointing with holy oil. The Sign of the Cross shows we believe that our rescue from the darkness of sin and our entry into the life of grace come from the redemptive death of Jesus on the cross. By accepting the mark of the cross on our foreheads, we are declaring our willingness to carry the cross of Christ in our own lives and to remain faithful to him no matter what obstacles are placed in our way.

Confirmation is not absolutely necessary for salvation (as is Baptism), but it makes it much easier for us to get to heaven. It would be a serious sin to refuse to be confirmed out of contempt for the sacrament or out of spiritual laziness. As in the case of Baptism, the candidate for Confirmation should choose the name of a saint and a sponsor who is a practicing Catholic and who has been confirmed. Since Confirmation completes Baptism, it would be appropriate to choose a baptismal godparent for a Confirmation sponsor. The sponsor's role, as in Baptism, is to help the one confirmed, by prayer and example, to live the life of a faithful Catholic.

A Soldier of Christ

One of the most enduring comparisons for a newly confirmed person is to a soldier about to go into battle. Baptism makes us citizens in the kingdom of Christ; Confirmation enlists us in the army of Christ. The warfare that we will face was described by St. Paul, who said that we must "put on the armor of God so that you may be able to stand firm against the tactics of the devil. Our battle is not against human forces but against the principalities and powers, the rulers of this world of darkness, the evil spirits in regions above" (Ephesians 6:11-12).

In this same vein, Pope John Paul noted that since the Middle Ages, the Church "has not hesitated to highlight the strength given by Confirmation to Christians who are called to serve as soldiers for God." He said that the grace conferred by the sacrament "corresponds to the need for greater zeal in facing the spiritual battle of faith and charity, in order to resist temptation and give the witness of Christian word and deed to the world with courage, fervor, and perseverance. This zeal is conferred in the sacrament by the Holy Spirit" (General Audience, April 1, 1992).

This strength and zeal is necessary, the Pope pointed out, noting that it was our Lord himself who warned of the danger of being ashamed to profess the Faith: "If a man is ashamed of me and my doctrine, the Son of Man will be ashamed of him when he comes in his glory and that of his Father and his holy angels" (Luke 9:26). According to Pope John Paul, "being ashamed of Christ is often expressed in those forms of 'human respect' by which one hides one's own faith and agrees to compromises which are unacceptable for someone who wants to be Christ's true disciple. How many people, even Christians, make compromises today" (*Ibid.*)?

Instead of making compromises, we must follow the courageous example of the Apostles, who acted on the power given them by the Holy Spirit and went forth fearlessly to proclaim Christ to all, "full of joy that they had been judged worthy of ill-treatment for the sake of the Name" (Acts 5:41).

Confirmation increases sanctifying grace in our souls, provided we are in the state of grace when we receive it. If we are not, the sacrament is still valid, but we commit a sin of sacrilege and the grace of the sacrament does not take effect until we have gone to the sacrament of Penance and had our sins forgiven. In addition to the sacramental grace conferred by Confirmation, we also receive **seven important gifts of the Holy Spirit**. The first four of those gifts – wisdom, understanding, knowledge, and counsel – help us to know and understand the meaning of the truths of the Catholic Faith. The last three – fortitude, piety, and a reverent fear or awe of the Lord – give us the grace and strength that our will needs to do what God wants us to do.

The soul can be compared to a boat, with the seven gifts the sails and the other helps we get from the Holy Spirit the winds. At Baptism, the soul was given its first small sails; at Confirmation, those small sails are enlarged so that the person may more readily progress along the ocean of life. This voyage is not always easy or pleasant. There are rough seas and stormy days ahead of us. What Confirmation does is to prepare us to sail through those seas and storms unharmed, to practice our faith openly even amidst difficulties, and to fight successfully against the devil, who "is prowling like a roaring lion looking for someone to devour" (1 Peter 5:8). On our own, we would be no match against the allurements of the world, the flesh, and the devil. But with the strength of Christ's Sacraments, particularly Confirmation, we need fear no temptation and no enemy.

An Indelible Character

Though the person newly confirmed may look the same on the outside, an interior change has been effected. The Apostles on the first Pentecost were in hiding, fearful that they would suffer the same fate as their crucified Master. With the coming of the Holy

Spirit, they went out boldly in front of people who were ridiculing them and accusing them of being drunk and baptized three thousand new Christians before the day was over. Confirmation may not give us the power to be understood in many languages, as the Apostles were that day in Jerusalem, but it will give us the knowledge and the courage to battle the enemies of Christ, to live as loyal Catholics, and to bring others into the fold. With God on our side, who can stop us?

One of the invisible but very real effects of this sacrament is the character, the spiritual and indelible sign, that is imposed on our souls. This mark distinguishes us for all eternity from those who were not confirmed. It is the badge of a full-fledged Catholic that will last forever. "As with Baptism," said Pope John Paul, "a special character is also impressed on the soul by the sacrament of Confirmation. It brings to perfection the baptismal consecration and is conferred by two ritual acts: the imposition of hands and the anointing."

He said that the "ability to participate in worship, which was already received in Baptism, is strengthened by Confirmation. The universal priesthood is more deeply rooted in the person and can be exercised more effectively. The specific function of the character of Confirmation is to put into practice Christian witness and action" (*Ibid.*).

Strength for the Apostolate

"He who is not with me," our Lord said, "is against me" (Matthew 12:30). There is no middle course. We must choose either the side of good or the side of evil. There are no spectators in this battle; we are all on the battlefield, on one side or the other. Confirmation gives us the strength to choose the right side, even if everyone else appears to be on the other side. It is actions that count, not words. Remember that Peter promised Christ, "Even though I have to die with you, I will never disown you" (Matthew 26:35). But a few hours later, when the first challenge came, Peter three times denied that he even knew Jesus. This was all changed when he received the Holy Spirit on Pentecost, and Peter later was crucified for his belief in Jesus. That is what Confirmation will do for us.

The sacrament will also give us an extra push to put pride or spiritual laziness behind us, and to reach out to those in our homes, schools, offices, factories, and social circles and invite them to make

Christ a vital part of their lives. How many times when we finally get around to inviting someone to become a Catholic, or to come back to the Church after many years of being away from the Sacraments, do we learn that they would have responded favorably a long time ago if only someone had asked them? Lay people travel in circles not accessible to priests or religious, so it is up to the laity to gain converts for Christ in their travels. In the words of Vatican II:

"On all Christians therefore is laid the splendid burden of working to make the divine message of salvation known and accepted by all men throughout the world. For the exercise of this apostolate, the Holy Spirit who sanctifies the People of God through the ministry and the sacraments gives to the faithful special gifts as well (cf. 1 Corinthians 12:7), 'allotting to everyone according as he will' (1 Corinthians 12:11). Thus may the individual, 'according to the gift that each has received, administer it to one another' and become 'good stewards of the manifold grace of God' (1 Peter 4:10), and build up thereby the whole body in charity (cf. Ephesians 4:16)" (*Decree on the Apostolate of the Laity*, n. 3).

There is a story about Alexander the Great, the brilliant military strategist who lived four centuries before Christ. One day while watching his men in battle, Alexander saw a soldier leave his post and run away from the battle. When the soldier was finally caught and brought before Alexander, the general asked his name. "Alexander," the young man said in a quavering voice. "What did you say?" the general roared. "Alexander, sir," the soldier replied. "Well," the general barked, "I suggest that you either change your name or change your conduct." So, too, any person who has been confirmed in the Catholic Church has a solemn obligation to live up to the name Catholic.

A Call to Holiness

At the end of the second century, the Christian writer Tertullian had this to say about the Sacraments of Initiation – Baptism, Confirmation, and the Holy Eucharist:

"The body is washed, that the soul may be cleansed; the body is anointed, that the soul may be consecrated; the body is signed, that the soul too may be fortified; the body is overshadowed by the laying on of hands, that the soul too may be enlightened by the Spirit; the body is fed on the Body and Blood of Christ, that the soul too should be nourished by God."

These sacraments, which make us members of Christ's Church, and which strengthen and nourish us to be holy and zealous members of that Church, bring personal spiritual benefits to the individuals who receive them. But Confirmation also has a social dimension that obliges us to serve other people, especially the poor and the needy. We are expected to spread the Catholic Faith to others, but we are also to perform the corporal and spiritual works of mercy, to witness to Christ by helping the least of his brothers and sisters, realizing that whatever we do for them, we do for him (Matthew 25:40).

Some have the mistaken notion that once they have been confirmed, no further religious instruction or practice is necessary. They could not be more wrong. Confirmation is not the end of one's religious training; it's the beginning. Thus, the person confirmed is called to learn more about Christ and his Church by studying Scripture, reading about the saints, and gaining as much knowledge about Catholic beliefs and practices as possible. The person confirmed is called to keep the Commandments, to make the principles enunciated in the Beatitudes and the Sermon on the Mount a part of his or her life, and to avoid sin at all costs. The person confirmed is called to worship God faithfully and enthusiastically by actively participating in the Holy Sacrifice of the Mass every weekend, by frequenting the sacraments of Penance and the Holy Eucharist, and by praying with the same fervor and perseverance that Jesus did.

Our connection with the Holy Spirit must not be a one-time thing at the moment of our Confirmation, but rather a lifelong relationship. We need to work closely with the third Person of the Blessed Trinity if we are to be more Christ-like in our actions. The potential is there, but we must build on it. We must help let the light of Christ shine before the world so that others "may see goodness" in our acts "and give praise to your heavenly Father" (Matthew 5:16). St. Paul reminds us that "the Spirit God has given us is no cowardly Spirit, but rather one that makes us strong, loving, and wise" (2 Timothy 1:7). We must allow this Spirit to work in us and through us so that we can lead ourselves, and all those who come in contact with us, in the direction of heaven.

Chapter 16

He Is There

The Eucharist is "the source and summit of the Christian life." "The other sacraments, and indeed all ecclesiastical ministries and works of the apostolate, are bound up with the Eucharist and are oriented toward it. For in the blessed Eucharist is contained the whole spiritual good of the Church, namely Christ himself, our Pasch." – *Catechism of the Catholic Church*, n. 1324

After presenting his little daughter with a crucifix on the occasion of her First Holy Communion, the father asked her if she knew the difference between the figure of Jesus on the cross and the Host which the priest holds up at Mass. "When I look at the cross," the child said, "I see Jesus and he is not there. When I look at the Host, I do not see Jesus and he is there." Sometimes we can learn a profound lesson from the lips of children. This is so often true of the mystery of Christ's Real Presence in the sacrament of the Holy Eucharist, which only a sincere act of faith can help us to understand and appreciate.

G.K. Chesterton was one of the greatest converts to the Catholic Church in this century. Recalling what it was that led him to become a Catholic, Chesterton said that as a boy he was strangely attracted to the Catholic church in his town. Although that church was not as inviting as some of the other churches, he often visited it secretly, feeling in some way that the light that burned night and day in the sanctuary somehow made this church different from those that were more beautiful and more imposing. It wasn't until years later that Chesterton realized that it was not the sanctuary lamp that made the difference between the Catholic Church and all others, but rather the presence of Jesus in the tabernacle.

The Hungry Multitude

During our Lord's public life, he performed many miracles. He cured the sick and the handicapped, he changed water into wine, he walked on water, he expelled demons, and he brought dead people back to life on three occasions. As a result of these wonders, increasingly large numbers of people followed him. Not all of these people were friendly toward Jesus. Some, of course, were devoted to him, but some could not make up their minds, some were curious, some were disbelievers who thought that his miracles were the result of self-hypnosis or mob psychology, and some even hated him and came only to embarrass him or to try to trip him up. But whatever reason brought people to see Jesus, they came by the hundreds and the thousands, so that Christ hardly had time to eat or rest.

On one particular day, after being followed by an enormous crowd, Jesus and his Apostles got into their fishing boat and sailed across the Sea of Galilee to the opposite shore. The sea is eighteen miles long and about three miles wide. Jesus and his friends landed at the foot of a beautiful hillside, with rather high mountains behind it. The spot is a few miles north of the town of Tiberias, then newly built and occupied mostly by Romans. It was a fishing town as well as a vacation place.

As usual, the news traveled fast that Jesus was nearby, and soon a steady stream of people approached our Lord from the region of Tiberias until more than five thousand had gathered around him. They were all there – the devoted women, the doubters, the curiosity seekers, the tax collectors, the hecklers, the prostitutes who saw a ray of hope, the fishermen who knew Peter and some of the other Apostles, the children who had tagged along with the adults. They had all come together on the sloping hillside.

Ever conscious of the needs of his flock, Jesus knew that the people were hungry, so he asked Philip the Apostle, "Where shall we buy bread for these people to eat?" Jesus knew what he planned to do, but he asked the question to test Philip, who responded, "Not even with two hundred days' wages could we buy loaves enough to give each of them a mouthful." The Apostle Andrew, Peter's brother, had canvassed the crowd and had come up with five loaves of bread and two fish, but said, "What good is that for so many" (John 6:5-9)?

The Miracle of the Loaves and Fishes

Our Lord put the Apostles to work getting everybody seated on the grass, which was thick and tall and made a good cushion. He then blessed the meager food supply, gave thanks, and began distributing both bread and the fish to those who were reclining there, giving each person as much as they wanted. When everyone had had enough to eat, Jesus ordered the Apostles to gather up any crusts that were left, and there was enough to fill twelve baskets.

It may have been easy in the past to mock and to doubt when the deaf heard and the blind saw, and to talk about self-hypnosis and mob psychology, but the people on that hillside knew a good piece of smoked fish when they tasted it, and they knew that there was nothing psychological about a nourishing chunk of bread. Jesus had performed a tremendous miracle that was both heavenly in its origin and earthly in its reality.

What had just taken place soon dawned on the crowd. "This is undoubtedly the Prophet who is to come into the world!," some of them said. Everyone was enthusiastic and excited. Shouts were heard, "He deserves to be king! Make him king!" Some were pushing their way forward, trying to reach Jesus. "At that, Jesus realized that they would come and carry him off to make him king, so he fled back to the mountains alone" (John 6:14-15).

The crowd slept on the hillside that night, hoping that Christ would return in the morning. But Jesus had crossed the lake again while it was still dark, walking on the water and calming the waves that were tossing about the boat carrying the Apostles. Meanwhile, word of the great miracle had reached Tiberias, and many more people came to the place where it had occurred. When they learned that Jesus had left, someone apparently suggested that he might be in the fishing town of Capernaum. After all, his friend Peter lived there, and he was always welcome at the house of Peter's mother-in-law. And besides, there was a big synagogue there, and everyone knew that Jesus was a devout Jew.

So there was a rush to board the boats, and soon a large flotilla was heading toward Capernaum, loaded with many of those who had witnessed the miracle of the loaves and fishes. Sure enough, they found Jesus in Capernaum and asked, "Rabbi, when did you come here?" Jesus answered them, "I assure you, you are not looking for me because you have seen signs but because you have eaten your fill of the loaves. You should not be working for perishable food but for food that remains unto life eternal, food which the Son of Man will give you" (John 6:25-27).

"So that we can put faith in you," they asked our Lord, "what sign are you going to perform for us to see? What is the 'work' you do? Our ancestors had manna to eat in the desert; according to Scripture, 'He gave them bread from the heavens to eat.' " Jesus said to them: "I solemnly assure you, it was not Moses who gave you bread from the heavens; it is my Father who gives you the real heavenly bread. God's bread comes down from heaven and gives life to the world." They pleaded with him, "Sir, give us this bread always" (John 6:30-34).

The Promise of the Eucharist

Jesus explained to them: "I myself am the bread of life. No one who comes to me shall ever be hungry, no one who believes in me shall ever thirst .... I am the bread of life. Your ancestors ate manna in the desert, but they died. This is the bread that comes down from heaven for a man to eat and never die. I myself am the living bread come down from heaven. If anyone eats this bread he shall live forever; the bread I will give is my flesh, for the life of the world."

At this the Jews quarreled among themselves, saying, "How can he give us his flesh to eat?"

Thereupon Jesus said to them: "Let me solemnly assure you, if you do not eat the flesh of the Son of Man and drink his blood, you have no life in you. He who feeds on my flesh and drinks my blood has life eternal and I will raise him up on the last day. For my flesh is real food and my blood real drink. The man who feeds on my flesh and drinks my blood remains in me, and I in him. Just as the Father who has life sent me, and I have life because of the Father, so the man who feeds on me will have life because of me. This is the bread that came down from heaven. Unlike your ancestors who ate and died nonetheless, the man who feeds on this bread shall live forever" (John 6:48-58).

After hearing these words, many of his disciples remarked, "This sort of talk is hard to endure! How can anyone take it seriously?" And from that time on, many of his disciples broke away from Jesus and would not remain in his company any longer. Jesus then said to the Twelve, "Do you want to leave me too?" Simon Peter answered him, "Lord, to whom shall we go? You have the words of eternal life. We have come to believe; we are convinced that you are God's holy one" (John 6:66-69).

Over the past two thousand years, from every true follower of Jesus Christ comes a thunderous echo of those words of Peter: "Lord, to whom shall we go. You have the words of eternal life. We have come to believe; we are convinced that you are God's holy one."

The Promise Fulfilled

About a year later, at his last meal with the Apostles the night before he died, Jesus fulfilled his promise to give himself as a gift to the world. Toward the end of that ritualistic meal of the Jewish religion, Jesus took bread, blessed it and broke it, and said, "This is my body to be given for you. Do this as a remembrance of me" (Luke 22:19). Then he took the cup of wine and said, "This cup is the new covenant in my blood. Do this, whenever you drink it, in remembrance of me" (1 Corinthians 11:25).

In St. Matthew's account of the institution of the Eucharist, Jesus blessed and broke the bread and gave it to his disciples, saying, "Take this and eat it, this is my body." He then took the cup, gave thanks, and said to them, "All of you must drink from it, for this is my blood of the covenant, to be poured out in behalf of many for the forgiveness of sins" (Matthew 26:26-28).

However difficult it may have been for the Apostles, and for those who would come after them, to understand what Jesus had said at the Last Supper, there can be only one meaning to his words: he was giving his body and blood for the spiritual nourishment of the world. He didn't say, "This is a symbol of my body," or "This represents my blood," but rather, "This *is* my body .... This *is* my blood." No language could be simpler. And if we try to put any other meaning on those words, as many have tried to do down through the centuries, then it becomes impossible to attach any meaning to them at all.

We must see, as the Apostles saw, that the words spoken by Christ at the Last Supper were the fulfillment of the promise he had made in Capernaum a year earlier. When many of his listeners in Capernaum walked away because they could not stomach the idea of eating the flesh of Jesus and drinking his blood, our Lord did not say, "Wait a minute! Come on back! I didn't really mean you had to eat my flesh and drink my blood. I was only speaking metaphorically." No, Jesus let those disciples walk away because his words meant exactly what the doubters thought they meant.

Moreover, Christ at the Last Supper gave the Apostles, his first priests, the power to do what he had just done – to change bread and wine into his body and blood. He commanded them to "do this as a remembrance of me." And so in every Mass, on every altar in every nation of the world, at every time of the day, when the priest repeats those earth-shaking words of Christ, "This is my body .... This is my blood," Jesus becomes present on that altar under the appearances of bread and wine. The Host still looks the same and tastes the same, but it is no longer bread but rather the Body of Christ.

In the *Credo of the People of God*, Pope Paul summarized this miracle in these words:

"We believe that as the bread and wine consecrated by the Lord at the Last Supper were changed into his Body and Blood which were to be offered for us on the cross, likewise the bread and wine consecrated by the priest are changed into the Body and Blood of Christ enthroned gloriously in heaven, and we believe that the mysterious presence of the Lord, under what continues to appear to our senses as before, is a true, real, and substantial presence."

Transubstantiation

In many material things there is a hidden quality that we cannot see. If we put an imitation diamond worth a relatively small amount of money next to a diamond worth a fortune, they might look the same to an uninformed person. But if we take them to a jeweler, the vast difference between the two stones will be pointed out to us. So it is with the Eucharist. Before and after the words of consecration spoken by the priest, the host appears to be the same color, weight, taste, and shape. But there is a world of difference because in place of the substance of the bread there is now the substance of Christ. Pope Paul's *Credo* explains how we are to understand this miraculous change in substance:

"Christ cannot be thus present in this sacrament except by the change into his body of the reality itself of the bread and the change into his blood of the reality itself of the wine, leaving unchanged only the properties of the bread and wine which our senses perceive. This mysterious change is very appropriately called by the Church *transubstantiation*. Every theological explanation which seeks some understanding of this mystery must, in order to be in accord with Catholic faith, maintain that in the reality itself, independently of our mind, the bread and wine have ceased to exist after the Consecration, so that it is the adorable Body and Blood of the Lord Jesus that from then on are really before us under the sacramental species of bread and wine, as the Lord willed it, in order to give himself to us as food and to associate us with the unity of his Mystical Body."

As was true for many Catholics before us, we must take a stand for or against Christ and his teaching on the Eucharist. Many still find this teaching too difficult and once again repeat the words: "This sort of talk is hard to endure!" (John 6:60), and turn away from Christ. Many others, however, without fully understanding the mystery, give their assent in a spirit of faith, repeating with St. Peter, "Lord ... you have the words of eternal life" (John 6:68).

When Jesus instituted the sacrament of the Holy Eucharist at the Last Supper, he gave the power to the Apostles, his first priests, and to priests for all time, to "do this as a remembrance of me." Obeying the Lord's command, the Apostles went forth, not giving plain bread and wine to their fellow Christians, but rather making Christ really present under the appearances of bread and wine. "Is not the cup of blessing we bless a sharing in the blood of Christ?" St. Paul asked the people of Corinth. "And is not the bread we break a sharing in the body of Christ" (1 Corinthians 10:16)?

After repeating the words of institution that Christ spoke at the Last Supper, Paul said that "every time, then, you eat this bread and drink this cup, you proclaim the death of the Lord until he comes! This means that whoever eats the bread or drinks the cup of the Lord unworthily sins against the body and blood of the Lord" (1 Corinthians 11:26-27).

But how could a person be guilty of sinning against the Body and Blood of the Lord by eating a little bread or drinking a little wine in an unworthy manner unless it was no longer bread and wine but the Lord himself? Would a person be accused of assault if he did violence to a portrait or a statue of the President of the United States? Of course not. So Paul took the words of our Lord literally, and so did all the Popes and saints and doctors of the Church in its early centuries. It wasn't until many centuries later that people began to deny the Real Presence of Christ in the Eucharist, but their denials are refuted by the overwhelming evidence of Scripture and history (cf. *Catechism of the Catholic Church*, nn. 1373-1381).

Thomas Merton, the best-selling author who became a Catholic as a young man, said that before his conversion he had no idea that there existed such a thing as the Blessed Sacrament. "I thought churches were simply places where people got together and sang a few hymns," he wrote in *Seven Storey Mountain*. It wasn't until after he came into the Church that he learned what even some Catholics do not fully appreciate – the power of Christ in the Blessed Sacrament to influence individuals and the world. There is an awesome power of light and truth in the tabernacles of Catholic churches, even over those who have never heard of the hidden Christ, and Catholics ought to spend as much time as possible praying before the Blessed Sacrament.

Proving His Love for Us

"There is no greater love than this: to lay down one's life for one's friends," Jesus said at the Last Supper (John 15:13). And he did just that for us the following day, demonstrating once again that he would never ask us to do anything that he had not done himself. After his ascension into heaven, Christ was separated from us, but he had promised that he would not leave us alone and that he would be with us "always, until the end of the world!" (Matthew 28:20). He has remained with us as spiritual food in the Holy Eucharist, nourishing us with his Body and Blood. But how many people truly appreciate this great gift?

Toward the end of his life, Napoleon was held prisoner on an island by English soldiers. One day a friend came to visit him and asked what had been the happiest day of his life. The friend was probably expecting to hear Napoleon speak of the glory of the military conquests he had made and of the days when all of France hailed him as a great ruler. But there was no mention of any of these triumphs. Instead, Napoleon's mind ranged back to his childhood, to a little church in Corsica, where he remembered the happiest day of his life as having been "the day of my First Communion."

Many people have fond memories of their own First Communion day. But how many of them still have the same feeling of awe and reverence toward Jesus in the Eucharist? We can receive Communion every day of the year, and some people do. A larger number receive Communion weekly, but that is only about fourteen percent of the year. If someone got a grade of fourteen percent on a history or math test, they wouldn't brag about it to their family and friends, would they? So what about those who receive Jesus only once or twice a year, or worse still, the large number of Catholics who don't bother going to church at all and never meet their Lord and Savior in the Eucharist.

If someone offered these people a gift of one million dollars, you can be sure that they would gladly accept it. Jesus in the Holy Eucharist is a gift beyond price, but many people pass up the most valuable gift they will ever receive and, in turning their backs on our Lord, they jeopardize their salvation. For as Jesus said, "If you do not eat the flesh of the Son of Man and drink his blood, you have no life in you" (John 6:53).

Those Who Appreciated the Eucharist

There is an old saying that you never really miss something until you lose it. Those who have spent years in prisoner-of-war camps can attest to how much they valued their freedom once they had it taken away from them. And those who were unable to go to Mass or to receive the Sacraments for a long time because their countries were taken over by evil forces that sought to obliterate any mention or worship of God can describe the great joy that they experienced when freedom of religion was restored. There are also some stirring stories of people who risked their lives for a brief taste of the Lord in the Eucharist.

From the martyrs in the catacombs in the first centuries after Christ, to those who gave their lives for the faith in England in the sixteenth century, to those who have suffered persecution for their faith in our own time, there are some inspiring examples for our edification. In Mexico during the 1920s and 1930s, when Mass and Holy Communion were forbidden, lay people volunteered for the risky duty of keeping the Eucharist in their homes so that individuals and small groups could come and receive Communion. A priest in hiding would offer Mass and consecrate the sacred Hosts, and men, women, and even children would bring them to places designated as "Eucharistic Centers," where passwords were used to admit Catholics who were willing to risk their lives to receive Jesus in Holy Communion.

During World War II, some four hundred Catholic priests were held prisoner in a Nazi concentration camp. Then a new group of priests was brought to the camp, one of whom had managed to smuggle in many Hosts in a small leather pouch. Over two consecutive nights, all four hundred priests were able to receive Communion, an event that one of them later called the most exhilarating experience of his life.

During his imprisonment by the Communists in Budapest, Jozsef Cardinal Mindszenty, the Primate of Hungary, recalled in his memoirs the time that he noticed a small glass of wine on a stand in the interrogation room. "I took a small piece of bread I was brought for breakfast and concealed it," he wrote. "When the guards left me alone for a moment, I poured half of the wine into my water glass, spoke the words of consecration over the bread and wine, and communicated. In this way I was able to celebrate Mass twice."

There are many other stories of similar experiences, which makes it all the more ironic that there are people who have never been deprived of the opportunity to receive the Holy Eucharist but who seem to have so little appreciation for this wonderful gift from heaven. Let us pray for those people, and for ourselves, that we will always be willing and worthy to take the second Person of the Blessed Trinity into our mouths and hearts.

Questions About the Eucharist

Around the year 700 A.D., a priest in Italy who had begun to doubt the presence of Jesus in the Eucharist held up the Host during Mass one day and saw it change into flesh, while the liquid in the chalice became clots of blood. This treasure was guarded by monks until 1970 when Church authorities gave a team of scientists permission to study the substances. After taking samples and putting them through a variety of tests, the scientific team concluded that the flesh was really human flesh and the clots were human blood. The team found no trace of any preservative or embalming agent, yet the flesh and blood were just as fresh then as they were thirteen centuries earlier.

Very few of us will ever have the privilege of witnessing such a miracle. Most of us accept the Real Presence of Christ on faith, that is, we believe it because Jesus, the Son of God, revealed it to us. But questions come up frequently about the Eucharist. For instance, a Catholic bishop was once asked by a non-Christian, "How is it possible for bread and wine to become the Body and Blood of Christ?" The bishop replied: "You have grown since childhood and today you have more flesh and blood than you had then. Your body changed the food you ate into flesh and blood; if the human body can do that, God can do it also."

Satisfied with this answer, the non-Christian posed another question: "How can it be possible for the whole Body and Blood of Christ to be present in all your churches, in every host and every part of each host?" The bishop answered: "To God nothing is impossible. I will however show you something similar in everyday life. In a large mirror you see your image reflected only once. When you break the mirror into a hundred pieces, you see the same image of yourself in each piece. This may help you to understand how Christ may be present in many places at the same time."

Despite these answers, the Holy Eucharist remains one of the most profound mysteries of our faith, and some people find such mysteries very hard to accept. Why should that be so? In every other aspect of our lives, we are confronted with mysteries that we accept without question. Put a high-sounding scientific name on a mystery and people seem satisfied. For example, gravity causes all things to fall to the ground, yet sap runs upward. Tell someone that the phenomenon is the result of "capillary action," and they won't ask any more questions. Or take the case of a magnet which can affect objects without even touching them. Use the term "magnetic attraction" to explain what happens, and many people no longer consider the situation a mystery.

But leave the field of the physical and material and mysteries become a stumbling block. Men and women who would never think of questioning a scientific concept feel no reluctance at all to challenge spiritual concepts. No matter how infinite the mystery, those with finite intellects do not hesitate to question things that are beyond their comprehension. And while the use of some technical scientific term will satisfy their curiosity in the realm of physics, they are not as easily swayed by a technical religious term like "transubstantiation."

But be that as it may, it is a teaching of the Catholic Church that Christ is fully present in every Host and in every part of each Host. Just as the light of a candle is not weakened no matter how many other candles are lighted from it, so the Eucharistic Host is not weakened no matter how many tiny particles are broken off it. Or look at it this way. Suppose a person writes a book and has a thousand copies printed. There are two elements that make up that book. First of all, there are the ideas that are expressed in the book. This element the philosophers call the "substance," the important thing. Second, there is the paper, the printing on the pages, and the cover. These elements are known as the "accidents." They are less important because the same ideas could have been expressed in a speech, or on television, or in some other way.

So it is with Holy Communion. There may be a thousand Hosts, yet each person receives the same entire substance of Christ. Jesus is present wholly and entirely under the appearance of bread or wine alone. Remember what St. Paul said: "Whoever eats the bread *or* drinks the cup of the Lord unworthily sins against the body *and* blood of the Lord" (1 Corinthians 11:27). Thus, Catholics should have no difficulty in expressing their belief that what they receive in Holy Communion is the Body, Blood, Soul, and Divinity of Jesus Christ.

House of Bread

The place where our Lord was born two thousand years ago is called Bethlehem. The name of that small town comes from a Hebrew phrase made up of two words that mean "House of Bread." Is it something more than a coincidence that the One who would someday come to us as the "Bread of Life" should be born in a place called the "House of Bread"? Every Catholic church is another Bethlehem, for it is indeed a "House of Bread" wherein dwells the Bread of Life.

On that first Christmas night when the shepherds approached their Lord in Bethlehem, they were greatly privileged and blessed. But we are privileged even more, for in a Catholic church we not only come close to Christ, but he gives us himself as spiritual food, uniting himself to us in a union greater than that of two pieces of wax melted together. This unity was remarked by St. Paul, who said that "because the loaf of bread is one, we, many though we are, are one body, for we all partake of the one loaf" (1 Corinthians 10:17).

The purpose of food is to strengthen and nourish our body, to keep our resistance high and ward off disease, and to restore energy to our body. All that material food does for our body, the Eucharist does for our soul. As material food builds us up to be able to handle our daily duties, so the Eucharist accomplishes these things for us spiritually by increasing sanctifying grace – God's life – in us. Without this grace, we cannot get to heaven. For our body, food and rest are necessary to restore energy burned up by physical activity, and to repair any minor breakdown of tissues.

For our soul, the reception of the Eucharist restores our spiritual energy and repairs any minor damage caused by venial sin.

There is still another way that Holy Communion is important for our spiritual health. Just as natural food builds up our physical strength and helps us to resist disease, so the Eucharist builds up our spiritual strength and helps us to resist the disease of sin. We are exposed every day to a large number of temptations, or invitations to commit sin, and we will not be able to say no to those temptations unless we have built up our resistance. Frequent reception of Holy Communion will give us the extra strength that we need.

Receiving the Eucharist Worthily

In order to receive Holy Communion worthily, we must be in the state of grace, we must fast from all food and drink (except water) for one hour, and we must have the right intention.

(1) *We must be in the state of grace.* This means that we must have no mortal sins on our soul, that we must not have deliberately disobeyed any of God's laws. If we are conscious of having committed a mortal sin, we cannot go to Communion until we have received the sacrament of Penance and obtained God's forgiveness.

(2) *We must fast for the required time.* The period that we must fast from food and drink, with the exception of water and medicine, has been greatly decreased in recent decades – from midnight the previous night to three hours to one hour before Communion. The purpose of the Eucharistic fast is to prepare us to receive the Lord, so there is no reason why one cannot fast *longer* than required as a way of showing our love for Christ and our appreciation for the great gift he is to us.

(3) *We must have the right intention.* This means that we must want to receive our Lord for the right reason, e.g., to unite ourselves more closely to him, to build up resistance to sin, to seek God's help for ourselves and others. A person who receives Communion because everyone else is doing it, or to impress other people, or because he or she would be embarrassed to remain in their seat does not have the right intention.

Furthermore, a person going to Communion should act in a holy and reverent manner. They should be dressed in clean and modest clothes, their mind should be on the great privilege that they are about to experience, they should not be talking or fooling or chewing gum on the way to or from Communion, and they should take a few moments after returning to their places to talk quietly with God. We can praise him, thank him for all that he has done for us, ask him to help those in need, and offer up our prayers and good works in reparation for our own sins and the sins of the world.

The Fruits of the Eucharist

"Holy Communion is the shortest, surest way to heaven," said Pope St. Pius X, who lowered the age at which children could receive Jesus in the Eucharist. He didn't mean that the mere receiving of Communion is a sure guarantee of salvation, for there are many people receiving Communion in a very lackadaisical and perfunctory manner. And one can't help but notice that as the Communion lines have become much longer, the lines for Confession are virtually non-existent. It would be naive in our sin-filled society to think that the decline in those approaching the sacrament of Penance is attributable to a corresponding decline in the number of sins committed.

St. Cyril of Jerusalem declared that when we receive the Eucharist, we become Christ-bearers. And not only do we become bearers of Christ personally, but if we appreciate what Christianity is all about, then we become bearers of Christ to all whom we meet. The reception of Communion is not just a private experience, but it is supposed to prepare us to reach out to others (cf. *Catechism of the Catholic Church*, nn. 1391-1398).

"It can be said that according to Jesus' intention in formulating the new commandment of love at the Last Supper, Eucharistic Communion enables those who receive it to put into practice: 'Love one another as I have loved you,'" Pope John Paul II told those at a general audience on April 8, 1992. "Participating in the Eucharistic Banquet testifies to their unity, as the Council points out in writing that the faithful, 'strengthened by the Body of Christ in the Eucharistic Communion, manifest in a concrete way that unity of the People of God which this holy sacrament aptly signifies and admirably realizes'" (*Dogmatic Constitution on the Church*, n. 11).

The Holy Eucharist should have a very definite effect on our daily life, on our relationship with others, if we receive it frequently and worthily. For as the Second Vatican Council said: "No Christian community can be built up unless it has its basis and center in the celebration of the most Holy Eucharist" (*Decree on the Ministry and Life of Priests*, n. 6).

Chapter 17

The Greatest Prayer of All

When the Church celebrates the Eucharist, she commemorates Christ's Passover, and it is made present: the sacrifice Christ offered once for all on the cross remains ever present. "As often as the sacrifice of the Cross by which 'Christ our Pasch has been sacrificed' is celebrated on the altar, the work of our redemption is carried out." — *Catechism of the Catholic Church*, n. 1364

Caught up in a conversation with a well-educated atheist one evening, a priest was asked, "Even if God existed, why should I worship him? What would it get me? How would I benefit?" They were not easy questions to answer because the atheist had put the emphasis in the wrong place. He was so concerned with himself that it never occurred to him that religion and worship might be a two-way street, that perhaps we might have some obligations toward God apart from any benefits that we might get from God.

Unfortunately, the attitude of the atheist is rather commonplace today, even among people who believe that there is a God. Some think that God should do all the giving without expecting anything from us in return. Although the purposes of prayer include adoration, thanksgiving, petition, and reparation, many people engage exclusively in petition, in asking God for favors. They seldom offer adoration and praise to God, or express thanks to him for the blessings they have received, or try to make up for sins by prayer and good works.

There is nothing wrong, of course, in asking favors of God. It is perfectly natural to do so, especially since Jesus himself told us,

"Ask and you will receive" (Matthew 7:7). He told us to consider God our Father and to make our needs known to him. A child will ask a parent for something desirable, and we, as children of God, should not hesitate to ask our Father in heaven for things that would be good for us. But just as we would discourage a child from always asking for things, and would scold a child who never expressed any gratitude for the things provided by a loving parent, so, too, God expects more from us than just prayers of petition.

The best way that we can show our love and gratitude to God is by faithfully worshiping him at Mass every week. The Mass is the greatest prayer of all, the central act of worship for a Catholic, and the source of uncounted blessings in our spiritual life. And yet, as many polls, and the empty seats on Sunday, indicate, a lot of Catholics do not go to Mass. Some are too lazy; some say that they don't get anything out of the Mass; some say that the Mass is boring; and some say that they can worship God in their own way, that they don't need to go to Church.

The problem with that kind of thinking is that God expects us to go to Mass. He provided us with this way of worshiping him, and he will not look kindly on those who deliberately ignore his command to keep holy the Lord's Day. The night before Jesus died on the cross for our sins, he asked us to "do this as a remembrance of me" (Luke 22:19). How anyone can so easily dismiss this simple request from a Person who was about to lay down his life for them is hard to fathom. Jesus didn't ask us to die in the same horrible way that he did; only to take part in an unbloody renewal of his sacrifice on the cross. That doesn't seem like too big a favor to ask, does it? Especially when you consider all that Jesus did for us.

It is one thing to be lazy and careless about Mass participation, but it is quite another to claim to be a follower of Jesus and then to disregard totally the most important thing he asked us to do in memory of him. Using stronger words than that, Pope John Paul II said that "it would be a pernicious illusion to claim that one is acting in accordance with the Gospel without receiving its strength from Christ himself in the Eucharist, the sacrament he instituted for this purpose. Such a claim would be a radically anti-Gospel attitude of self-sufficiency" (General Audience, May 12, 1993).

How Did the Mass Come About?

To understand the Mass completely, and to find out why it is considered such a serious obligation, it is necessary to gather some historical background information. We learned some things in the previous chapter about the Eucharist and its place in the Mass. What we need to do now is to explore the origins of the Mass as a sacrifice. To do that, we must go back to the beginning of human history.

The Bible and the Church tell us that Adam and Eve, our first parents, were created in a state of perfect happiness. They were not subject to pain or suffering or death and they had a right to heaven. However, at the tempting of the devil, they disobeyed God and lost their state of perfect happiness and their right to heaven. They were then subject to pain, suffering, and eventual death. But God did not abandon them, and he promised one day to send a redeemer who would atone for their sin (Genesis 3:15).

For many centuries, the descendants of Adam and Eve tried to win God's forgiveness and to regain their right to heaven by means of sacrifice, that is, by destroying and offering up to God some animal or crop. Thus, Abel offered a lamb to God (Genesis 4:4); Melchizedek, the high priest who was king of Salem, brought out bread and wine to welcome back Abram from his rescue of Lot (Genesis 14:18); Abraham was prepared to sacrifice his beloved son Isaac when an angel of the Lord stopped him; he sacrificed a ram instead (Genesis 22:12). And so on throughout the Old Testament. But these offerings were not enough to make up for the sins of Adam and Eve and their descendants.

God loves us so much, however, that two thousand years ago he sent his only Son, Jesus Christ, to offer himself as a sacrifice for the sins of the world. Because Jesus is God, he could offer the perfect sacrifice to his Father and make up for the sin of our first parents. Because Jesus was also a man, a human being like us in all things but sin, he could represent us, stand in our place, and make reparation for our sins. That is why we call Jesus the "Lamb of God," because he sacrificed himself for us and restored our friendship with God.

Jesus wanted us to have a share in his perfect sacrifice, so on the night before he died, he instituted the Mass. At the Last Supper, he changed bread and wine into his Body and Blood ("This is my body .... This is my blood"), and gave the Apostles, his first priests, the power to effect that same transformation. He also commanded them to "do this as a remembrance of me." So every time a Catholic priest celebrates Mass, he is following Jesus' instructions and making it possible for us to share in the sacrificial banquet handed on to us by the Lord himself.

At Mass, said the bishops of Vatican II, priests act "in the person of Christ" and "join the offering of the faithful to the sacrifice of their Head. Until the coming of the Lord (cf. 1 Corinthians 11:26), they re-present and apply in the Sacrifice of the Mass the one sacrifice of the New Testament, namely the sacrifice of Christ offering himself once and for all to his Father as a spotless victim" (*Dogmatic Constitution on the Church*, n. 28).

Pope John Paul II also commented in this same vein when he said: "In the Eucharist the presbyter [priest] reaches the high point of his ministry when he pronounces Jesus' words: 'This is my body .... This is the cup of my blood....' These words concretize the greatest exercise of that power which enables the priest to make present the sacrifice of Christ. Then the community is truly built up and developed – in a sacramental way and, thus, with divine efficacy" (General Audience, May 12, 1993).

The Mass is not merely the prayer of the priest. It is the prayer of the People of God, offered through the priest. That is why the priest during the Mass calls it "our sacrifice." And all members of Christ's Church share in the fruits of every Mass. No matter how unknown or forgotten a follower of Christ may be, no matter where he or she is on this planet, the Church does not forget her people. Upon thousands of altars every day, in majestic cathedrals in large cities and in tiny chapels in remote jungles, the Church prays for every member of the flock of Christ, using the same prayer that Jesus said on Holy Thursday and reenacting the same sacrifice that Jesus offered on Good Friday.

What Is the Mass?

The poet Henry Wadsworth Longfellow once wrote of "the precious keepsakes into which is wrought the giver's loving thought." All of us have precious keepsakes – perhaps an old photo album, or a mother's ring, or a father's watch, or some medal or piece of jewelry that may not be worth much in a monetary sense, but which is priceless in sentimental value. We should think of the Mass as the most precious keepsake that our Lord and Savior could have given to us. The reasons why can be found in the following paragraph from Vatican II:

"At the Last Supper, on the night when he was betrayed, our Savior instituted the Eucharistic Sacrifice of his Body and Blood. He did this in order to perpetuate the sacrifice of the cross throughout the centuries until he should come again, and to entrust to his beloved spouse, the Church, a memorial of his death and resurrection: a sacrament of love, a sign of unity, a bond of charity, a paschal banquet in which Christ is consumed, the mind is filled with grace, and a pledge of future glory is given to us" (*Constitution on the Sacred Liturgy*, n. 47).

Thus, the Mass is both a re-presentation of the Last Supper and a reenactment of Calvary. Christ could die only once, but his sacrifice is perpetuated for us in an unbloody manner at Mass. A sacrifice requires a priest, an altar, and a victim. Christ is the priest and victim both on Calvary and at Mass, although he offers himself at Mass through the ministry of the priest, and the cross was his altar on Calvary, where he poured out his blood of behalf of many (Mark 14:24). It was the will of the Father that Christ leave this world, that by his death our redemption would be accomplished. But "he had loved his own in this world" (John 13:1) and wanted to find a way to remain, and yet not remain. So Jesus solved this dilemma by leaving the world in his bodily existence, while leaving us with his Real Presence in the Eucharist.

The Mass is a memorial of his death and resurrection. "I received from the Lord what I handed on to you, namely, that the Lord Jesus on the night in which he was betrayed took bread, and after he had given thanks, broke it and said, 'This is my body, which is for you. Do this in remembrance of me.' In the same way, after the supper, he took the cup, saying, 'This cup is the new covenant in my blood. Do this, whenever you drink it, in remembrance of me.' Every time, then, you eat this bread and drink this cup, you proclaim the death of the Lord until he comes!" (1 Corinthians 11:23-26).

The Mass is a sacrament of love. "As the Father has loved me, so I have loved you. Live on in my love .... There is no greater love than this: to lay down one's life for one's friends. You are my friends if you do what I command you .... The command I give you is this, that you love one another" (John 15:9-17).

The Mass is a sign of unity. "Having been nourished by the Lord himself, the Christian should with active love eliminate all prejudices and all barriers to brotherly cooperation with others. The Eucharist is a sacrament of unity. It is meant to unite the faithful more closely each day with God and with one another" (*Basic Teachings for Catholic Religious Education*, n. 12).

The Mass is a bond of charity. "The liturgy in its turn inspires the faithful to become 'of one heart in love' when they have tasted to their full of the paschal mysteries; it prays that 'they may grasp by deed what they hold by creed.' The renewal in the Eucharist of the covenant between the Lord and man draws the faithful into the compelling love of Christ and sets them afire" (*Constitution on the Sacred Liturgy*, n. 10).

The Mass is a paschal banquet. "The Eucharist is a meal which recalls the Last Supper, celebrates our unity together in Christ, and anticipates the messianic banquet of the kingdom. In the Eucharist, Jesus nourishes Christians with his own self, the Bread of Life, so that they may become a people more acceptable to God and filled with greater love of God and neighbor" (*Basic Teachings for Catholic Religious Education*, n. 12).

Why Go to Mass?

As we said earlier, we should not go to Mass primarily to feel better, or to get an emotional uplift, or to "get something out of it," although all three wishes can come about if we take part in the celebration intelligently and enthusiastically. The main reason for going to Mass, in addition to fulfilling Jesus' request to "do this in memory of me," is to give our Creator the worship that is due to him from his creatures. We go to church not to get something, but to give something. If we are to love God with all our hearts, all our minds, all our souls, and all our strength, then there is no better way to demonstrate that love than by participating in the Holy Sacrifice of the Mass.

By doing so we not only receive the grace and strength that the Mass provides, but we also fulfill the four ends or purposes of the greatest prayer of all:

Adoration – Our first duty and obligation is to praise and adore God because he is our Creator and Sustainer, the One who brought us into this world and who watches over us every minute of every day. Notice how many prayers in the Mass offer adoration to God the Father and the Son, particularly the Gloria, in which we say, "Lord God, heavenly King, almighty God and Father, we worship you, we give you thanks, we praise you for your glory ... for you alone are the Holy One, you alone are the Lord, you alone are the Most High...."

Thanksgiving – If we did a big favor for someone, and they never said thank you, we would be hurt and disappointed. Who has done more favors for us than God? God has given us our life, our families and friends, and our talents. A person would have to be very thoughtless and ungrateful to refuse to attend Mass for one hour out of the 168 hours in a week to thank God for all the blessings he has showered on us.

Petition – Attendance at Mass gives us the opportunity to ask God to help ourselves and others. For instance, during the Prayers of the Faithful, the Eucharistic Prayer, the Our Father, and the thanksgiving after Communion, we can put our needs before the Lord. He already knows everything we need or intend to ask for, of course, but we must do our part in petitioning him. And remember that we make these requests not by ourselves but along with the priest and the People of God in the church with us.

Reparation – Part of our responsibility as believers in God and followers of Jesus is to repair or make up for our own sins and the sins of others. If Jesus willingly suffered and died for our sins, can't we go to Mass at least once a week and join our prayers, works, joys, and sufferings with those of our Lord to bring us closer to him and to try to make up for some of what is going on in the sinful world around us?

The Parts of the Mass

It is not the function of this chapter to give a complete picture of the Mass in all its aspects. But to add to our understanding of what the Mass is all about, it might be well to give a brief summary of the principal parts of the celebration. The two primary divisions of the Mass are the Liturgy of the Word and the Liturgy of the Eucharist, and here are some of the key parts of those divisions:

Pentitential Rite – When we call to mind our sinfulness and ask God for his mercy and forgiveness. This rite can take away venial sins, but those in mortal sin must avail themselves of the sacrament of Penance.

Gloria – As noted earlier, this is a prayer of praise and thanksgiving to the three Persons of the Blessed Trinity, Father, Son, and Holy Spirit.

Liturgy of the Word – Readings from the Bible, with the first reading usually from the Old Testament, the second reading usually from the letters of Paul, and the third reading always from one of the four Gospels. The readings are arranged in a three-year cycle so that a person who attends Mass every Sunday for three consecutive years will hear read from the altar a very substantial portion of the Bible.

Homily – A brief talk by the priest or deacon to explain to us how the readings from Scripture apply to our lives here and now. The homily should instruct us, inspire us, and challenge us to do the will of God.

Profession of Faith – A statement from the fourth century of the basic beliefs of the Catholic Church. We ought to think about what we are saying and profess our adherence to those beliefs.

Prayers of the Faithful – Petitions to God for the Church and its leaders, for the world and its leaders, for the sick and the deceased, for ourselves and our loved ones, and for all those in need of God's help.

Preparation of the Gifts – An offering to God of the gifts of bread and wine for the sacrifice, and an offering of money to support our parish, the Church in our diocese and worldwide, and those in need of assistance.

Eucharistic Prayer – The most solemn part of the Mass during which the priest repeats the words of our Lord at the Last Supper ("This is my body .... This is my blood") and makes Jesus present on the altar at the Consecration of the elements of bread and wine.

Our Father – The prayer that Jesus himself taught us in which we pledge to do God's will on earth as it is done in heaven and promise to forgive others as God has promised to forgive our sins and transgressions.

Sign of Peace – An expression of love and good will towards others at Mass with us.

Holy Communion — The awesome experience of receiving Jesus Christ in his Body, Blood, Soul, and Divinity, giving us the spiritual food we need to live as his witnesses and disciples in the world.

Dismissal – When the priest sends us forth with the reminder that we are called upon to spend the rest of the week loving and serving the Lord and others.

Brothers and Sisters in Christ

To be rightly understood, the Mass must point in two directions: vertically up to God and horizontally out to our brothers and sisters in the Lord. Worship of God has social implications. It was Jesus who said, "If you bring your gift to the altar and there recall that your brother has anything against you, leave your gift at the altar, go first to be reconciled with your brother, and then come and offer your gift" (Matthew 5:23-24). In a similar vein, St. Paul told the Christians at Corinth that they had better straighten out their uncharitableness and lack of consideration for others because "whoever eats the bread or drinks the cup of the Lord unworthily sins against the Body and Blood of the Lord" (1 Corinthians 11:27).

It is not surprising that throughout the centuries there has been an emphasis on one aspect or another of the Mass. In the early days of the Church, the memory of the crucified and risen Lord was of greatest importance. After the Council of Trent in the sixteenth century, the true presence of Christ in the Mass was stressed because of the widespread denial of the Real Presence by the Protestant reformers.

In our own century, there has been emphasis on social action and concern for our brothers and sisters in need. While there are good reasons for focusing on each of these aspects, we must remember that all of them are important. We must stress the whole picture of the Mass: sacrifice, memorial of the Savior's death and resurrection, sacrament of love, sign of unity, bond of charity, and paschal banquet.

We must also remind the faithful of their share in the mission of Christ. It is not just the responsibility of priests; the laity are called to a priesthood of their own by virtue of the outpouring of the Spirit in Baptism and Confirmation. "The lay faithful participate, for their part, in the threefold mission of Christ as Priest, Prophet, and King," said Pope John Paul in *Christifidelis Laici*.

He explained that the laity share in the priestly mission of Christ "in the offering they make of themselves and their daily activities"; in the prophetic mission by their "ability and responsibility to accept the Gospel in faith and to proclaim it in word and deed, without hesitating to courageously identify and denounce evil"; and in the kingly mission by engaging in "spiritual combat in which they seek to overcome in themselves the kingdom of sin (cf. Romans 6:12), and then to make a gift of themselves so as to serve, in justice and charity, Jesus who is himself present in all his brothers and sisters, above all in the very least" (n. 14).

The lay faithful, the Holy Father said in the same section of his apostolic exhortation, "are called to restore to creation all its original value." He traced the source of the laity's participation in the threefold mission of Christ back to the anointing of Baptism and recalled the words of St. Peter: "You, however, are 'a chosen race, a royal priesthood, a holy nation, a people he claims for his own to proclaim the glorious works' of the One who called you from darkness into his marvelous light" (1 Peter 2:9).

A Lesson from the Past

In the sixteenth century, the sparsely populated Danish territory of Greenland underwent a vicious persecution. Enemies of the Catholic Church tried their best to destroy the Church and its believers on that island by massacring or exiling every priest. Their annihilation of the Church appeared to be complete and, for fifty years, no priest reached the shores of Greenland, and no Mass was celebrated there.

Yet a few courageous Catholics managed to keep the seed of Catholicism alive. Every Christmas Eve they met among the ruins of their old church almost buried in the snow. After a fervent prayer, young and old waited in expectant silence as the old sacristan prepared for a strange ceremony. Slowly he hobbled to a niche in the wall where the Blessed Sacrament had once been reserved. With trembling hands he eagerly probed the niche, aided by the muted glow of a torch which gave him some light in the midnight darkness, Suddenly, the face of the sacristan beamed with exultation. Slowly he brought forth a faded yellow cloth and, with tears in his eyes, kissed it reverently and laid it upon the broken stones of the former altar. One after another, those in the small community came to press their lips to the cloth. When asked why, the old man explained:

"Fifty years ago, Mass was last said in this country. I served that last Mass. Let us thank God for this precious relic on which rested the Body and Blood of Jesus, and let us pray that God may send us priests to offer the Holy Sacrifice in our midst again." The precious cloth was a corporal, the linen cloth on which the Host and the chalice rest during Mass, and for half a century it was the only visible connection with the reenactment of our Lord's death on Calvary. Wouldn't it be wonderful if every Catholic in our own time had the same love and reverence for the Mass and all that it signifies?

How to Get the Most Out of Mass

The Mass has come down to us over twenty centuries because Jesus, at the Last Supper, commanded his Church to "do this as a remembrance of me." During every moment of every day, somewhere in the world, Mass is being celebrated from the rising of the sun until its setting (cf. Malachi 1:11). It has survived wars, persecution, and indifference. It will last as long as the Church of Jesus Christ lasts, which means until the end of time. It should be the most important thing in our life. But is it? Each one will have to answer that question in the quiet of his or her own heart.

If you want to make the Mass the most important thing in your life, you must put yourself completely into the Mass. That means arriving on time, genuflecting properly, watching what the priest does and listening to what he says, saying the responses clearly, singing the songs fervently, trying to get from the Scripture readings and the homily just one point that would make a difference in your life, paying particularly close attention during the Eucharistic Prayer, especially at the Consecration of the bread and wine, receiving Holy Communion devoutly, taking time to say your thanksgiving to God after Communion, and vowing as you leave the church at the end of Mass to live the rest of the week as God would want you to live.

The Second Vatican Council gave this advice for getting the most out of Mass:

"The Church, therefore, earnestly desires that Christ's faithful, when present at this mystery of faith, should not be there as strangers or silent spectators. On the contrary, through a proper appreciation of the rites and prayers they should participate knowingly, devoutly, and actively. They should be instructed by God's word and be refreshed at the table of the Lord's Body; they should give thanks to God; by offering the Immaculate Victim, not only through the hands of the priest, but also with him, they should learn to offer themselves too. Through Christ the Mediator, they should be drawn day by day into ever closer union with God and with each other, so that finally God may be all in all" (*Constitution on the Sacred Liturgy*, n. 48).

Chapter 18

Christ's Easter Gift to Us

"Those who approach the sacrament of Penance obtain pardon from God's mercy for the offense committed against him, and are, at the same time, reconciled with the Church which they have wounded by their sins and which by charity, by example, and by prayer labors for their conversion." – *Catechism of the Catholic Church*, n. 1422

One day when Jesus was visiting a small town in Palestine, a group of influential men invited him to dinner at the house of Simon the Pharisee. While they were eating, an unusual thing happened. A woman known in the town as a notorious sinner suddenly appeared at the door. That such a woman should present herself at the house of a man as important as Simon was incredible enough, but she startled the invited guests even more by throwing herself at Christ's feet. She wet his feet with her tears, dried them with her hair, and finally perfumed them with a special oil.

When Simon saw what was happening, he said to himself, "If this man were a prophet, he would know who and what sort of woman this is that touches him – that she is a sinner." In answer to his thoughts, Jesus said: "You see this woman? I came to your home and you provided me with no water for my feet. She has washed my feet with her tears and wiped them with her hair. You gave me no kiss, but she has not ceased kissing my feet since I entered. You did not anoint my head with oil, but she has anointed my feet with perfume. I tell you, that is why her many sins are forgiven – because of her great love. Little is forgiven the one whose love is small."

Jesus then told the woman, "Your sins are forgiven .... Your faith has been your salvation. Now go in peace" (Luke 7:36-50).

All of Christ's life on earth has been studied and reflected on by Christians, but certain incidents stand out as unforgettable. This is one such incident, when a group of influential citizens stared in astonishment as a sinful woman sought the mercy of the Lord, and he told her that because of her great love and faith, "Your sins are forgiven."

The men in the house were indignant when they heard those words and declared that only God could forgive sins. They were right, but this Prophet at table with them was God. And since the purpose of his life was to free the human race from its sins, not only the people of his own day but all those throughout history, he extended that forgiveness to the penitent woman. But Jesus did not stop there. He knew that many other men and women, boys and girls, would need that same forgiveness, so he delegated the power to forgive sins to the Apostles and their successors in the priesthood.

From Bethlehem to Calvary, Christ offered mercy and forgiveness to a suffering and sinful humanity. He began his public life with a call to "reform your lives and believe in the Gospel!" (Mark 1:15). He told parables like the Lost Sheep (Luke 15:4-7) and the Prodigal Son (Luke 15:11-32) to illustrate the mercy of God. And when the Pharisees complained about his association with sinners, Jesus told them, "People who are healthy do not need a doctor; sick people do. I have come to call sinners, not the self-righteous" (Mark 2:17).

Our Lord went around doing good, giving sight to the blind and curing all types of ailments. But though he spent much of his time bringing relief to those suffering from physical and mental infirmities, Jesus' main purpose on earth was to cure a humanity that was spiritually sick from sin. His mission on earth was summed up shortly before he was born, when an angel told Joseph concerning Mary: "She is to have a son and you are to name him Jesus because he will save his people from their sins" (Matthew 1:21). And Christ carried out that mission by forgiving those who were sorry for their sins, such as the penitent woman, the woman caught in adultery (John 8:1-11), and the good thief on the cross (Luke 23:43).

Christ's Remedy for Sin

Since Jesus established a Church on earth to carry on his work, one of the principal tasks of that Church, if it is to be true to its Founder, is the reconciliation of sinners with God. In the words of Pope John Paul II: "To evoke conversion and penance in man's heart and to offer him the gift of reconciliation is the specific mission of the Church as she continues the redemptive work of her divine Founder. It is not a mission which consists merely of a few theoretical statements and the putting forward of an ethical ideal unaccompanied by the energy with which to carry it out. Rather it seeks to express itself in precise ministerial functions, directed toward a concrete practice of penance and reconciliation" (*Reconciliation and Penance*, n. 23).

How were we to obtain forgiveness of sins after Jesus returned to heaven? Why he would appoint human agents – the Apostles and their successors in the priesthood – to carry on this essential work. There are those who insist that they don't have to confess their sins to a priest, that they can deal directly with God. But to say that is to ignore Christ's specific commission to the Apostles and those who would take their place. There can be no mistake about the intentions of Jesus on this vital matter.

On the Sunday after the death of Jesus, when the city of Jerusalem was filled with rumors of his resurrection, the Apostles were gathered behind locked doors, fearful of what might happen to them, when suddenly Jesus stood in the middle of the room. "Peace be with you" was his greeting to them, but the Apostles were terrified. They thought at first that Jesus was a ghost. He repeated the greeting, "Peace be with you," and then said: "As the Father has sent me, so I send you. Receive the Holy Spirit. If you forgive men's sins, they are forgiven them; if you hold them bound, they are held bound" (John 20:19-23).

Some time earlier in his public life, Christ had assured the Apostles, "Whatever you declare bound on earth shall be held bound in heaven, and whatever you declare loosed on earth shall be held loosed in heaven" (Matthew 18:18). When a soul is bound by the chains of sin, he was telling them, I give you the power to release that soul. And now on the first Easter Sunday night, he was telling them that they would have the power to forgive sin and reconcile sinners with God. Sin would always be in the world, but the remedy for sin would always be in the Church. He was telling his first priests and all those who would come after them that when they pronounced the words of forgiveness, he would ratify their action in heaven and make sins that had been as red as scarlet become as white as wool.

Following Christ's Directions

Sin is not just simple human error, said Pope John Paul II. "It is an offense against God in that the sinner disobeys the law of the Creator and Lord, and thus offends his paternal love. Sin cannot be considered merely from the point of view of its psychological consequences: sin draws its significance from the person's relationship to God .... It is an offense against the divine majesty, in regard to which St. Thomas Aquinas does not hesitate to say that 'the sin committed against God has a certain infinity in virtue of the infinity of the divine majesty' " (General Audience, April 15, 1992).

Those who say that they can seek God's forgiveness directly are right up to a point, but they must go that one step farther and follow the directions spelled out by Jesus. We must go to God in the way that Jesus determined. Why would he give the power to forgive sins to priests if sins could be just as well forgiven without these ministers of reconciliation? If someone gives you the key to his house, authorizing you to admit or bar those whom you choose, that would be a useless favor if you later discovered that everyone possessed a key to the house and could enter when they pleased.

To those who ask how a priest can forgive sins since "he is only a human being," we concede that a priest is only human, with all the shortcomings of our fallen humanity. But we might ask: "Can an ordinary citizen grant a pardon to a person about to be executed for a crime?" The answer, of course, is that he cannot. But the governor of that state has that power. Why? After all, he or she is only human, the same as we are. But the governor has the power to grant a pardon by virtue of being elected to that office.

The situation is similar with reference to a priest. True, he is only a human being, but in virtue of his office as priest he can grant forgiveness. Christ gave him this power with his office: "If you forgive men's sins, they are forgiven." There are many ways that Christ could have granted us his pardon, but he chose to do it through his priests in the sacrament of Penance/Reconciliation.

Actually, there are a number of good reasons for confessing our sins to a priest besides the fact that this is what Jesus told us to do:

(1) Since Jesus said that priests could hold someone's sins bound, that is, not forgive them, they would first have to be told the sins by the penitent in order to know what sins to forgive or not forgive.

(2) Telling our sins to a priest teaches us humility, something we would not learn if we confessed our sins privately to God. We might even refrain from committing a sin if we know that we will have to tell a priest about it. There would be no such inhibition if we only had to speak directly to God.

(3) We receive graces from the sacrament of Penance.

(4) The priest can give us sound advice on how to avoid sin in the future, while the person praying in private receives no helpful instructions.

(5) There may be an attempt on our part to rationalize the sinfulness of some act, to convince ourselves that it really wasn't a sin, without the intervention of a priest who can force us to be more honest with God and with ourselves.

(6) By absolving us of our sins, the priest, who is representing Christ, gives us the assurance that our sins have been forgiven. There is no such assurance for those who claim to be dealing directly with God. "If we acknowledge our sins," said the Apostle, "he who is just can be trusted to forgive our sins and cleanse us from every wrong" (1 John 1:9).

As Pope John Paul II reminded those who think that they can bypass the sacrament of Penance: "It would therefore be foolish, as well as presumptuous, to wish arbitrarily to disregard the means of grace and salvation which the Lord has provided and, in the specific case, to claim to receive forgiveness while doing without the sacrament which was instituted by Christ precisely for forgiveness" (*Reconciliation and Penance*, n. 31).

What the Sacrament Does

Knowing human nature as he does, Jesus gave us the sacrament of Reconciliation because we all feel the need for forgiveness at times, even on the natural level. If we have hurt a family member or a friend in some way, we experience anxiety and concern until we have obtained that person's forgiveness. The same is true in our relationship with God. How many people spend thousands of dollars going to psychiatrists when one visit to a compassionate and understanding priest might dispel the doubts and feelings of guilt?

It is not easy to go to Confession, especially if one has committed serious sins, but the feeling of relief and gratitude to God in getting those sins wiped from the slate is one that many Catholics have experienced over the years. Catholics go to the sacrament of Penance not because it is easy, but because they experience there the compassion and consolation of the Savior himself, and because they get the graces to avoid sin in the future and remain in God's friendship. It seems that repentant sinners cause considerable jubilation in heaven, too: "I tell you, there will likewise be more joy in heaven over one repentant sinner than over ninety-nine righteous people who have no need to repent" (Luke 15:7).

Whether it's called Confession, Penance, or Reconciliation, the sacrament of forgiveness is as complete in its effects as we are willing to let it be. Mortal sin, venial sin, punishment due to sin can be removed, and sanctifying grace and helpful advice on how to avoid sin in the future may be obtained. The disposition of the penitent is a key factor, of course. If the penitent is only half-hearted in seeking forgiveness, then some of the punishment attached to forgiven sins may still remain. Or, God forbid, if some sins are knowingly concealed from the priest, the penitent is in worse shape than before because now he or she has added the sin of a bad Confession to the sins deliberately concealed. And the next time one approaches the sacrament, the bad Confession must be revealed as well as those sins not previously confessed.

The sacrament of Penance is the ordinary way of obtaining forgiveness and the remission of serious sins committed after Baptism. While many people today have lost their sense of sin and are staying away from Penance because they do not consider themselves sinners, we know only too well from a glance at the newspapers or the news programs on television that the number of sins committed has not decreased. The lines of penitents may have diminished, but unfortunately that is due not to fewer sins but to fewer people who honestly recognize their failure to love God and others. That is why recent Popes have tried so hard to restore in the People of God a sense of sin, and to call them back to the sacrament given to us by the Lord himself to obtain forgiveness for sin.

It was G.K. Chesterton, the convert to Catholicism, who once said that "there is no need to be so ashamed of our blunders .... It is human to err, and the only final and deadly error among all our errors is denying that we have erred." The Apostle John put it more bluntly: "If we say, 'We are free of the guilt of sin,' we deceive ourselves; the truth is not to be found in us" (1 John 1:8).

Eternal Life Insurance

We hear a lot today about insurance. People are very concerned about having insurance on their life and health and property in case anything goes wrong. Well, we are speaking for the "Eternal Life Insurance Company," and the policy concerns the last moment of your life. The premiums are sorrow for sin and a good Confession. When people take out a life insurance policy, they are not around to collect the benefits. On our policy, however, we will collect peace of soul and eternal life.

As we saw in the chapter on the Commandments of the Church, Catholics are required to go to Confession at least once a year if they are conscious of having committed a mortal sin. But we ought to take advantage of the merciful love of God more often than that, whether we are guilty of mortal sin or not. We clean our homes more than once a year, don't we? Shouldn't we therefore clean our spiritual houses frequently too? Even Voltaire, an atheist and no friend of the Catholic Church, once made this amazing statement: "There is not perhaps a more useful institution than Confession."

Similar acknowledgements of the great value of this sacrament given to us by Christ have come from Catholics and non-Catholics alike. Penance has come down through the ages as the great remedy for sin and a wonderful solace for sinners. What a shame that more people do not take advantage of this sacrament! Perhaps part of the reason is that the sacrament is misunderstood. Let us therefore review and explain the principal elements of the sacrament of Penance: contrition, confession, absolution, and satisfaction.

The Element of Contrition

The confession of sins is not the only thing necessary to obtain forgiveness. No offense against God is forgiven without sorrow and, unless we have a sincere desire to make up to God for our sin, we are not really sorry. **Contrition is a sincere sorrow for having offended God.** It is, said Pope John Paul II, "a clear and decisive rejection of the sin committed, together with a resolution not to commit it again, out of the love which one has for God and which is reborn with repentance. Understood in this way, contrition is therefore the beginning and the heart of conversion" (*Reconciliation and Penance*, n. 31).

Sorrow is an act of the will; it need not be felt. People may feel more sorrow at the death of a loved one than they feel for their sins, but that does not lessen the value of their sorrow in the sacrament of Penance. Feelings have nothing to do with the efficacy of Confession. The real test of our sorrow is in the will, in our decision to avoid sin in the future.

If critics of the sacrament understood this, they would not be so quick to say that Catholics are free to sin, confess it to the priest, and then go right out and sin again. In order for sins to be forgiven, the penitent must truly intend while receiving the sacrament not to commit those sins again. If there is any conscious intention to sin again, then those sins would not be forgiven. This is not to say that the penitent will never again commit the same sins, only that the penitent will do all in his or her power to avoid those sins in the future.

Our attitude ought to be that we acknowledge sin to be the greatest evil in the world, and are prepared to endure anything rather than turn our backs on God in the future. That may seem like an impossible ideal, but it is an ideal based upon the truth that there is no greater evil, no greater injustice, than sin. And, as we know, nothing is impossible with God's help.

The motive for our sorrow must be a supernatural one – either love of God or the fear of his punishment. Merely natural motives, such as the fear that we will be fined or even sent to jail for stealing or for lying under oath, are not sufficient. So there are two kinds of contrition: **Perfect contrition is sorrow because sin offends the God whom we love; imperfect contrition is sorrow because we fear that God will punish us by sending us to hell.** Either kind is sufficient for the sacrament of Penance, but we should at least aim for perfect contrition.

The friendship that we have injured with our sins is the greatest of all friendships, and we ought to be sorry for our sins primarily because they have offended our best Friend, even if at the beginning we are sorry because they have hurt us. And our sorrow must come from the heart, not merely from our lips.

The Element of Confession

The second essential element in receiving the sacrament of Penance worthily is the actual telling of our sins to the priest. This is so important, said Pope John Paul, "that for centuries the usual name of the sacrament has been and still is that of Confession. The confession of sins is required, first of all, because the sinner must be known by the person who in the sacrament exercises the role of judge. He has to evaluate both the seriousness of the sins and the repentance of the penitent; he also exercises the role of healer, and must acquaint himself with the condition of the sick person in order to treat and heal him" (*Reconciliation and Penance*, n. 31).

In Confession, as the Holy Father indicated, the priest is not only a spiritual father, but a spiritual doctor. His role is to restore, in the name of Christ, spiritual health to the penitent. When a person goes to the doctor, he must tell him the symptoms. Before the doctor can begin the healing process, he must know what is wrong. A prisoner writing to the governor for a pardon would have to state the crime committed and what the sentence was. Otherwise, the governor could not intelligently judge the appeal.

Confession of sins means telling the priest what sins were committed, how many times they were committed, and what the circumstances were. In the case of serious sins, all of these must be told, for if even one mortal sin is knowingly omitted, the whole situation is changed; no forgiveness is granted for any of the sins confessed, and a new sin of sacrilege has been committed. If a door has a double or triple lock, and all the locks except one are unlocked, the door still cannot be opened. If one is adding up a series of figures and one wrong number is punched into a calculator, the whole sum will be wrong, and the process must begin all over again.

So, too, if one mortal sin is knowingly held back from the priest, the penitent must return to the sacrament and tell all his or her sins, plus the fact that a mortal sin was omitted during the previous Confession. (If the penitent truly forgets to tell a mortal sin, then it would be sufficient merely to mention that sin the next time one goes to Confession.)

It was St. Bonaventure who gave this advice to Catholics who might be hesitant to tell their sins because of shame or fear: "Begin with the sin which it costs you most to confess, and afterwards all the rest will come easy to you." Bear in mind, too, that there is no sin you can tell the priest that he has not heard before. There are no new sins, only old ones committed over and over again.

Though all mortal sins – those involving grave matter, sufficient reflection, and full consent of the will – must be told, no venial sins need be confessed, although the Church urges us to do so. (Venial sins can be forgiven by acts of sorrow, works of charity, prayer, and the Penitential Rite at the beginning of Mass.) If the person has no mortal sins to tell, venial sins may be confessed in order to receive the grace of the sacrament. If no venial sins can be recalled since one's last Confession, a sin already forgiven in the past may be mentioned. There is no reason why we cannot express sorrow more than once for some serious offense we committed in the past against a gracious and loving God. Pope John Paul once summarized this element of the sacrament:

"It is good to recall that all that we have said is true of the sin which breaks our friendship with God and deprives us of 'eternal life'; that is why it is called 'mortal.' Recourse to the sacrament is necessary when even only one mortal sin has been committed (cf. Council of Trent, DS 1707). However, the Christian who believes in the effectiveness of sacramental forgiveness has recourse to the sacrament with a certain frequency, even when it is not a case of necessity; in it he finds the path for an increasing sensitivity of conscience and an ever-deeper purification, a source of peace, a help in resisting temptation and in striving for a life that responds more and more to the demands of the law and love of God" (General Audience, April 15, 1992).

The Element of Absolution

Acting as judge and healer, the confessor gives absolution to the penitent. **Absolution is the words and gestures by which the priest remits the guilt and penalty of sin.** The gestures include the imposition of the hand and the Sign of the Cross made over the penitent while the priest says the formula of the sacrament that includes the essential words, "I absolve you from your sins in the name of the Father, and of the Son, and of the Holy Spirit." It is at this moment that the contrite sinner comes into contact with the power and mercy of God, all sin is blotted out, and a state of innocence is restored through the intervention of our Savior Jesus Christ. Even though the priest himself is a sinner, he is empowered to grant to the penitent this sign of God's pardon and peace.

The Element of Satisfaction

For every sin committed, satisfaction must be made in this life or in the next. **Satisfaction involves the willingness of the person to perform the penance imposed by the priest as a**

token sacrifice to God in sorrow for sins committed. By carrying out the penance, we help to pay our debt to God. A person who breaks a civil law, say, by driving a car while drunk, must perform many hours of community service to atone for his illegal actions. So the person who breaks the law of God must perform a certain penance to make up for the offenses against the Creator. The greater the offense, the greater the debt of punishment that must be paid.

In the early days of the Church, very severe penances were imposed on sinners, and they often had to be carried out in public. Today the priest imposes comparatively light penances, usually consisting of a few short prayers, that are not really proportionate to the punishment we deserve for sin. So we really should not be satisfied with completing the relatively easy penance given by the priest, but should take on some additional good works in our life – Bible reading, recitation of the rosary, prayers before the Blessed Sacrament, visits to the sick, etc. – to shorten our time in purgatory.

Noting that acts of satisfaction "should not be reduced to mere formulas to be recited, but should consist of acts of worship, charity, mercy, or reparation," Pope John Paul said that these acts "include the idea that the pardoned sinner is able to join his own physical and spiritual mortification – which has been sought after or at least accepted – to the Passion of Jesus who has obtained the forgiveness for him.

"They remind us that even after absolution there remains in the Christian a dark area, due to the wound of sin, to the imperfection of love in repentance, to the weakening of the spiritual faculties. It is an area in which there still operates an infectious source of sin which must always be fought with mortification and penance. This is the meaning of the humble but sincere act of satisfaction" (*Reconciliation and Penance*, n. 31).

How to Make a Good Confession

Here are the steps involved in receiving the sacrament of Penance in a worthy and fruitful manner:

(1) There must be a good examination of conscience, that is, one must spend some time recalling any faults or sins committed since the last good Confession. Actually, Catholics ought to examine their consciences every night before going to sleep, asking them-

selves how they may have failed to love God and neighbor that particular day, saying an Act of Contrition, and promising God to get to Confession as soon as possible if a serious sin has been committed. The examination of conscience should be based on the ten Commandments, the Commandments of the Church, the Sermon on the Mount (including the Beatitudes), the corporal and spiritual works of mercy, the theological and moral virtues, and the seven capital or deadly sins.

(2) We must have contrition or sorrow for our sins and what the Church has called a firm purpose of amendment, that is, a sincere intention not to sin again.

(3) We must tell our sins to the priest honestly and completely. If there is something we are not sure about, we should ask the priest about it. It is important to indicate how many times a sin was committed so that the priest can evaluate our spiritual condition. Getting drunk once a month is wrong, but getting drunk ten times a month means that the penitent has a much more serious problem with alcohol.

(4) We must listen carefully to the advice the priest gives us, recite an Act of Contrition or some prayer of sorrow, and faithfully carry out the penance he imposes.

When we walk out of that confessional box or reconciliation room (the penitent must always be given the option of confessing sins anonymously or face to face with the priest) after hearing the words of absolution, our sins are pardoned just as effectively as if we had knelt or sat in the presence of Christ himself. That is why when a confessor once addressed King Louis IV of France as "Your Majesty," the monarch replied: "I am not a king here nor are you a subject; I am a child and you are my spiritual father."

The Seal of Confession

Thus far we have been looking at the sacrament of Penance primarily from the viewpoint of the penitent. What about the man on the other side of the screen or the room? In many cases, the priest does not know who the penitent is and may never come in contact with the person again. It is in this impersonal atmosphere that the priest usually exercises the power of Christ in reconciling sinners with God. The priest has been prepared for this task of guiding souls with many years of study and training. "This is undoubtedly the most difficult and sensitive, the most exhausting and demanding ministry of the priest, but also one of the most beautiful and consoling," said Pope John Paul in his apostolic exhortation *Reconciliation and Penance.*

The Holy Father went on to stress that for the effective performance of this ministry, "the confessor must necessarily have human qualities of prudence, discretion, discernment, and a firmness tempered by gentleness and kindness. He must likewise have a serious and careful preparation, not fragmentary but complete and harmonious, in the different branches of theology, pedagogy, and psychology, in the methodology of dialogue, and above all in a living and communicable knowledge of the word of God."

Furthermore, the Pope said, "it is even more necessary that he should live an intense and genuine spiritual life. In order to lead others along the path of Christian perfection, the minister of Penance himself must first travel this path. More by actions than by long speeches he must give proof of real experience of lived prayer, the practice of the theological and moral virtues of the Gospel, faithful obedience to the will of God, love of the Church, and docility to the Magisterium" (*Reconciliation and Penance*, n. 29).

For examples of priests who were holy and sensitive confessors, and who spent sixteen to eighteen hours a day in the confessional, one ought to read about the lives and spiritual heroism of St. John Vianney, the parish priest in France who was known as the Cure of Ars, and Padre Pio, the Italian monk who bore the five wounds of Christ in the hands, side, and feet for fifty years.

But what about parish priests who do know many of the penitents who come to Confession on a regular basis? Will there be embarrassment if the penitent who told the priest about a grave sin on Saturday runs into Father after Mass on Sunday? There shouldn't be since the priest is forbidden to speak of the sin to the penitent outside Confession unless the penitent has given him permission to do so.

It is one of the great boasts of Catholicism that anything heard in the sacrament of Penance may never under any circumstances be revealed by the priest to anyone. The smallest item of confessional matter may not be made known by the confessor, even at the price of his own life, or even if the information might save a nation from being annihilated.

These things not only may not be revealed, they may not even be hinted at by the priest. If a penitent told the priest in Confession that he was going to rob the priest's room in the rectory that night, the priest could not go out and buy a lock for his room. Such is the integrity of the Seal of Confession. Canon 1388 of the *Code of Canon Law* says that any priest who violates this seal is automatically excommunicated, that is, cut off from the Church.

Martyrs to the Seal of Confession

The Catholic Church has a long and glorious tradition of martyrs who have shed their blood for the Faith, and not least among those martyrs are the priests who died preserving the Seal of Confession. St. John Nepomucene was one of those courageous priests. This holy man, who lived in the fourteenth century, was the confessor to Queen Jane of Bohemia, whose husband, King Wenceslaus, was a wicked man. He was jealous of the good life his wife was leading and he attempted to find out from Father John what she had told him in Confession. The king thought that with his royal authority he could demand the information regardless of the secrecy of the confessional.

But the king was wrong. Father John refused to tell him anything and he was thrown into prison and tortured. Finally, during the night, John was bound hand and foot and drowned in a river. Three hundred years after his death, John's tomb was opened and those present were startled to see that, although the saint's body had turned to dust, his tongue remained as it had been in life. At the base of a statue erected in his honor at the spot of his death there is this inscription: "Here died a martyr to the Seal of Confession."

Closer to our own time, there was a French priest named Father Demoulin who in 1899 was charged with the crime of murder. The sexton of the parish church had actually committed the crime and, in order to throw suspicion on the priest, he had put the murder weapon in Father Demoulin's room. Then to seal the lips of the priest, the sexton went to Confession to him and admitted having committed the murder. The priest stood trial for the crime, knowing every day that he was innocent but not being able to reveal the real murderer's name even to save his own life. He was sentenced to life imprisonment on the infamous Devil's Island.

Father Demoulin went there as a young man and, twenty-five years later, the brutal life of convict labor had left him old, weak, and broken in body. Meanwhile, many miles away, the sexton lay dying and called for a priest. He revealed on his death bed that he had committed the murder. And then he sought forgiveness through the very same sacrament whose inviolable secrecy he had abused to send an innocent priest to prison.

Even more recently, in 1973, a West German priest was threatened with a jail term if he did not identify the man who had confessed to him that he had mailed bombs to West German government leaders. The state prosecutor warned Fr. Richard Schneider that action would be taken against him if he refused to reveal confessional information. The government backed down, however, when a spokesman for Cardinal Doepfner issued this statement: "The priestly obligation to maintain the secrets of the confessional is one of the most ironclad rules of the Church. All legal authorities everywhere know this."

Forms of Celebration

There are three ways in which the sacrament of Penance may be celebrated. The first and most common way is *reconciliation of individual penitents*. This is the only normal and ordinary way of celebrating the sacrament. It is preferred because it links the person with spiritual direction, and it must not be allowed to fall into disuse or neglect. The second form is *reconciliation of a number of penitents*, say, at a Penance Service, with individual confession and absolution after the service. This form allows the group to listen to the word of God and a homily before approaching the priest, and it can be effective if there are a sufficient number of confessors present. The third and least common way is reconciliation of a number of pentitents with *general confession and absolution*. Though some priests have used this latter form indiscriminately, it is only to be used in cases of grave necessity and with the permission of the local bishop.

Cases of grave necessity would include those in danger of imminent death, such as soldiers going into battle without sufficient time for individual confessions, or people living in a remote area who because of the unavailability of priests would be forced to go for a long time without sacramental grace or Holy Communion.

Only the bishop can decide whether the circumstances justify general confession and absolution. And if permission is given, the penitents, to receive valid absolution, must be properly disposed and truly sorry for their sins, must intend to confess individually their serious sins as soon as possible, and must confess them individually before a second general absolution takes place. Before granting general absolution, the priest must instruct the faithful about these conditions and their obligation to observe them.

Pope John Paul gave this cautionary statement regarding general confession and absolution: "The exceptional use of the third form of celebration must never lead to a lesser regard for, still less an abandonment of, the ordinary forms, nor must it lead to this form being considered an alternative to the other two forms" (*Reconciliation and Penance*, n. 33).

Our Easter Gift From Christ

There was a story in the newspapers not long ago about a new telephone service in South Africa that would give people the opportunity, for two dollars a minute, to "Dial a Confession" and seek forgiveness for crimes committed during that nation's long struggle over the policy of racial separation called apartheid. The story did not say how popular the new service was, but it did quote some critics as saying that it would not be effective because there was no way of determining whether there was true contrition, and there would be no penances imposed.

Many Catholics might wish that they could call up a priest and receive the sacrament of Penance over the telephone. It sure would be a lot easier than dealing with a priest in person. It requires considerable humility to admit to another human being that you have done wrong, but humility is a good thing because it helps us to see ourselves as we really are, and as people who are dependent on God. Pride is at the root of all sin. We decide that we know better than God what is right and wrong. The sacrament of Reconciliation leaves no room for pride; it forces us to humble ourselves and to ask God to "be merciful to me, a sinner" (Luke 18:13).

The parable of the Pharisee and the tax collector reminds us, in the words of Jesus, that "everyone who exalts himself shall be humbled while he who humbles himself shall be exalted" (Luke 18:14).

But whatever sins we have committed, Christ has provided us with a means of obtaining pardon for them. He intended this sacrament to be one of peace and joy, not fear or unpleasantness. Think of all the times in his public life that our Lord forgave sin. All these incidents were accompanied by the kindness of Jesus and peace of soul for those who were sorry for their sins.

Recall, too, the scene in the upper room on Easter Sunday night, when the risen Christ gave us the sacrament of Penance. The Apostles were anxious and fearful when Jesus suddenly came right through the locked door. But after he twice said to them, "Peace be with you," the Gospel tells us that "at the sight of the Lord the disciples rejoiced" (John 20:20). And in this atmosphere of peace and joy, the Son of God gave us the sacrament of Penance, the ordinary and best means of reconciling ourselves with God and of restoring peace and joy in our own lives. What a marvelous gift from the sinless Christ to a sinful humanity!

Chapter 19

Christ's Gift to the Sick

The Church believes and confesses that among the seven sacraments there is one especially intended to strengthen those who are being tried by illness, the Anointing of the Sick. – *Catechism of the Catholic Church*, n. 1511

During the French Revolution, one of the most bloodthirsty revolutionists swore that he would never ask a priest to enter his house and, that if one ever entered, the priest would never leave the house alive. The man later became dangerously ill, and someone summoned a priest to his bedside. The priest knew who the man was, and about his violent hatred of priests, but he went without hestitation to the man's house.

The man in bed was furious at the presence of the priest and shouted for a gun. With a fierce hatred in his eyes, he said to the priest: "I have strangled twelve such as you with my own hands."

"You are wrong," the priest replied calmly. "You killed only eleven. The twelfth did not die. God kept him alive that he might save your soul. I am the twelfth."

Then the priest opened his cassock at the neck and showed the man the marks of his hands, where some years before he had attempted to strangle the priest. At this manifestation of love, the revolutionist quieted down, expressed sorrow for his many sins, and received absolution from the priest.

In our own time, you may recall hearing about the ship filled with explosives that blew up in a Texas harbor, setting off other explosions and causing fires that threatened nearby oil tanks. Hundreds were killed or injured. After the initial explosion, Father William Roach, pastor of the only Catholic church in the area, hastened to the scene in his car. Police warned him of the danger, but he rushed through the smoke and flames to administer the sacraments to the dying. As he was performing his priestly duties, preparing others for their journey to eternity, an explosion killed him.

Such stories are not uncommon, and they illustrate a striking point: that in the sick room and at the deathbed, on highways and in places where disaster has struck, priests have performed heroically and have won the grateful love of Catholics, as well as the admiration of non-Catholics. Ministering to the sick and the dying is one part of the priest's work that is seen and appreciated by those of all religions, and those of no religion.

Priests are on call twenty-four hours a day, 365 days a year. It is not unusual to see a priest making his way through the dark, in all kinds of weather, en route to a sick person. No fear of contagion can keep him away; no peril is worthy of consideration when a soul is at stake. They are chaplains in hospitals, in police and fire departments, and in the branches of the military. When the alarm sounds, when someone is in a life-threatening situation, the priest is there. In this ministry to the sick, to the elderly, and to the dying, the priest is only following the example of Christ himself, who went about doing good, forgiving people's sins, imparting his blessing to them, and sometimes even healing them.

The Divine Physician

Since it is a sacrament, the Anointing of the Sick is a visible sign or ceremony that owes its existence not to the Church but to Christ himself. The grace and strength that it brings are just like the grace and strength that our Lord and the Apostles brought to the people of Palestine: "Jesus summoned the Twelve and began to send them out two by two, giving them authority over unclean spirits .... With that they went off, preaching the need of repentance. They expelled many demons, anointed the sick with oil, and worked many cures" (Mark 6:7-13).

Our Lord promised his followers that "signs like these will accompany those who have professed their faith: they will use my name to expel demons, they will speak entirely new languages, they will be able to handle serpents, they will be able to drink deadly poison without harm, and the sick upon whom they lay their hands will recover" (Mark 16:17-18).

One of Jesus' disciples, St. James, who was a cousin of Christ, gives us the clearest picture of the origins of the sacrament of the Anointing of the Sick. In his letter, James writes: "Is there anyone sick among you? He should ask for the presbyters [priests] of the church. They in turn are to pray over him, anointing him with oil in the Name of the Lord. This prayer uttered in faith will reclaim the one who is ill, and the Lord will restore him to health. If he has committed any sins, forgiveness will be his" (James 5:14-15).

Here we have a prescription from the Divine Physician himself – a spiritual remedy that lessens the difficulties of death, comforts the dying, strengthens the soul for its final passage into eternity, and sometimes brings about physical healing. How grateful we should be for this wonderful sacrament! How much it has meant over the centuries to Catholics facing illness, death, or just the trials of old age to have its special healing qualities. In as few as ten minutes, or as many as forty minutes, the rite is performed, with the key elements being the anointing with oil and the prayers of the priest.

Once again we see a sacrament that features the healing properties of oil, a sacrament that accomplishes spiritually what oil symbolizes materially. Oil has long been recognized for its medicinal and healing effects, as Jesus indicated in his parable of the Good Samaritan, where the Samaritan used oil to heal the wounds of the man beaten by robbers (Luke 10:34). Through the Anointing of the Sick, spiritual wounds are healed, the soul is cleansed from the remains of sin, temporal punishment due to sin is taken away, venial sins are forgiven, and even mortal sins can be taken away if the person is unable to confess his or her sins.

Since oil has been used by athletes to strengthen their bodies for a contest, it is a fitting symbol for Christ to express the spiritual strength given for the conflict with Satan. There is no time that is more important for the devil than the last moments of a person's life. It is the devil's last chance to claim that person's soul. "Sickness is never a mere physical evil; it is also a time of moral and spiritual testing," said Pope John Paul II. "The sick person has great need of interior strength in order to triumph over his trial" (General Audience, April 29, 1992). That interior strength comes from the Anointing of the Sick.

"Father Did It!"

The priest-authors of this book have during their years of ministering to the sick, not only in parishes, but also in hospital and police and fire emergency work, witnessed frequent and remarkable results from the holy anointing. That includes both spiritual results (reconciliation with God) and physical results (sometimes instant improvement). We have seen anxious and fearful patients become peaceful and resigned to the will of God. We have heard non-Catholic doctors say, "Whatever you are doing, Father, keep on doing it." And we remember a Jewish nurse walking up and down a hospital corridor, shaking her head and repeatedly saying, "The doctors couldn't do it, but Father did it."

These remarks were made because of amazing physical results. Imagine how great must be the effects of this sacrament on the soul! Never, never be afraid of this marvelous sacrament. Some people were afraid of it when it was called "Extreme Unction" because of the connotation that one would receive it only at the extreme moments of life, when death was imminent. Changing its name after the Second Vatican Council has helped many more people see what a wonderful gift from God this sacrament is.

The administering of the sacrament is reserved to a priest because the rite includes absolution for sins, which is a privilege of the priesthood. It also presupposes the presence of grace, since in order for all the fruits of the rite to be obtained mortal sins should already have been forgiven through the sacrament of Penance.

But the primary purpose of the sacrament is not to forgive sin but to strengthen the soul and purify it. It accomplishes the "tidying up" of the soul before its appearance at the throne of God. If it should happen that the person is unconscious when the priest arrives, and is unable to receive the sacrament of Penance, then we may pray that the person had at least imperfect sorrow for his or her sins and that the anointing will restore the patient to sanctifying grace.

At the last moments in a Catholic's life, just as throughout one's life, the Church is working not to put off death but to usher in eternal life. And just as Satan tries his hardest at the moment of death, so the Church expends her greatest energy and treasures at that same time. Because this moment is so important, a priest is ready, day or night, good weather or bad, to rush to the side of the dying person. That is why he will risk disease or danger to bring the grace of God through a sacrament that only he can administer.

Ancient and Modern Apostles

We know from the Scripture verses cited earlier that the Apostles anointed the sick with oil and worked many miracles. That same anointing has continued since their time. One modern example occurred in Dublin not long ago when a priest was called to assist a traveler lying ill in a hotel in the Irish capital. It was a stormy night and through the rain and wind the priest trudged to bring the sacraments to the sick man. After he had finished, the innkeeper remarked about the storm that had not kept the priest from his duties, and then began to speak of the comfortable life of the bishops and other higher-ranking clergy.

"I am sure," the innkeeper said, "that while you were walking through the rain on this sick call, the cardinal was in his comfortable house by a fire."

"I think you are wrong," said the priest.

"Why?" the innkeeper asked.

"Because I am the cardinal," the priest replied.

Concern for and care of the sick has always been a vital part of the Church's life from its earliest days. The record of Catholic hospitals and health care facilities through the years has been a living witness to the love and compassion of Christ and those who believe in him. However, the Church is not merely interested in physical healing but in spiritual healing as well. In a word, the Church seeks "total patient care," body, mind, and soul. Doctor and priest, medical staff and family, all work together for the complete healing of the patient.

The holy anointing often brings about a change of heart whereby the sick person gains reassurance and support needed at a time of sickness and suffering and in the throes of pain. It helps the sick to see the value of suffering when it is united with the suffering of Christ on the cross and to face that suffering courageously, even to the point of offering it up for one's own sins and for the sins of the world.

The new rite of anointing teaches us about the meaning of suffering in these words: "Suffering and illness have always been among the greatest problems that trouble the human spirit. Christians feel and experience pain as do all other people; yet their faith helps them to grasp more deeply the mystery of suffering and to bear their pain with greater courage. From Christ's words they know that sickness has meaning and value for their own salvation and the salvation of the world. They also know that Christ, who during his life often visited and healed the sick, loves them in their illness."

Jesus was a minister of healing throughout his public life. He made the blind see, the deaf hear, the crippled walk. But his physical healings always had a spiritual purpose. So, too, the new sacramental rite expresses a strong concern about both the physical and spiritual needs of the sick. The Church calls on everyone – doctors, nurses, medical and professional staff, family, and friends – to show the same love and compassion for the sick that Jesus showed when he walked the earth. Every loving act on behalf of the sick and every sincere effort to improve their physical, mental, and spiritual well-being is a participation in the healing ministry of Christ himself.

Speaking in this same vein, Pope John Paul II said that "the Church has made her own the special concern which Jesus had for the sick. On the one hand, she has promoted many endeavors of generous service to their care. On the other hand, with the sacrament of Anointing she has given and continues to give them the healing touch of Christ's own mercy" (General Audience, April 29, 1992).

Who May Be Anointed?

As mentioned earlier, the Anointing of the Sick is no longer considered to be a sacrament only for those in danger of death. That change in thinking was prompted by the revision of the sacramental rites which came out of Vatican II. Regarding this sacrament, the Council said:

" 'Extreme Unction,' which may also and more fittingly be called 'Anointing of the Sick,' is not a sacrament for those only who are at the point of death. Hence, as soon as any of the faithful begins to be in danger of death from sickness or old age, the appropriate time for him to receive this sacrament has certainly already arrived" (*Constititution on the Sacred Liturgy*, n. 73).

All that is needed is a prudent judgment that the beginning of the danger of death is present. We should not be too scrupulous about this, but should give the person the benefit of the doubt. One who is to undergo surgery, elderly people in a somewhat weakened condition, a person with a serious chronic condition who develops a viral infection – all of these should be anointed. Infants (or those so mentally retarded that they are equivalent to infants) should not be anointed since they have no need of this sacrament. Children who have reached the age of reason, around seven years of age, may be anointed. Unconscious persons who are in serious condition should be anointed if they can be presumed to have the desire to receive the sacrament. The anointing can be administered to the same person twice, either if the sick person recovers and later becomes ill again, or if, during the same illness, the danger of death becomes more serious.

To make older people more aware of the benefits of this sacrament, even when one is not at the point of death, provisions have been made for group anointings once or twice a year. These ceremonies may take place in the parish church or in hospitals, nursing homes, elderly housing complexes, or any place where there are sick people or senior citizens. Those who are not Catholics may be inspired to join the rite, although they would not be able to receive the sacrament itself. All of the benefits for an individual who is anointed are possible for those who receive the sacrament in a group.

The key elements of the Anointing of the Sick are the imposition of the hands and the anointing with holy oil of the forehead and hands of the sick or elderly. When the Sign of the Cross is made on the forehead, the priest says: "Through this holy anointing may the Lord in his love and mercy help you with the grace of the Holy Spirit." The person responds, "Amen." When he anoints the palms of the hands, the priest says: "May the Lord who frees you from sin save you and raise you up." And the response is "Amen."

When there is time, the longer rite may be used. This includes the sprinkling of holy water, an opening prayer and a Penitential Rite, readings from Scripture, a homily, general intercessions, laying of hands on the head of the sick, blessing of oil if it is not already blessed, the actual anointing of the person or persons, recitation of the Lord's Prayer, distribution of Holy Communion, and a final prayer and blessing.

Many Benefits from Anointing

Every sacrament is meant for our spiritual good, and every effort should be made to encourage people to utilize these special helps from God. This is particularly true of the Anointing of the

Sick, which may be unfamiliar to some people or which may still be associated only with those on the verge of death. We need to banish this association and emphasize that the sacrament should be given whenever a person is in most need of its fruits. These fruits may be summarized as follows (cf. *Catechism of the Catholic Church*, n. 1532):

– the uniting of the sick person to the passion of Christ, for his own good and that of the whole Church;

– the strengthening, peace, and courage to endure in a Christian manner the sufferings of illness or old age;

– the forgiveness of sins, if the sick person was not able to obtain it through the sacrament of Penance;

– the restoration of health, if it is conducive to the salvation of his soul;

– the preparation for passing over to eternal life.

When a person is sick or weakened by age, could they ask for more?

Chapter 20

Ambassadors of Christ

Holy Orders is the sacrament through which the mission entrusted by Christ to his apostles continues to be exercised in the Church until the end of time: thus it is the sacrament of apostolic ministry. It includes three degrees: episcopate, presbyterate, and diaconate. – *Catechism of the Catholic Church*, n. 1536

There is a story of a non-Catholic who sent in a letter requesting some literature on the Catholic Church. He began his letter: "Gentlemen: Please send me some pamphlets, etc...." When he received the literature and discovered that the senders were priests, the man quickly wrote this letter of apology: "Dear Fathers: I regret that in my previous letter I addressed you as gentlemen. I did not know that you were priests." The story, though humorous, reminds us that many people consider priests to be different from other men.

There is another story about a young man in a small African country who wanted to study for the priesthood. In order to pay for his studies, he went to work for three years in a copper mine. He saved enough money for the seminary training, but found that he had contracted an incurable disease while working in the mine. Instead of bemoaning his fate, the young man, realizing that the priesthood was out of the question for him, gave the money he had saved to another young man who was preparing for the priesthood and went back to work in the mine for another three years before the disease ended his life. How great was his esteem for the priesthood, and how strange are God's ways of supplying priests to work for the good of souls.

The calling of men to the priesthood over the centuries is the fulfillment of Christ's own words: "It was not you who chose me, it was I who chose you" (John 15:16). Jesus chose the twelve Apostles to carry out his work on earth and granted them his power. They in turn chose other priests who, as successors of the Apostles, inherit their spiritual power. In the words of Pope John Paul II:

"The participation in Christ's one priesthood, which is exercised in several degrees, was instituted by Christ, who wanted differentiated functions in his Church as in a well-organized social body, and for the function of leadership he established ministers of his priesthood. He conferred on them the sacrament of Orders to constitute them officially as priests who would work in his name and with his power by offering sacrifice and forgiving sins" (General Audience, March 31, 1993).

In their quest to gain souls for Christ, priests have braved unknown wilderness, sailed unexplored rivers, and courageously exposed themselves to plague and disease in the pursuit of their ordinary duties. They have been pioneers in education and in works of charity. From their ranks have come great musicians, artists, writers, even statesmen. Yet it is not from any of these accomplishments that the priesthood gets its unique dignity. No, the dignity of the priesthood springs from one thing: the reception of the sacrament of Holy Orders. For it is through this sacrament that the power comes to forgive sins and to bring down to earth on the altar at Mass the second Person of the Blessed Trinity himself under the appearances of bread and wine.

What Is a Priest?

The exalted dignity of the priest is derived not from any personal merits with which he may be endowed, but from the powers he has been given by Christ and from the duties he has been charged to perform. In truth, a priest exercises powers not given even to angels, who are very powerful in their own right. What angel was ever given the power to change bread into the Body of Christ? Not all the angels together could grant pardon for one sin.

That is why St. Francis said: "If I were to meet at the same moment one of the blessed come down from heaven and a poor priest, I should go first to the priest in order to honor him, and I should hasten to kiss his hands because they handle the Word of Life and are something superhuman."

The priest is an *ambassador of Christ*. If it is a great privilege to represent one's country in a foreign land, how much greater a privilege it is to represent the court of heaven among the nations of the earth! It was Jesus himself who said to his first priests, "As the Father has sent me, so I send you" (John 20:21).

The priest is a *shepherd*, feeding Christ's flock and dispensing his graces through the Sacraments.

The priest is a *spiritual father* to those under his care.

The priest is a *spiritual physician*, healing the wounds of sin.

The priest is a *merciful representative of Christ*, vested with power to prepare the dying for eternal life with God.

How could any mere man fulfill all of these duties without the help of God? These tasks are far above the capabilities of human nature, so God has given a pledge of his special help in the sacrament of Holy Orders. In that sacrament there is given a special grace through which the priest is granted God's assistance not only on his day of ordination, not for several years, but for a lifetime. On his ordination day, there is imprinted on the soul of a priest a spiritual character, like that of Baptism and Confirmation, that is an invisible but very real badge of authority that distinguishes a man as a priest. Pope John Paul II explained it this way:

"This character, in those who receive it through the sacramental anointing of the Holy Spirit, is a sign of: a special consecration, in relationship to Baptism and Confirmation; a deeper configuration to Christ the Priest, who makes them his active ministers in the official worship of God and in sanctifying their brothers and sisters; the ministerial powers to be exercised in the name of Christ, the Head and Shepherd of the Church [cf. *Catechism of the Catholic Church*, nn. 1581-1584].

"In the presbyter's soul, the character is also a sign and vehicle of the special graces for carrying out the ministry, graces related to the sanctifying grace that Holy Orders imparts as a sacrament both at the time it is conferred and throughout his exercise of and growth in the ministry. It thus surrounds and involves the presbyter in an economy of sanctification, which the ministry itself implies both for the one who exercises it and for those who benefit from it in the various sacraments and other activities performed by their pastors" (General Audience, March 31, 1993).

Through Holy Orders, the priest is made an official representative of Christ on earth, another Christ empowered to act in his name. This sublime dignity is within the reach of ordinary men. Most of Christ's first priests were humble fishermen and, since that day, rich men and poor men, men from high places and from lowly abodes have served the Lord and his people side by side in the ranks of the priesthood.

St. Paul, one of the first priests, saw his place in God's plan when he spoke of himself and his fellow priest, Apollos, laboring in the vineyard of Christ: "I planted the seed and Apollos watered it, but God made it grow. This means that neither he who plants nor he who waters is of any special account, only God, who gives the growth" (1 Corinthians 3:6-7).

The priest is an instrument in the hands of Christ. It is God alone who grants the grace and spiritual aid to help us get to heaven. The priest is the instrument that Jesus uses to bring us to God and to bring God to us, especially in the sacrament of the Holy Eucharist. He is the bridge between heaven and earth.

The Permanent Diaconate

Holy Orders is the sacrament administered by a bishop through which men receive the power and grace to perform their sacred duties. The word "orders" is plural because it involves bishops, priests, and deacons. It should be pointed out that the first step toward the priesthood is ordination to the diaconate. But there is also what is known as the permanent diaconate, a rank in the hierarchy that was restored by the Second Vatican Council and can be conferred upon men of mature age, even men who are married. In the words of the Council:

"At the lower level of the hierarchy are deacons, upon whom hands are imposed 'not unto the priesthood, but unto a ministry of service.' For strengthened by sacramental grace, in communion with the bishop and his group of priests, they serve the People of God in the ministry of the liturgy, of the word, and of charity. It is the duty of the deacon, to the extent that he has been authorized by competent authority, to administer Baptism solemnly, to be custodian and dispenser of the Eucharist, to assist at and bless marriages in the name of the Church, to bring Viaticum to the dying, to read the sacred Scripture to the faithful, to instruct and exhort the people, to preside at the worship and prayer of the faithful, to administer sacramentals, and to officiate at funeral and burial services" (*Dogmatic Constitution on the Church*, n. 29).

The Brilliant Jewel of Celibacy

While permanent deacons may be married men, priests may not marry. The modern world has trouble understanding priestly celibacy, which Pope Paul VI called "a brilliant jewel" (*Sacerdotalis Caelibatus*, n. 1), but then the modern world has trouble understanding any practice of self-denial for love of God. Often the refrain is heard that if the Catholic Church allowed priests to marry, as the clergy of other religions are allowed to marry, there would be no shortage of vocations. That is a very dubious conclusion. In any case, celibacy has been practiced in the Catholic Church since the fourth century for a number of very good reasons:

(1) It follows the example of Christ himself, who promised great rewards to those who have "given up home, brothers or sisters, father or mother, wife or children or property for my sake" (Matthew 19:29).

(2) It allows priests to focus exclusively on serving Christ and the Church, without at the same time worrying about wives and children. They are called to a higher fatherhood and have many more "spiritual children" than in an ordinary family. Married clergy in other religions, torn between their family and their congregation, have expressed appreciation for the celibacy required of Catholic priests.

(3) It provides space and time for serious prayer and development of a deep bond with Christ, whom the priest is called to share with the world.

(4) It is a foreshadowing of heaven where there will be no marriage.

(5) It is a wonderful example of commitment and sacrifice under difficult circumstances; it gives credibility to priests who ask their people also to make great sacrifices for God.

It should also be noted that no man is required to become a priest; that celibacy is not forced on priests but is freely chosen by them after years of training, reflection, and prayer; that celibacy is no more responsible for unfaithful priests than marriage is responsible for unfaithful husbands and wives; and that a great number of priests, Religious, and laity all over the world are today living inspiring lives of voluntary and consecrated celibacy.

A Sacramental Priesthood

In order that a man may receive the sacrament of Holy Orders worthily, there are several requirements. He must be in the state of grace and be of upright moral character; he must have reached the determined age and be in reasonably good health; he must have sufficient learning and training; he must have the desire to devote his life to the work of Christ in the priesthood; and he must be called to this sacrament by the bishop. The priesthood is a calling, a vocation.

"It was not you who chose me," said Jesus. "It was I who chose you" (John 15:16). An officer in the service of his country is commissioned by his superiors and ultimately by the President. A priest is commissioned by his bishop and ultimately by God.

Why can't women be ordained to the priesthood? It is the constant tradition of the Church since the time of Christ that the Church does not feel authorized to ordain women because Jesus himself did not do so, even though he was surrounded by some very holy and competent women, including his own mother. Furthermore, our whole sacramental system is based on natural signs that people can recognize with ease.

These signs, said St. Thomas Aquinas, "represent what they signify by natural resemblance." And the Church has said that "the same natural resemblance is required for persons as for things: when Christ's role in the Eucharist is to be expressed sacramentally, there would not be this 'natural resemblance' which must exist between Christ and his minister if the role of Christ were not taken by a man; in such a case it would be difficult to see in the minister the image of Christ. For Christ himself was and remains a man" (*Declaration on the Admission of Women to the Ministerial Priesthood*, n. 5).

This is no reflection on the worthiness or capability of women to serve the Church. Women have served Christ and his Church in extraordinary fashion for 2,000 years, and some of them are recognized as great saints. But while women are called to many roles in the Church, the priesthood is not one of them.

Pope John Paul made it clear that this teaching will never change when he stated in his apostolic letter *Ordinatio Sacerdotalis*:

"Wherefore, in order that all doubts may be removed in a matter of great importance, a matter which pertains to the Church's divine constitution itself, in virtue of my ministry of confirming the brethren (cf. Lk. 22:32), I declare that the Church has no authority whatsoever to confer priestly ordination on women and that this judgment is to be definitively held by all the faithful" (n. 4).

What Does a Priest Do?

In carrying out the mission of Christ on earth, the priest is expected to fulfill many roles. The priest is to *teach the doctrine of Christ* to the world, with the authority of Christ behind him: "He who hears you, hears me" (Luke 10:16).

The priest is to *forgive sins*: "If you forgive men's sins, they are forgiven them" (John 20:23).

The priest is to *offer a sacrifice*: "Do this as a remembrance of me" (Luke 22:19). The central act of a priest's day is the offering of the Holy Sacrifice of the Mass. It was meant to be the prayer *par excellence*, the highest and best way by which adoration, thanksgiving, petition, and reparation can be offered through the priest to God.

The priest is to *pray constantly*: "He told them a parable on the necessity of praying always and not losing heart" (Luke 18:1). "Consecrated in the image of Christ, the priest must be a man of prayer like Christ himself," said Pope John Paul II. "This concise definition embraces the whole spiritual life that gives the presbyter a true Christian identity, defines him as a priest, and is the motivating principle of his apostolate. The Gospel shows Jesus in prayer at every important moment of his mission....

"Indeed, we learn from Jesus that a fruitful exercise of the priesthood is impossible without prayer, which protects the presbyter from the danger of neglecting the interior life for the sake of action and from the temptation of so throwing himself into work as to be lost in it" (General Audience, June 2, 1993).

The sacrament of Holy Orders was instituted at the Last Supper. After making his Body and Blood present under the appearances of bread and wine, Christ told the Apostles to do what he had just done until the end of time: "Do this as a remembrance of me." In the early days of the Church, the Apostles celebrated the Sacrifice of the Mass and ordained other men to carry on the work of Christ. For instance, in each church that they visited, Paul and Barnabas "installed presbyters and, with prayer and fasting, commended them to the Lord in whom they had put their faith" (Acts 14:23). Every priest ordained by a bishop forms one more link in the chain that began on the first Holy Thursday, when Jesus ordained his first priests.

Everybody knows that to become a doctor, lawyer, chemist, teacher, or computer programmer, one has to pass through a certain period of preparation. A priest, who is called to be a spiritual leader and to do God's work effectively, must also be trained spiritually, mentally, and physically; his character must be formed and strengthened. And after those years of preparation have been successfully completed, the candidate for ordination comes before his bishop and the bishop gives the outward sign of the sacrament – the imposition of hands on the candidate and then the anointing of the new priest's hands with oil.

Something Divine and Human

Little wonder that Catholics and non-Catholics alike look with respect toward the Catholic priesthood, not because of *who* the priest is, but because of *what* the priest is. There is no higher dignity on earth than the priesthood. The priest's work is to be the liaison between God and his people. From God he brings supernatural gifts to us; from us he brings prayers and satisfaction for sin to God. No wonder the powers and duties of a priest put the work of presidents and kings in the background. For as St. John Chrysostom remarked: "The power of kings is only over the bodies of men, whereas that of the priest is over their souls."

We must remember that, in spite of their ordination, priests remain human beings, subject to the same temptations and trials as Religious and laity. Christ chose men, not angels, to lead his Church, and allowances must be made for human frailties. Priests will differ in personality, character, and other ways and, even if an individual priest may not personally deserve the respect due his position, respect is still due his priesthood. And if some priests do not live up to their calling, that should not reflect on the many holy and zealous priests who do indeed function as "other Christs" among us.

"I will close my eyes to their faults, and only see in them God's representatives," said St. Francis de Sales. And St. Augustine asked: "Are we to think slightingly of Christ and the Apostles because there was a Judas among them? Who will show me any body of men on earth who are without faults?" Actually, the Catholic Church is proud of the glorious tradition of men in the priesthood for almost two thousand years and will not let the failures and transgressions of a small minority besmirch the wonderful example of the vast majority.

There was a decline in vocations to the priesthood in some parts of the world in the years following the Second Vatican Council, but in other parts of the globe "an authentic spring is underway, rich in hope and promise for the Church and humanity," said Pope John Paul II. "The Spirit of the Lord acts with all the more power when consecrated persons and the whole Christian family are more decisive in refusing to adapt to the spirit of this world and more generous in accepting the mystery of the cross." He said that God "will not fail to give the Church holy and courageous persons totally consecrated to the glory of God and the true good of their brothers and sisters, shining witnesses of the Gospel message" (General Audience, February 2, 1993).

The Priest as Prophet

When many people hear the word "prophet," the first thing that comes to mind is the foretelling of future events. But the primary meaning of the word is "a person who speaks for God." Such were the biblical prophets, men like Amos, Isaiah, and Jeremiah in the Old Testament, and John the Baptist in the New Testament. They were not mostly concerned with foretelling the future, although they did that very accurately with regard to the Messiah, but rather with calling people to reform their lives and turn back to God. The priest is called to this same prophetic role, in season and out of season, whether his listeners want to hear the message or not.

In his thought-provoking book *Whatever Became of Sin?*, psychiatrist Karl Menninger said that he considered the place of the clergyman of the greatest importance in denouncing sin and restoring morality to society. But he also wondered whether the clergy had lost its moral leadership: "Have they been diverted or discouraged from their task? Have they succumbed to the feeling that law and science and technology have proved morality and moral leadership irrelevant?"

If he were writing today, Menninger might also ask: "Is it true that many priests give uninspiring homilies because they fear offending those in the congregation? Is it true that the lack of being specific about sin and guilt leaves people unsatisfied and without true and practical moral guidance?" In a word, do many priests fail to be prophets? Have you ever heard a homily on *Humanae Vitae*, Pope Paul VI's courageous and prophetic defense of human life against the evils of contraception, sterilization, and abortion? Have you ever heard a homily on the sinfulness of homosexual acts, not on homosexual orientation, which is not sinful, but on homosexual behavior?

Christ did not hesitate to condemn the evil and perversions of his day. Isn't the world in need of bishops and priests to fulfill this prophetic role today? Are we going through another time like that described by John Milton, where "the hungry sheep look up and are not fed"? Do some priests hold back on their prophetic role because they fear rejection? Or the loss of popularity? Priests today may not be called to physical martyrdom, but they may be called to a spiritual or social martyrdom for speaking the truths of Christ. And in so doing, they will be following in the steps of the Master, who said that "they will harry you as they harried me" (John 15:20).

The sense of sin has been deadened today. It is brushed aside as a sickness, a disease, a quirk of the brain, or a relic of a former unenlightened time. The psychiatrist, the sociologist, the counselor, the lawyer, the doctor, the advice columnist, the talk-show host – all these at times have taken over the prophetic role of the priest and are telling people, not to reform their lives, but to accept what used to be called sin as normal and even proper conduct.

So the role of the priest as prophet is a key one in our time. If a priest casts aside this role, who will denounce immorality in society and among individuals? We need some modern Jeremiahs and John the Baptists. The priest has a cure for modern society that no other person can give. He can bring the sinner to acknowledge and seek pardon for his sinfulness, and thus to find inner peace while making the atmosphere around him more peaceful. And there is a reward attached to being a prophet for Christ: "Blessed are you when they insult you and persecute you and utter every kind of slander against you because of me. Be glad and rejoice, for your reward is great in heaven" (Matthew 5:11-12).

The Unworldly Priest

There is an old saying that a priest – and lay people, too – should be in the world but not of the world. A worldly person is one devoted to the things and pleasures of the world, and neglectful of the things of God; an unworldly person is one who is not caught up in material pursuits but seeks to make the world a better place by turning people's attention back to God. But it is not sufficient merely to enunciate pious platitudes. People today are enmeshed in sin and are searching for spiritual help in making moral decisions. Therefore, a priest must be involved in the things of the world, but *as a priest*. He must never forget what he is and what his vocation is. If he makes his priesthood a sideline, a part-time job, he has lost his way.

If you look through the New Testament, you will find that there is hardly a subject of public interest not alluded to or discussed by our Lord and the Apostles. To those concerned about *matters of church and state*, Jesus said, "Give to Caesar what is Caesar's, but give to God what is God's (Matthew 22:21). On *marriage*: "Everyone who divorces his wife and marries another commits adultery. The man who marries a woman divorced from her husband likewise commits adultery" (Luke 16:18). On *public immorality*: "Wicked designs come from the deep recesses of the heart; acts of fornication, theft, murder, adulterous conduct, greed, maliciousness, deceit, sensuality, envy, blasphemy, arrogance, an obtuse spirit" (Mark 7:21-22).

On *citizenship*: "Let everyone obey the authorities that are over him" (Romans 13:1). On *racism, sexism, and bigotry*: "There does not exist among you Jew or Greek, slave or freeman, male or female. All are one in Christ Jesus" (Galatians 3:28). On *employer-employee relations*: "Here, crying aloud, are the wages you withheld from farmhands who harvested your fields. The cries of the harvesters have reached the ears of the Lord of hosts. You lived in wanton luxury on the earth" (James 5:4-5). Surely if the great High Priest and the priests of the early Church could be concerned about these matters, so should priests today preach about them.

It is important, however, that while priests talk about the ethics and morality of public and political issues, that they not become enmeshed in politics itself. Noting that "Jesus never committed himself to any particular political movement; the liberation he offered to humanity was not of a political order but of a spiritual one," Pope John Paul II said that involvement in political activity is the responsibility of the laity and that "priests must give up this particular activity in order to keep themselves as men of service for all. They must always give unmistakable witness to spiritual fraternity and fatherhood. The task proper to the Church is the proclamation of the Gospel, thus offering her cooperation to whatever concerns the common good."

The Holy Father also said that "the priest certainly has the right to have his own opinion in what regards politics and in voting, but knowing that his priestly ministry is above what is contingent and that no ideology can evade the whole truth of the Gospel. He will do his best to avoid making enemies because of his political views, which may make him lose people's trust and may cause the faithful entrusted to his pastoral mission to become distanced from him" (General Audience, July 28, 1993).

Where Do We Come In?

If the priest fulfills his role as prophet, if he carries out his duty to lead people to God, then we have the obligation to follow his lead. Instead of smugly pointing the finger at the clergy, we need to look in the mirror and ask ourselves, "When God's prophet speaks, do I listen?" We also need to give our wholehearted support and prayers to those priests who are faithfully living their vocations. It is always easy to criticize and find fault. But why not compliment priests when they celebrate a reverent Mass or give an inspiring homily? We all need a pat on the back; we all need to know that our efforts are appreciated. This is especially true of priests who are loyal to Christ and to the Church, for they are often on the front lines in the battle for souls, and they need all the support and encouragement we can give them.

After Christ promised to be with his Church "until the end of the world" (Matthew 28:20), he sent out priests to be his ambassadors to all people of all time. Many priests have even given their lives doing the work of Christ because they were very cognizant of their divinely appointed task. In the words of St. Paul: "Men should regard us as servants of Christ and administrators of the mysteries of God. The first requirement of an administrator is that he prove trustworthy" (1 Corinthians 4:1-2). How many priests have indeed proved trustworthy over the centuries? We owe them a great debt of gratitude for being the bridge over which we may pass into heavenly glory.

Chapter 21

Together in Christ

The sacrament of Matrimony signifies the union of Christ and the Church. It gives spouses the grace to love each other with the love with which Christ has loved his Church; the grace of the sacrament thus perfects the human love of the spouses, strengthens their indissoluble unity, and sanctifies them on the way to eternal life (cf. Council of Trent: DS 1799). – *Catechism of the Catholic Church*, n. 1661

There used to be a custom among young people in Germany, it is said, that on the eve of the feast of St. Andrew, the youths would float small boats made of paper in water and invoke the name of St. Andrew, who in that country holds a similar place as St. Valentine does in other countries. On each boat was the name of one boy or girl and, according to tradition, if St. Andrew drew two of the boats together, the boy and girl whose names were on them would be married. If a boat drifted away alone, that person would never marry. How reliable this manner of finding a mate for life turned out to be, we don't know, but it gives us a glimpse of how some people view marriage.

What is the Catholic attitude toward the vocation of marriage? The best place to find the answer would be in such important Church documents as Pope Pius XI's encyclical *Casti Connubii* (1930), Vatican II's *Pastoral Constitution on the Church in the Modern World* (1965), Pope Paul VI's encyclical *Humanae Vitae* (1968), Pope John Paul II's apostolic exhortation *Familiaris Consortio* (1981), and the *Catechism of the Catholic Church* (1992).

In God's plan, as these documents show, some are called to be priests, Religious brothers or sisters, or to the single life. But the great majority of men and women are called to be husbands and wives, fathers and mothers.

Marriage has been part of the human race from the very beginning of the world (Genesis 2:24), and God thought so much of this institution that he raised it to the dignity of a sacrament. That is the difference between the marriage of Christians and the marriage of anyone else: any person may be married, but only baptized persons receive the blessings of the sacrament of Matrimony. **Matrimony is the sacrament by which a baptized man and woman bind themselves for life in lawful marriage and receive the grace to carry out their duties.** The teaching of the Catholic Church on the dignity of the vocation of marriage and its indissolubility is at complete odds with the attitude of modern society, which sees little problem with the skyrocketing divorce rate, and the Church is fighting to defend and spread its teaching for the good of families and society in general.

The Lesson of Cana

St. John tells us that Jesus performed his first miracle at the wedding feast in Cana at the behest of his mother, who informed her Son that they had run out of wine. While reluctant at first to demonstrate his divine power at that early stage of his public ministry, Jesus bowed to the wishes of the Blessed Mother and turned the water in six stone jars into wine. The significance of this miracle has been beautifully summarized by Pope John Paul II:

"He gives new wine, the symbol of new love. The episode in Cana shows us how marriage is threatened when love is in danger of running out. With this sacrament Jesus Christ reveals his own help in an effective way, in order to save and strengthen the couple's love through the gift of theological charity, and to give them the strength of fidelity. We can also say that the miracle worked by Jesus at the beginning of his public life is a sign of the importance marriage has in God's saving plan and the formation of the Church.

"Finally, we can say that Mary's initiative in asking and obtaining the miracle foretells her future role in the divine plan for Christian marriage: a benevolent presence, an intercession, and a help in overcoming the inevitable problems" (General Audience, May 6, 1992)

Help for Married Couples

Whenever God puts before us some end to be achieved, he always gives us the means necessary to attain that end. The purposes of marriage are to bring children into the world and prepare them for heaven, and to foster the mutual love and sanctity of husband and wife. In order to achieve these interwoven purposes, there are special graces that flow from the sacrament of Matrimony. First, sanctifying grace is increased if the husband and wife are already in the state of grace when they receive this sacrament. They are strengthened and confirmed in the grace they already have; it gives them, so to speak, a stronger title and claim to heaven. It is up to them never to do anything in the future to throw away that title to heaven.

Second, sacramental grace is given. This is a pledge by Christ of all the help the couple will need to accomplish the duties and obligations of married life. This grace does not cease when they leave the church after the ceremony, or within a week or month; it will last for all the years of their married life. It will help them to overcome difficulties and disappointments, to make the sacrifices demanded by real love, to raise and nurture children, and to deepen their love as the years go on. This is not just a pious hope; it is a binding promise from God. But the responsibility for cooperating with God in securing this grace belongs to the couple themselves.

The parties to the marriage begin their cooperation with God by administering the sacrament to each other. The outward sign is the giving and expressing of their consent. The priest does not administer the sacrament; he is the Church's official witness. "The couple administer the sacrament to one another by their mutual consent," said Pope John Paul. "The sacrament shows the value of the man's and woman's free consent, as a statement of their personality and an expression of mutual love" (General Audience, May 6, 1992).

Three Working Together

In light of this, when people ask why the Catholic Church has the right to make laws regulating the marriage of baptized persons, we can show that the Church has authority over the sacraments, and that Jesus himself raised marriage to the level of a sacrament. The state may make laws regarding the civil requirements of marriage, but that is as far as it may go. It is the Church that defines the high purposes of marriage, the cooperation of a husband and wife with God in bringing into the world new souls destined for heaven. God has decided that he will not create new lives without our cooperation, and so married couples, through the sacrament of Matrimony, work with the Creator in accomplishing this great goal. Francine M. O'Connor, the popular Catholic writer, summed up this cooperation in this way:

It only takes two to have a friendship,
And two can play catch or run a race.
Two are enough to start a special club
With a secret meeting place.

It takes just two to play checkers,
And you and God can make a prayer.
You don't need a crowd to be happy,
Just someone with whom you can share.

Every happy marriage begins with two,
One bride, one groom, very much in love.
But to stay in love their whole life through,
They need the special help of the Lord above.

They stand before the altar, hand in hand,
And they promise their love eternally.
Then they make God a partner in their plans,
And bride and groom plus God makes three.

Three to make the new marriage strong,
Three to raise a loving family,
Three to be together when things go wrong,
Three for all the happy years to be.

Two are not enough for a Christian family,
The sacrament of Matrimony starts with three.

Marriage Is for Life

In view of the purposes of Matrimony, God has endowed this institution with certain fundamental qualities, notably unity and indissolubility. Marriage is the union of one man and one woman only, and it is to last until the death of one spouse. While polygamy and divorce may have been permitted in Old Testatment times to avoid greater evils, Jesus clearly rejected both in the New Testament. To those who want the Church to change its teaching on the indissolubility of marriage, the response is that the sacrament of Matrimony cannot be dissolved because Jesus said so. The sanctity of the marriage contract is not human law; it is divine law.

Speaking to a crowd one day, Jesus told them: "Everyone who divorces his wife and marries another commits adultery. The man who marries a woman divorced from her husband likewise commits adultery" (Luke 16:18). On another occasion, when a group of Pharisees asked Jesus if a man could divorce his wife for any reason whatever, our Lord replied: "Have you not read that at the beginning the Creator made them male and female and declared, 'For this reason, a man shall leave his father and mother and cling to his wife, and the two shall become as one'? Thus they are no longer two but one flesh. Therefore, let no man separate what God has joined" (Matthew 19:4-6).

If anyone knew the mind of Christ in this matter, it was the Apostles and those who were associated with them. This included St. Paul, who made the attitude of Christ clear to the people of Corinth: "To those now married, however, I give this command (though it is not mine; it is the Lord's): a wife must not separate from her husband. If she does separate, she must either remain single or become reconciled with him again. Similarly, a husband must not divorce his wife" (1 Corinthians 7:10-11).

Twenty centuries later, the Catholic Church, faithful to its Founder, calls divorce a "plague" and a profanation of the sacrament of Matrimony (*Pastoral Constitution on the Church in the Modern World*, nn. 47, 49). And Pope John Paul said that "it is a fundamental duty of the Church to reaffirm strongly ... the doctrine of the indissolubility of marriage." He said that Christian spouses must "remain faithful to each other forever, beyond every trial and difficulty, in generous obedience to the holy will of the Lord" (*Familiaris Consortio*, n. 20).

This teaching on divorce, which seems so strict to the modern world, makes good sense in the practical order. The very nature of marriage and the family demands an indissoluble bond. The good of both husband and wife must stand or fall with the marriage tie. What happens to children when parents separate at their own pleasure is all too evident today. Divorce has brought with it more hardships and more unhappiness than marriage fidelity with all its trials and sacrifices. Whatever problems arise in marriage, couples must try to work them out with the help of God's grace rather than break a contract that has been ratified by God.

The Ideals of Christian Marriage

A drunk staggering along the street one day came across another drunk lying in the gutter. He studied the situation for a minute, tried lifting up the man from the gutter without success, and finally said, "Well, I can't lift you up, but what I'll do instead is to lie down there beside you."

Some people's attitude toward marriage is not unlike the remark of that man. Christ and his Church have presented the ideals of marriage that we are to strive for, but many people, looking at the situation in society today, say in effect, "Well, I really can't (or don't want to) do anything about it, so I'll just go along with the tide of easy divorce." What we must say, however, is a resounding no to that attitude. We must say, "Let's live the ideals of Christ in our own lives, and try to get others to practice those same ideals in their lives."

The standards of a marriage pleasing to Christ were set forth for us by St. Paul in the first century:

"Husbands, love your wives, as Christ loved the church. He gave himself up for her to make her holy, purifying her in the bath of water by the power of the word, to present to himself a glorious church, holy and immaculate, without stain or wrinkle or anything of that sort. Husbands should love their wives as they do their own bodies. He who loves his wife loves himself. Observe that no one ever hates his own flesh; no, he nourishes it and takes care of it as Christ cares for the church – for we are members of his body.

" 'For this reason a man shall leave his father and mother, and shall cling to his wife, and the two shall be made into one.' This is a great foreshadowing; I mean that it refers to Christ and the church. In any case, each one should love his wife as he loves himself, the wife for her part showing respect for her husband" (Ephesians 5:25-33).

What a high ideal God has set for those united in Matrimony! The bond of love between a husband and wife is compared to the bond between Christ and his Church. As Christ has only one Church, so husbands and wives will have only one spouse. As Christ loved his Church so much that he was willing to lay down his life for her, so husbands and wives are to sacrifice for each other and to love each other as Christ loved the Church.

The ideals of Christian marriage are so sublime that they exceed human achievement. But the union of Christian husband and wives is not merely human; it is a supernatural bond, supported by Christ, who gives his graces in abundance to those who seek his help. Married couples will attain these ideals by fulfilling the duties of married life – by being faithful to each other, by praying often together and with their children, by generously conceiving children and providing for their material and spiritual welfare, and by cooperating with God in getting themselves and their children to heaven.

Vatican II also spoke of these ideals: "Christian spouses, in virtue of the sacrament of Matrimony, signify and partake of the mystery of that unity and fruitful love which exists between Christ and his Church. The spouses thereby help each other to attain to holiness in their married life and by the rearing and education of their children. And so, in their state and way of life, they have their own special gift among the People of God" (*Dogmatic Constitution on the Church*, n. 11).

In view of the sublime dignity and the awesome responsibilities of married life, Catholics should prepare carefully for this vocation by asking God to help them in the choice of a good and holy partner, by seeking the guidance of parents and a priest, by receiving frequently the sacraments of Penance and the Holy Eucharist, and by familiarizing themselves with the ideals of marriage that have been spelled out in such Church documents as *Casti Connubii*, the *Pastoral Constitution on the Church in the Modern World*, *Humanae Vitae*, *Familaris Consortio*, and the *Catechism of the Catholic Church* (nn. 1601-1666).

A New Nazareth

There is a wonderful analogy that expresses well the meaning of the bond of Matrimony. We are familiar with the brilliance of the north star. Astronomers tell us that what we see is not one, but two stars so close together that their light merges and appears to all who look at them as a single star. Isn't this same brilliant merger what we hope to see when a man and woman join their lives together in marriage? People don't see two separate individuals, but only one happy and holy married couple.

That same brilliance was evident in the village of Nazareth many centuries ago, when the Son of God spent thirty of his thirty-three years on earth in the midst of a family. Just as Jesus brought many blessings on the family headed by Joseph and Mary, so today he will bring many blessings on those families who try to live according to the ideals lived by the Holy Family. We have our model family to emulate, and we have all the graces we will ever need to reach for the high ideals of Christian marriage. So instead of lowering our standards to conform to those of our troubled society, let us give society the example of the high standards of our own "new Nazareth."

(For a fuller treatment of the subject of marriage and the family, the reader is referred to a companion volume in this series, *Catholicism and Society*, by the same authors.)

Chapter 22

"You Are Mine"

"All Christians in any state or walk of life are called to the fullness of Christian life and to the perfection of charity." All are called to holiness: "Be perfect, as your heavenly Father is perfect." – *Catechism of the Catholic Church*, n. 2013

There are two basic factors influencing the minds and hearts of millions today: confusion and lack of a proper sense of values. Christ and the Catholic Church have the answer to both of these problems. The only way to end the confusion in human hearts, and to restore a sense of values that would stop men and women from searching for happiness in all the wrong places, is to bring God back into the world and to put Christ in his proper place in our own lives.

Christ is the source of the true happiness and peace that is missing in the hearts of so many today. "I am the way, and the truth, and the life," he has said (John 14:6). He alone can show us the way to final happiness; he alone can give us the truth that we desperately need; he alone can bring vitality into our spiritually sluggish lives.

Why then are Christ and his Church so maligned and persecuted today? The answer to that question was given by St. Augustine many centuries ago: "To ailing eyes the light is hateful which is loved by healthy ones." Those who are steeped in sin and darkness cannot stand the light of Christ, so they reject the light instead of welcoming it. They do not want to repent and change their lives, so they try to ignore or ridicule those who call for repentance and conversion. Loyal followers of Jesus cannot expect to be treated any differently than he was if they call people to believe in the Gospel.

Serving Christ in His Way

It is amazing, and somewhat discouraging, to realize how little the average person really puts his or her powers of reason to work. The pace of life is so fast, there are so many things that we think need to be done, that we seldom take time just to think. The noise, the speed, the tension of modern life all work against serious thinking. When you combine this with the growing tendency of people to be lazy, to shun serious effort, to spend much of their time being passively entertained by television, then you can understand why there is so little time devoted to applying religious principles to our daily lives.

And yet we know that the key to happiness is in the knowledge, love, and service of God. "Our heart is restless until it rests in you," said St. Augustine. We must not only know the teachings of Christ and his Church, but we must apply them in our own lives and spread them to others so that their conduct will be conformed to the will of Christ, too. Living up to and demonstrating those ideals will require considerable effort and sacrifice. It will not be easy; after all, the symbol of Christianity is the cross, not the easy chair. Jesus warned us, "If a man wishes to come after me, he must deny his very self, take up his cross, and begin to follow in my footsteps" (Matthew 16:24).

What kind of a potential soldier would tell the recruiting officer: "I want to join the Army, but I want you to guarantee that there will always be a soft bed, plenty of good food, an eight-hour day, weekends and holidays off, and triple pay for overtime"? But isn't that how many people approach religion today? They say that they want to be a follower of Christ, but on their terms, not his. Oh, they'll go along with the teachings of Christ that don't seem too hard to follow, but as for the difficult sayings, no way! But there is no halfway Christianity, no compromises in following Christ. We either follow him all the way, to Calvary if necessary, or we are not really his followers.

Supermarket Christians

In the modern supermarket, the customer can go up one aisle and down another and see literally hundreds of items from which to choose. We pick certain things because we like them, or because the price is right, and we leave other things on the shelves. Some people want to treat religion like a supermarket, where they are free to pick the doctrines and teachings they agree with or find not too burdensome, and to ignore or reject those they don't like. But religion is not a supermarket, it is a state of being. Jesus does not say, "Drop in and see me sometime," but, "Give me your heart." He does not want just a piece of our love; he wants all of it.

When a boy and girl are in love, their love affects everything they do. Religion is essentially the love relationship between God and us and, if we love God, it will affect everything we do. It will guide us in keeping the Commandments and in frequenting the Sacraments. When we are faced with a moral choice, we will ask ourselves what would God want me to do in this situation, rather than what would my friends want me to do. We must try to live the words of the Lord's Prayer: "thy will be done."

We cannot divide our lives into two separate spheres of activity — one natural (eating, working, recreation, etc.) and one supernatural (praying, going to church, receiving the Sacraments, etc.). Living our faith means raising natural activities to a supernatural level and offering up our daily routine of prayers, works, joys, and sufferings to God out of love and in reparation for sin.

A distinguished surgeon once said that, in his years of dealing with the pain and suffering of patients, he had found that people were able to bear physical pain far better with a strong faith in God than with drugs. This confirms that there are times in our lives when the only thing that will help us is not human consolation, or pity, or the friendship of others, but faith in God.

That is why in wartime, or in times of crisis or tragedy, people who hadn't been paying much attention to God suddenly resume praying or going to church. It seems that when problems arise and disaster strikes, we fall back on God. But when everything is going well, God is not as important in the lives of some people. That kind of attitude is false and foolish because God is always there for us, and we owe him not just petitions for favors when there is nowhere else to turn, but also adoration, praise, thanksgiving, and reparation.

An unknown author once illustrated God's continuing concern for us with a brief reflection entitled "Footprints in the Sand." It goes like this:

> One night I had a dream. I dreamed I was walking along the beach with the Lord. Across the sky flashed scenes from my life. For each scene, I noticed two sets of footprints in the sand: one belonging to me, and the other to the Lord.

When the last scene of my life flashed before me, I looked back at the footprints in the sand. I noticed that many times along the path of my life there was only one set of footprints. I also noticed that it happened at the lowest and saddest times in my life.

This really bothered me and I questioned the Lord about it. "Lord, you said that once I decided to follow you, you'd walk with me all the way. But I have noticed that during the most troublesome times in my life, there is only one set of footprints. I don't understand why when I needed you the most you would leave me."

The Lord replied: "My precious, precious child. I love you and I would never leave you. During your times of trial and suffering, when you see only one set of footprints, it was then that I carried you."

It Depends on Our Perspective

There is a story about a man who had heard about the beautiful stained glass windows of a famous church, and he went to see them himself. When he arrived at the church, he stood outside looking at the windows, but soon voiced his disappointment. A person standing nearby, who was familiar with the church, overheard the remark and told the man to go inside and look at the windows from there. When the man followed this advice, he was amazed at how different the windows looked. The glass, now illumined by sunlight, took on beautiful colors; the confusion of many small pieces now became a masterpiece of art.

When we look at the events of our life from the perspective of the world, things can seem confusing and jumbled. But if we look at those same events through the eyes of faith, that is, from God's perspective, the dark glass of daily difficulties can take on a bright new meaning. We must learn to see the hand of God in our lives. Christ meant us to do more with the truths he revealed to us than merely to acknowledge them but pay little attention to them. He wanted them to influence our lives for the better, so that one day they might lead us to eternal happiness with him in heaven.

What can faith do for us? The same thing that it did for the woman in the Gospels. One day as Jesus was walking through a town, great crowds milled around him and more and more people pressed in on him, brushing against him from time to time. There was one woman in the crowd who had suffered from hemorrhages for a dozen years, and no doctor had been able to help her. "If only I can touch his cloak," she thought, "I shall get well." When the woman touched the tassel on his cloak, Jesus turned to her and said, "Courage, daughter! Your faith has restored you to health" (Matthew 9:20-22). And at that very moment the woman got well.

As Christians we come often into contact with Christ – through prayer, the Bible, the Church, the Sacraments – and that is all to our good. But the ideal for which we strive, however, is a much deeper and more constant thing than just passing contact with Christ; what we need is a day by day, hour by hour spirit of faith in Christ our Lord, so that our life is an echo of the words of Scripture: "In him we live and move and have our being" (Acts 17:28).

A Religion of Happiness

John Ruskin, the social reformer and writer of the last century, once wrote to an acquaintance: "How can you ever be sad, looking forward to eternal life with all whom you love, and God over all? It is only so far as I lose hold of that hope that anything is ever a trial to me." Christ never said that we had to be gloomy in order to follow him. In fact, he promised those who keep his commandments that "my joy may be yours, and your joy may be complete" (John 15:11). He did say, however, that to be truly happy now and forever we must change our lives: "You will all come to the same end unless you reform" (Luke 13:3).

If we are loyal and loving Catholics, if we are living our faith, we will be happy even in a troubled world. Society often confuses happiness with pleasure, wealth, honor, and fame. While these things can give us momentary satisfaction, they cannot bring real happiness. Pleasure and money and fame are all exterior things that pass all too quickly. True happiness is interior, spiritual, and lasting.

The mother who gives all her energy every day taking care of a large family does not have time for much besides her daily routine, but she is closer to God and to real joy and happiness than the influential and wealthy person with plenty of leisure time who is not living up to the laws of God. Experience tells us that we derive more happiness from giving of ourselves to others than from being the recipient of the attentions and gifts of people.

The Dead Sea on the boundary of Israel and Jordan has many streams flowing into it but, unlike other bodies of water, there is no outlet. Water flows in, but the only way out is by evaporation.

The result is that the high salt content of the sea kills most of the surrounding vegetation and makes the area very desolate. Graces are constantly flowing into the soul of a Catholic, but do we have outlets for those graces? Do we serve God generously as a way of thanking him for the many blessings he has bestowed on us? Do we demonstrate our love for our brothers and sisters in Christ? Do we try to share the gift of faith with others? Or do we, like the Dead Sea, let those graces stagnate and evaporate, killing the life of God in ourselves and in those around us and leaving us and them in a state of spiritual desolation?

In every human heart there is a desire for happiness. That is Christ's plan for each of us. But working out that plan involves a partnership, and it will not come about unless each partner does his or her share. God is doing his share. What about you?

A Religion of Peace

In these days of violence, bloodshed, uprisings, wars, and rumors of wars, there is one title given to Christ centuries ago which may appear out of synch with our times, and the title is "Prince of Peace" (Isaiah 9:5). Peace is something for which human beings have been crying since the beginning of time because it is linked to happiness. Remember the demeanor of the Apostles on that first Easter Sunday night? They were locked in the upper room in fear and trembling, when suddenly Jesus stood in their midst. "Peace be with you," he said to them (John 20:19), and the room that had been filled with gloom and anxiety was now overflowing with peace and joy. Such is the peace that Christ can bring to our hearts and to the world.

Many people today are plagued by the same feelings the Apostles had before Christ came to them. There is fear, anxiety, and uneasiness in our world. The mad pursuit of noise, pleasure, and the diversions of modern living may be motivated in part by a desire to flee from the uncertainties of life. Like the boy who whistles while walking through the cemetery at night, not because he is happy or has a sense of security, but because he is afraid.

People today are afraid, and the only way they can banish that fear and obtain the peace of mind and heart they are seeking is to be in the presence of Jesus. Peace has three aspects: peace with oneself, peace with neighbor, and peace with God. We can be in a state of world unrest, but we will not be afraid if we possess peace within ourselves and peace with God. That is why when Christ sent the Apostles into a hostile Roman world, with all odds against them and where they would have to shed their blood, he could say paradoxically, "My peace is my gift to you" (John 14:27).

The world around us may be in turmoil, but we can enjoy a higher and more satisfying peace – with God. The human heart has a yearning for God, but also a desire for things that are opposed to God and contrary to his love and his laws. Those things we call sin. The further we get from Christ by sin, the less peace we will have.

So we must reject sin and move closer to our Lord if we are to experience the peace that drives away apprehension and anxiety. Christ's presence brought immediate peace to those in the upper room, and his presence in our lives, especially through the sacraments of Penance and the Holy Eucharist, will also bring an immediate and lasting peace. This is the peace that the world cannot give; it is the peace that is available only from the Prince of Peace.

Follow the Blueprint

There was a story in a London newspaper some time ago about an old woman from Scotland who was dying. She was well known for her quarrels and hard feelings toward some of her acquaintances. So on her deathbed she was asked if she forgave everyone. "Yes," she replied, "all except Mrs. McGregor." The woman was told that she must forgive even Mrs. McGregor because in the Lord's Prayer it says that we are to forgive others if we expect God to forgive us. "Surely you will forgive Mrs. McGregor when you say the Lord's Prayer," those at the bedside said. "No," the woman replied, "but you have reminded me of something. When I get better, I'll never say that prayer again."

Some people are like the old woman in Scotland. They think that they can pick and choose the religious principles they will follow. But just as the builder of a house must follow the blueprint exactly, so Christians must follow Christ's blueprint completely. The ten Commandments are not just a list of things we shouldn't do; they are a positive blueprint for personal sanctity and apostolic action. They are love letters from God that can be summarized in the two great commandments: love of God and love of neighbor. We may have to make sacrifices to live up to the blueprint given to us by God, but our reward will be great in heaven (Matthew 5:12).

A healthy sign of mental balance is a knowledge of who we are and where we are going. If that standard were applied to a lot of Christians these days, their mental health might be in doubt. We are human beings with a body and soul, and we are supposed to be trying to get to heaven. The best way that we can achieve that goal is to keep the Commandments, listen to the Church that Jesus left to guide us, and receive the Sacraments that he gave us to strengthen us along the road. We are not here merely to mark time or to "get the most out of life," but to follow Jesus, who is the way, the truth, and the life. Failing to do so would be like failing to cash in a winning lottery ticket. Although that would mean just losing money, while failure to follow Jesus will mean losing our soul.

But the choice is ours to make. God does not send anyone to hell. People send themselves to hell by deliberately choosing something other than God, whether it's money or power or pleasure or whatever, and making that their god. It would be one thing if we had to struggle through life with no blueprint to follow and no special helps from God. But we have been given both by a generous and loving God and how foolish we would be not to take advantage of them.

A Challenge to Change

The editor of a small-town newspaper was once in desperate need of copy as the deadline approached. So he had an assistant type out the ten Commandments without any introduction or editorial comment. Two days later, the editor got a letter which said: "Cancel my subscription. You are entirely too personal."

Those who just go through the motions of receiving the Sacraments, or who don't think the Commandments apply to them, will not be able to make much of a difference in improving the moral and spiritual climate. On the other hand, those who obey the Commandments and who fully appreciate and take advantage of the graces available through the Sacraments will not only transform their own lives, but also the lives of those around them.

A sign in front of a church asked, "If you were arrested for being a Christian, would there be enough evidence to convict you?" You may call yourself a Catholic, but do you talk and act like one? When people look at you and the way you live, do they come away with a good impression of the Catholic Church, or a bad one? We have been given a marvelous inheritance, but are we using it wisely, or are we squandering it? Christ once compared this inheritance to a buried treasure "which a man found in a field. He hid it again, and rejoicing at his find went and sold all that he had and bought that field" (Matthew 13:44).

Our Catholic Faith is like that treasure, an invaluable find for which we must pay a price and make many sacrifices, but the rewards will far outweigh the effort we expend. We can get the most out of that treasure by developing a close personal bond of friendship with Jesus Christ. This can be achieved by weaving the Commandments and the Sacraments into our daily existence and using them to bring us ever closer to the Lord.

What's in a Name?

In biblical times there was a close relationship between a name and a person's character, personality, and mission in life. Thus, Abram's name was changed to Abraham by God when he was given a special divine commission. Simon became Peter when he was made the first head of Christ's Church. And Saul became Paul before he began his missionary travels. So God evidently considers a person's name of great significance.

To call a person by their first name builds a stronger personal bond. Saying "Hello, Terry" instead of just "Hello" carries a note of warmth and friendship. So picture the scene of Mary Magadalene arriving at the tomb of Jesus and finding it empty on Easter morning. She sees a man standing nearby but does not recognize him. "Sir," Mary says, "if you are the one who carried him off, tell me where you have laid him and I will take him away" (John 20:15). Then Jesus calls her by name, "Mary!," and the whole scene changes. You can feel the warmth of the Master's love and the transformation of Mary Magdalene.

Such is the power of a name, and the symbolism underlying the act of calling a person by name! To each one of us who sanctifies his or her life through the Sacraments, and transforms his or her life through the Commandments, Jesus says in effect: "I have called you by name: you are mine" (Isaiah 43:1).

Bibliography

Alcorn, Randy. *Pro-Life Answers to Pro-Choice Arguments*

Balducci, Corrado. *The Devil ... Alive and Active in Our World*
Basic Teachings for Catholic Religious Education
Brennan, William. *The Abortion Holocaust*
Burke, Cormac. *Covenanted Happiness*

Catechism of the Catholic Church
Catholic Almanac
Catholic Encyclopedia. Edited by Fr. Peter M. J. Stravinskas
Cochini, Christian, S.J. *Apostolic Origins of Priestly Celibacy*
Code of Canon Law
Connell, Fr. Francis J. *Outlines of Moral Theology*
Cristiani, Msgr. Leon. *Satan in the Modern World*
Cruz, Joan Carroll. *Eucharistic Miracles*
_____. *Relics*

Dannemeyer, William. *Shadow in the Land: Homosexuality in America.*
DeMarco, Donald. *Biotechnology and the Assault on Parenthood*
Dictionary of the Liturgy. Edited by Rev. Jovian P. Lang, O.F.M.
Dictionary of the Saints. Edited by John J. Delaney
Dilenno, Joseph A., M.D., and Smith, Herbert F., S.J. *Homosexuality: The Questions*
Documents of Vatican II, The. Edited by Walter M. Abbott, S.J.
Drummey, James J. *Catholic Replies*

Encyclopedia of Church History. Edited by Matthew Bunson
Everett, Carol. *Blood Money: Getting Rich off a Woman's Right to Choose*

Flannery, Austin, O.P. *Vatican Council II: The Conciliar and Post Conciliar Documents* (2 vols.)
Fox, Fr. Robert J. *The Gift of Sexuality: A Guide for Young People*
_____. and Mangan, Fr. Charles. *Until Death Do Us Part*
Freze, Michael, S.F.O. *The Making of Saints*

_____. *Fundamentals of the Faith*
_____. *Love Is Stronger Than Death*
_____. *Making Sense Out of Suffering*
Kuharski, Mary Ann. *Raising Catholic Children*

Lawler, Ronald, Boyle, Joseph and May, William E. *Catholic Sexual Ethics*
LeBar, James J. *Cults, Sects and the New Age*

Marks, Frederick W. *A Catholic Handbook for Engaged and Newly Married Couples*
Marshall, R.G. and Donovan, C.A. *Blessed Are the Barren: The Social Policy of Planned Parenthood*
May, William E. *An Introduction to Moral Theology*
Menninger, Karl. *Whatever Became of Sin?*
Mindszenty, Cardinal Jozsef. *Memoirs.*
Myers, Bishop John. *The Obligations of Catholics and the Rights of Unborn Children*

Nathanson, Bernard N. *Aborting America*
_____. *The Hand of God*
Nerbun, Ann, Taylor, Ruth and Hogan, Richard. *Our Power to Love: God's Gift of Our Sexuality*

O'Connor, Cardinal John J. *Abortion: Questions and Answers*
Ott, Ludwig. *Fundamentals of Catholic Dogma*

Pacwa, Mitch, S.J. *Catholics and the New Age*
Paul VI, Pope. *Humanae Vitae*
Pius XI, Pope. *Casti Connubii*
Pius XII, Pope. *Mystici Corporis*
Pontifical Council for the Family. *The Truth and Meaning of Human Sexuality*
Pornography's Victims. Edited by Phyllis Schlafly

Reardon, David C. *Aborted Women: Silent No More*
Rice, Charles E. *50 Questions on Abortion, Euthanasia and Related Issues*
_____. *50 Questions on the Natural Law*
_____. *No Exception: A Pro-Life Imperative*

Sacred Congregation for the Clergy. *Only for Love: Reflections on Priestly Celibacy*

Sacred Congregation for Divine Worship. *Christian Faith and Demonology*

Sacred Congregation for the Doctrine of the Faith. *Declaration on Certain Problems of Sexual Ethics*

_____. *Declaration on Euthanasia*

_____. *Declaration on Procured Abortion*

_____. *Instruction on Respect for Human Life in Its Origin and on the Dignity of Procreation*

_____. *Letter to the Bishops of the Catholic Church on the Pastoral Care of Homosexual Persons*

Sattler, Vern. *Challenging Children to Chastity*

Sharing the Light of Faith: The National Catechetical Directory for Catholics of the United States

Sheed, Frank J. *Theology for Beginners*

_____. *Theology and Sanity*

_____. *To Know Christ Jesus*

_____. *What Difference Does Jesus Make?*

Smith, Janet E. *Humanae Vitae: A Generation Later*

Steffon, Fr. Jeffrey J. *Satanism: Is It Real?*

Steichen, Donna. *Ungodly Rage*

Stravinskas, Fr. Peter M.J. *The Bible and the Mass*

_____. *The Catholic Answer Book*

_____. *The Catholic Answer Book 2*

Why Humanae Vitae Was Right: A Reader. Edited by Janet E. Smith

Willke, Dr. and Mrs. J.C. *Abortion: Questions and Anwers*

Wuerl, Donald W., Lawler, Thomas C. and Lawler, Ronald, O.F.M. Cap. *The Catholic Catechism*

_____. *The Teaching of Christ*

Index